T
LIGHT OF
CHRIST

THE
LIGHT OF
CHRIST

THOMAS JOSEPH WHITE, OP

THE
LIGHT OF
CHRIST

AN INTRODUCTION TO
CATHOLICISM

The Catholic University
of America Press
Washington, D.C.

Library of Congress Cataloging-in-Publication Data
Names: White, Thomas Joseph, 1971– author.
Title: The light of Christ : an introduction to
Catholicism / Thomas Joseph White, OP.
Description: Washington, D.C. : Catholic University of
America Press, 2017. |
Includes bibliographical references and index.
Identifiers: LCCN 2017014454 | ISBN 9780813229713
(pbk. : alk. paper)
Subjects: LCSH: Catholic Church—Doctrines. |
Theology, Doctrinal—Popular works.
Classification: LCC BX1754 .W45 2017 | DDC 230/.2—dc23
LC record available at https://lccn.loc.gov/2017014454

Nihil Obstat:
Rev. Thomas Petri, OP

Imprimi Potest:
Very Rev. Kenneth R. Letoile, OP
Prior Provincial
August 11, 2016

Nihil Obstat:
Rev. Thomas Petri, OP
Censor Deputatus

Imprimatur:
Most Rev. Barry C. Knestout
Auxiliary Bishop of Washington
Archdiocese of Washington
Sept. 16, 2016

The *nihil obstat* and *imprimatur* are official declarations
that a book or pamphlet is free of doctrinal or moral
error. There is no implication that those who have
granted the *nihil obstat* and the *imprimatur* agree with
the content, opinions, or statements expressed therein.

CONTENTS

V

This book is
dedicated to R. R. Reno,
in friendship

The Church, though dispersed throughout the whole world, even to the ends of the earth, has received from the apostles and their disciples this faith: She believes in one God, the Father Almighty, Maker of heaven, and earth, and the sea, and all things that are in them; and in one Christ, Jesus the Son of God, who became incarnate for our salvation; and in the Holy Spirit who proclaimed through the prophets the dispensations of God: [announcing in prophecy] the birth from a virgin, and the passion, and the resurrection from the dead, and the ascension into heaven in the flesh of the beloved Christ, Jesus our Lord, and His future manifestation from heaven in the glory of the Father to gather all things in one, and to raise up anew all flesh of the whole human race.... As I have already observed, the Church, having received this preaching and this faith, although scattered throughout the whole world, yet as if occupying but one house, carefully preserves it. She also believes these points of doctrine just as if she had but one soul, and one and the same heart, and she proclaims them, and teaches them, and hands them down, with perfect harmony, as if she possessed only one mouth. For, although the languages of the world are dissimilar, yet the content of the [apostolic] tradition is one and the same. For the churches which have been planted in Germany do not believe or hand down anything different, nor do those in Spain, nor those in Gaul, nor those in the East, nor those in Egypt, nor those in Libya, nor those which have been established in the central regions of the world. But as the sun, that creature of God, is one and the same throughout the whole world, so also the preaching of the truth shines everywhere, and enlightens all men that are willing to come to a knowledge of the truth.

Irenaeus (ca. 180 A.D.)

Irenaeus, *Against Heresies* I, 10, 1–2, trans. A. Roberts and W. Rambaut, in *Ante-Nicene Fathers*, vol. 1, ed. A. Roberts, J. Donaldson, and A. C. Coxe (Buffalo, N.Y.: Christian Literature Publishing, 1885); translation slightly modified.

꧁

Modern Catholicism is nothing else but simply the legitimate growth and complement, that is, the natural and necessary development, of the doctrine of the early Church.

John Henry Newman (1845 A.D.)

John Henry Newman, *An Essay on the Development of Christian Doctrine* (Notre Dame, Ind.: University of Notre Dame Press, 1989), 169.

THE
LIGHT OF
CHRIST

INTRODUCTION

THE CATHOLIC
INTELLECTUAL
LIFE

Intellectus means to "read from within." To be intellectual—to be an intellectual—means to seek to see into the depths of reality. This is something we should all want to do and be. In fact, to a great degree we do not have much of a choice. Human beings are made with the capacity to "read from within." We tend inevitably to seek the truth about what makes things the way they are. Why is the natural world so beautiful? Why is it marked by an intelligible order that the sciences discover progressively? Are the forces that gave rise to the universe entirely impersonal, and ultimately indifferent to human life? Why is there a world at all? If everything around us has a cause, does that mean there is a cause of all causes?

Not everyone ponders metaphysical questions. In fact, they are very likely of pressing concern for only a few people. Far more wonder about moral goodness. Nearly everyone is concerned to discern how he should live. This is not so much a concern about moral rules, though they are important. It is an attempt to penetrate the depths of our own existence. Is this the right person to marry? Should I marry? Is this the subject to major in or right job

1

to take? Have I devoted myself to what really matters? We want to see ourselves "from within," as it were, taking hold of the final meaning or purpose of our lives.

This concern to know life's purpose is closely related to our fascination with beauty. This is not something we typically seek to know, at least not in the usual sense of knowing. But "knowing" translates the ancient Greek word *episteme*, which means being around or intimate with. It is this sense of the word that allowed early modern translators of the Bible to use "knowing" as a euphemism for sexual intercourse: "Adam knew Eve his wife, and she conceived."[1] We seek to know beauty in this way, wishing to draw close to that which is beautiful, seeking to make beauty part of our lives. The prehistoric tools made by our distant ancestors were formed not just to function, but also to please. From earliest times humans decorated their bodies.

The spiritual quest of the human person for truth, goodness, and beauty can be deferred and even denied for a time. It can be stunted and stymied by lack of education, corrupt social influences, and subservience to the idols of money, status, and other forms of worldly success. But it cannot be eradicated. Our souls will not be satisfied with mere information, as if our hunger for knowledge could be quelled by uploading data. Google provides endless facts, available in an instant. But we want understanding, insight, and wisdom. We want to know why and what for. We wish to perceive all in the unending light of what is and cannot not be. Our hearts are restless with the desire to know the truth.

We see this all around us, not least in the paradoxes of our anti-metaphysical age. A number of scientists and philosophers have concluded that what we imagine to be a noble quest for truth is in fact an odd offshoot of various mental functions associated with the development of our brains in the evolutionary process. If we look into the depths of reality we find … neurons, electrons,

1. Gn 4:1.

2

protons, and other bits of matter. Yet, these very same intellectuals seem oddly driven to evangelize us and debunk our (to them) illusions about truth, goodness, and beauty. The same goes for literary professors convinced that "truth" is an army of metaphors commanded by the powerful. It's a nihilistic conviction nearly always pressed forward as a liberating truth. The zeal of the skeptics, materialists, and reductionists of our time bears witness to our lasting desire for and devotion to truth, even as their words deny it.

Although perennial and unavoidable—or perhaps because perennial and unavoidable—we often feel our deepest longings for knowledge to be perilous. They can give rise to frustration, disgust, and despair. When we try to see into the depths of the Gulag or the gas chamber, we enter into a dark chasm of brutality. The human condition is opaque. Every earthly city is marred by injustices, perhaps less grotesque and demonic, but pervasive and dehumanizing nevertheless. Yes, history testifies to heroism, nobility of soul, and the human capacity for self-sacrifice. But like everything human, it is stained by original sin. Human beings are often most inhuman—most not themselves—in the way they treat their fellow human beings.

Moreover, we are always haunted by the knowledge that we can be deceived, perhaps by our own doing, or by the wiles of others, or simply by society's conventional view of things. This is not a modern awareness. Again and again the Old Testament warns of idolatry's many seductions. We are tempted by what is convenient. We are intimidated by what is powerful and popular. In his dialogues Plato warns of sophistry. Logical arguments may seem a reliable guide, but they can be manipulated by the unscrupulous. Bad arguments can be made to seem good by those skilled at rhetoric. St. Paul warns against those who would be wise according to the world. By this he does not mean knowledge of nature, the created world, but instead an outlook on life defined by "worldly" assumptions: that God is remote and inaccessible, that death is final, that power and wealth provide the only reliable means to achieve happiness in this life, and so forth. All this may seem true, but the ways of God are not the ways of men. In Christ the wisdom of the wise is destroyed, and the cleverness of the clever thwarted.[2]

Our acute sense of vulnerability is heightened all the more when we venture into religious questions. For God, however near he may draw, is not accessible like other realities around us. Even when we feel him near, he eludes our grasp. And at the same time, in his hiddenness God is at the core of our being, more interior to us than we are to ourselves. Moreover, the question of God has implications for our lives. To believe something—anything—about the ultimate source of reality and summit of truth affects our convictions about how we should live and what we should live for. It is for this reason that we approach the question of God with such a perplexing combination of urgent desire and profound hesitation. It could be the most important question of all, but it could lead us down the path into serious error and delusion. But in that case, it is the most dangerous question to ignore, and the most dangerous question to answer wrongly!

For this reason, any sincere effort to seek religious truth must address simultaneously our rightful fear of arbitrary religious manipulation and our genuine thirst for transcendent knowledge of the true, good, and beautiful.[3] Our quest for God must

2. 1 Cor 1:19.
3. Joseph Ratzinger, *Behold the Pierced One: An Approach to a Spiritual Christology*, trans. Graham Harrison (San Francisco: Ignatius Press, 1986), 28–29: "There has always been a kind of basic evidence for the reality of God ... [but] the basic certainty of the existence of God was and is always accompanied by a sense of its being an immense riddle. Once we attempt to name and describe this God in more detail, once we try to relate human life to him and respond to him, the image of God falls apart in contradictory aspects .... A consideration of the history of religion yields a further result: the theme of revelation crops up regularly. Negatively, this shows that man is not in a position to produce a relationship to God on his own account .... Positively it means that the existing means of relating to God go back to an initiative on the latter's part, the tradition of which is passed on within a community as the wisdom of the ancients. To that extent, even the awareness that religion must

be both judicious and risk-taking, meditative and ready to abandon all for the opportunity to see God himself "from within," if only through a glass darkly. Questions of faith require critical reflection. It is a foolish, convenient, and ill-informed conceit of the modern secular world that religious faith is based on a childish, credulous mentality. The critical apparatus of Western intellectual life was first developed in order to guide faith's affirmation with care, guarding against idolatry, against an anthropomorphic projection onto God of human values, against simple-minded literalisms, and against a zealous mentality quick to turn to the sword to defend the truths of faith. But it is equally foolish to imagine that deep truths can be known if one stands forever at the edge, never willing to commit. There must be a moment of abandonment, however carefully guided. We cannot be romanced by a truth we lack the courage to embrace.

Every person has to accept risk in truth's call to us. Even religious indifference is a kind of risk, perhaps the greatest of all, for if nothing is ventured, nothing is gained. The mind is reason's instrument, but the heart is its seat. Faith shares a commonality here with romance. In opening our hearts to the search for God, we set out in hope and trust, acknowledging all the while the serious possibility of failure. Here we naturally try to avoid the two extremes of excessive skepticism and facile credulity. Excessive skepticism can lead to despair, which is a hidden form of self-aggrandizement. Facile credulity can lead to ideology, which is a not so hidden form of idolatry. And no person, whether the most ardent atheist or the most convicted believer, should refuse to take seriously the arguments of opposing viewpoints. How indeed can we enter more deeply into the truth if we do not consider why and how our convictions may be false?

---

rest on a higher authority than that of one's own reason, and that it needs a community as a 'carrier,' is part of mankind's basic knowledge, though found in manifold forms and even distortions."

Finally, the wisest recognize their need for companions on the journey to truth, especially religious truth. We need reliable guides. No one person can cover all the fronts of argument, analysis, and investigation. Physics, chemistry, and the other modern sciences are necessarily team efforts. The same goes for philosophy and theology. Indeed, all the more so in these domains, for in our search for knowledge of the highest truths we need wisdom's guidance and not just the voice of expertise.

John Henry Newman once observed that reason's powers of proof and argument diminish as the subject matter becomes greater and more consequential.[4] Geometry runs on proofs. Especially gifted young people can teach themselves mathematics and learn foreign languages on their own. These are worthy enterprises, and the remarkable ability of some to make such rapid progress on the basis of pure aptitude testifies to the extraordinary propulsive power of our desire for truth. However, education of the young typically requires structure and discipline, which are meant to liberate people for the service of the truth. Like training spirited horses that already seek to gallop, one of the great joys of teaching comes from the fact that one is releasing and guiding the innate hunger for learning that energizes young minds.

Questions of God, right worship, and righteous living cannot be answered with syllogisms alone. The modern myth of the noble savage conjured up the illusion that knowledge of the good is innate, spoiled by education rather than developed by it. But to be unformed by a moral tradition is to be feral, not "natural." Moreover, there is no "natural" religious outlook that a talented autodidact can work out on his own in the same way as he can teach himself algebra. A deep knowledge of the truth, the good, and the beautiful involves the use of reason. But a great deal turns on the first principles, initial assumptions, and deep intuitions

4. John Henry Newman, *An Essay in Aid of a Grammar of Assent* (Notre Dame, Ind.: University of Notre Dame Press, 1979), 300–303.

that ground reflection. As a result, we need teachers we can trust to help us discern which to affirm, which to cultivate. And in our moral and religious teachers we often (and quite rightly) prefer sound character to shining brilliance, wisdom to erudition, depth of piety to breadth of learning. In this there is peril yet again, for often we must choose our teachers before we know enough to make an expert decision. Or as is more often the case, they are chosen for us by our parents or community. And once again we must accept the risk, not failing to use our critical faculties as best we can, but not dithering on the sidelines of truth's quest for so long that we fail to make the journey.

This is a book that offers itself as a companion. I do not presume to argue the reader into the truths of the Catholic faith, though I will make arguments. Logical arguments sometimes fail to move a person to God, but they do often help us take the next step to discover God eventually. I do not offer these chapters as homilies, though they do seek to bear witness to a supernatural faith. At times we need to see before us the truth we do not yet believe, or only half believe. My goal is to make explicit in a few broad strokes the shape of Catholicism. I hope to outline its inherent intelligibility or form as a mystery that is at once visible and invisible, ancient and contemporary, mystical and reasonable. Throughout I do not seek primarily to present my own individual ideas, but to represent the wisdom of the Catholic Church. For she has been for us what Christ himself promised she would be: the trustworthy teacher of truths both human and divine.

1

REVELATION AND
REASON

Human Search for an Unknown God

At the starting point there is no ambiguity: apostolic Christianity is based on an appeal to divine revelation. "The Word became flesh and dwelt among us, full of grace and truth."[1] This founding statement is not the conclusion of philosophical argument, nor is it a first principle of natural reason. It is a statement of the truth about God, an uncovering or unveiling. (Revelation is a Latin-derived word for the Greek term *apocalypsis*, which means uncovering or unveiling.) And the reality revealed is God himself, and what God in his freedom has done for us in Christ. As something "from the beginning," this is as fundamental for our human destiny as the creation of reality itself.

Jesus of Nazareth is a person, not the conclusion to a syllogism. Christ's crucifixion is not something we can deduce from first principles of philosophy or mathematics. We can only know the truth about Christ because we are told about it, and not just by anyone, but by trustworthy sources who testify to us about him. The author of the Gospel of John follows up the announcement

1. Jn 1:14.

8

of the Incarnation in precisely this way: "John bore witness to him, and cried, 'This was he of whom I said, 'he who comes after me ranks before me, for he was before me.'"[2] There are many internal reasons why we come to faith. Some are spurred on by philosophical questions, or a personal search for meaning. Others identify with the mystery of Christ suffering on the Cross. Still others are inspired by the example of friends whose faith seems to make them generous or peaceful. There are as many paths to Christ as there are types of people and moments in history. But he is only available to us because he is proposed to us, because he is put forward by others as the Christ—because others bear witness to him.

The idea of organizing our lives around a truth received on the testimony of others received on trust is often thought to be at odds with universal human reason. How can we base our beliefs about a transcendent God on the words of someone like an itinerant desert ascetic and preacher, John the Baptist, which after all depend on the trustworthiness of the testimony of John's Gospel where they are recorded, which in turn depends on the trustworthiness of the small Christian community that decided to take the Gospel as an authoritative truth? Our beliefs about the ruler of the universe should flow from universal human reason, should they not? Put somewhat differently, given the supreme importance of God—this is a truth we desire most deeply—don't we want to be especially careful to get things right, which means trusting not this prophet or seer or even religious tradition, but relying on the testimony of the reason all human beings share?

Well, no. Universal human reason *is* capable of coming to considered conclusions about God. We have been deliberating about God for as long as human beings have sought to discipline their wonder with the considered use of reason. But we are not capable of determining the free decisions of God. Reason cannot deter-

2. Jn 1:15.

mine whether the transcendent God chooses to remain hidden from us—or concerns himself with human destiny and reveals himself personally, and not just in the distant past, but here and now, in your life and mine. This is why, if we are thinking clearly, we can conclude that it is *rational* to be open to the religious search for God. For reason is in no position to know conclusively whether or not God may come in search of us! In fact, it is reasonable to be open to the suggestion of divine revelation, and arbitrary and unreasonable simply to exclude this possibility.

We nevertheless feel a tension between our normal ways of thinking and the claims of revelation, even when it is authentic. This is because revelation clashes with human convention. Christian revelation is not opposed to reason. It surpasses reason. But it contradicts conventional ideologies.

Religious Pluralism and "The True Philosophy"

From the very outset Christianity was at odds with what at the time seemed to be a very successful way of approaching the question of God. Ancient Greco-Roman culture was religiously pluralistic, composed of diverse tribes and nations, and admitted a fairly broad range of incompatible viewpoints, both philosophically and religiously. The political unity of the Roman Empire was maintained not by forging a universal consensus about truth, but by adopting a multiplicity of religions into an ever-increasing pantheon of gods. Conventions of various conquered cultures were not abolished but assimilated. This civilization differed in many ways from today's multiculturalism, but it shared with contemporary sensibilities a flexible attitude toward theological truth-claims, and pragmatic commitment to the basic good of social unity.

Ancient Romans considered this a strength, not a weakness. The great pagan orator Symmachus, writing after Christianity had become politically powerful, deplored the abolition of the pagan cults. He argued on practical grounds: every society needs to maintain continuity with its ancestors. The Greco-Roman system that assimilated diverse religious cultures had provided centuries of stability and peace. Moreover the resulting pluralism encouraged a more humble approach: "What does it matter with what philosophy each individual seeks the truth? It is not possible to reach so great a secret by a single route."[3] Better, then, to cultivate many different paths to God.

The audacity of ancient Judaism and early Christianity was to claim that this system of political assimilation of "every truth" was a betrayal of our most fundamental vocation as seekers of truth. We should be concerned to protect social unity and promote peace, and that may require compromise and a humility that comes from recognizing that our own views might be mistaken. But we were made primarily for conviction in the truth, not doubt, for knowledge, and not only for questioning. At some point the authority of truth itself must govern, not the pragmatic needs of the moment. At times we are arrested by insights and persuaded by arguments so strong and so fundamental that to set them aside compromises our integrity and violates our conscience. Only shared truths can unite human beings in an enduring way.

Ancient Rome endured for so long because it subordinated our search for God to the Roman quest for glory. *That* ideology was the shared truth behind the supposed humility of their religious pluralism. A refusal to accept this subordination of religious and intellectual conscience was the reason why the earliest Christians made common cause with another group that criticized popular pagan religion organized around civic life: the philosophers.

3. Symmachus, "Third Relatio to the Emperor Valentinian II" (382), c. 10, in *Ambrose of Milan: Political Letters and Speeches*, trans. John Hugo Wolfgang Gideon Liebeschuetz (Liverpool: Liverpool University Press, 2005), 69.

Already in sixth-century B.C., Xenophanes of Colophon attacked the religious myths of the poets. He claimed that they attributed immorality to the deity, and depicted God in an irrational, anthropomorphic fashion. "Homer and Hesiod have attributed to the gods everything that is a shame and reproach among men, stealing and committing adultery and deceiving each other."[4] Heraclitus attacked the notion that blood sacrifice could alleviate guilt.[5] Sophocles criticized state obligations of Greek religion in *Antigone*, suggesting that his heroine's decision to bury her brother was an act of true justice and piety. Most famously, Socrates was accused in his trial, among other things, of denying the gods of the city, and of therefore being an atheist.[6] Plato responds by reversing the charges. In the *Republic* he says that if a dramatic poet, the muse of the city's gods, comes to visit the ideal state, he should be "crowned with wreaths and sent away to another city."[7] Aristotle in the *Metaphysics*, in the midst of his own discussion of divine attributes, says that the poets have portrayed the gods mythologically for reasons of political expediency and rhetorical persuasion.[8] They and other spokesmen for the city's pantheon are silver-tongued propagandists.

The earliest Christian apologists took up this tradition of vigorous critique of Greco-Roman paganism to promote Christianity as "the true philosophy." This appeal to reason's power and dignity appears already in the New Testament. In Romans 1:19–25, St. Paul tells his readers that all human beings can come to recognize that God exists. Human reason can know something of the creator from the consideration of his creatures, which are his effects. However, human beings typically have "exchanged the

---

4. Xenophanes, fr. 11 and 14, from *The Presocratic Philosophers*, ed. and trans. G. S. Kirk and J. E. Raven (Cambridge: Cambridge University Press, 1957), 168.

5. Heraclitus, fr. 5 (*The Presocratic Philosophers*, 211).

6. Plato, *Apology* 18c.

7. Plato, *Republic* III.398a, from *Plato: Complete Works*, ed. John M. Cooper, trans. G. M. A. Grube (Indianapolis, Ind.: Hackett, 1997).

8. Aristotle, *Metaphysics* XII.8.1074b1–14.

truth about God for a lie ... and served the creature rather than the Creator," by treating physical objects in the creation as absolute causes, or by worshiping God with images of reptiles, birds, animals, and mortal men.

Here Paul echoes the literature of Hellenistic Judaism. In the book of Wisdom (from around 100 B.C.) the rationality of belief in God is contrasted to those who believe the universe to be itself divine, or upheld in being by the mere power of the stars. "They supposed that either fire or wind or swift air, or the circle of the stars, or turbulent water, or the luminaries of heaven were the gods that rule the world." Against this seduction of errant reason, the book of Wisdom proposes a view of God as the transcendent creator of everything rather than a particularly powerful or sublime force within the world. "If through delight in the beauty of these things men assumed them to be gods, let them know how much better than these is their Lord, for the author of beauty created them .... For from the greatness and beauty of created things comes a corresponding perception of their Creator."[9] God is not the greatest or most powerful force within the cosmos. He is not even "beyond" the cosmos in the sense of being outside or above. He is the source of the very fabric of existence, the transcendent cause of the intelligibility that we discover in all that exists.

St. Paul exposits this view of God in his discourse to the Athenians at the Areopagus in Acts 17. This hill in the northwest of the city was a place for philosophical debates. "Men of Athens I perceive that you are in every way religious. For as I passed along, and observed the objects of your worship, I found also an altar with this inscription, 'To an unknown god.' What therefore you worship as unknown, this I proclaim to you."[10] Fundamentally, Paul stipulates that the unknown God of the Greeks is he in whom "we live and move and have our being," "the God who

9. Wis 13:2–3, 5.
10. Acts 17:22–23.

made the world and everything in it."[11] God exists beyond the realm of finite realities we can identify and categorize. For that reason he cannot be found and known in the way we can find and know a new continent or develop a new scientific theory. But he can be known as the source of all finite reality, the ground of being. The truly supreme and transcendent source of all reality is above the cacophony of local religions collected together and harmonized by Roman society for its own political purposes. Sound philosophy itself can show that many conventional religious views of God fail to speak his true name.

Greek philosophy was a powerful ally in the Christian criticism of Rome's ideological subordination of the search for God to the needs of the earthly city. But it too promoted its own conventional wisdom. St. Paul speaks of the Cross of Christ as foolishness to the Greeks.[12] This is because Greek philosophy took it as axiomatic that the infinite, immaterial, and unchangeable supreme being is antithetical to the finite, material, and changeable world of human life. And what could be a more poignant and bitter sign of changeability than death? Therefore, the metaphysical imagination of the ancient world found it absurd to think of God as incarnate, and even more absurd to think that his humiliating death could be "good news" preached by Christians.

Our metaphysical imaginations have not changed much. On occasion one hears a religiously interested person recoil from the dogmatic nature of Christianity. "The mystery of God is too great to put into a box," he says. This resembles the Greek intuition. Transcendence is unlimited. Finite existence is limited. Therefore, the finite historical life of Christ cannot reveal the infinite God. Stated differently, in this way of thinking all particular views about God, including the Christian view, become idolatrous if they are taken as final and ultimate.

11. Acts 17:28, 17:24.
12. 1 Cor 1:23.

In his *Confessions*, Augustine recognized that this view is erroneous, and that it springs from a crucial weakness in ancient philosophy.[13] The key error is to oppose the transcendence of God with his real presence in the world. Religious awe is set in opposition to spiritual intimacy. Against this false opposition, the Church Fathers developed a deeper understanding of the mystery of creation. God's transcendent mystery is distinct from the finite world, but not antithetical to it. In fact, it is precisely because God is the cause of all that exists that he can be intimately present to all that is. By contrast, the idea of an intrinsic antithesis between God and the finite world implies a paradoxical limit on God, as if he were somehow excluded from his creation. The Church Fathers recognized that the mystery of God is present all around us. God is "He Who Is," the hidden transcendent source who gives existence to all things, and that accounts for their being, goodness, and beauty. This transcendence is not only consistent with God being immanently present in all things as creator, but even entails that it is so. It is God in whom we live, and move, and have our being, because there is nothing he does not sustain in existence. Therefore, God can become human without changing in himself. He can reveal who he truly is to us *in a singular human life* without diminishing himself in any way. God can become intimately present to humanity by grace and make himself known to us personally, while remaining incomprehensible, transcendent, and omnipotent.

St. Paul also spoke of the Cross as a scandal to the Jews.[14] This sense of scandal stems from a different kind of conventional thinking, one that concerns how we read the scriptures of Israel rather than how we engage in philosophical speculation. Ancient Jews were not religious syncretists. True, they were tempted by

13. Augustine, *Confessions*, VII.ix(13)–xii(18), trans. H. Chadwick (Oxford: Oxford University Press, 1991), 121–25.
14. 1 Cor 1:22–24.

the politically convenient pluralism that characterized Greek and Roman religion. The Old Testament presents us with numerous instances when the leaders and people of Israel adapted themselves to the cults and practices of their more powerful neighbors, clearly hoping to juggle theological commitments for the sake of political goals. But the Old Testament prophets, unlike Roman apologists, denounced these strategies as base betrayals of Israel's vocation to be a people uniquely chosen by God, a monotheistic light to the nations.

Nor did the Jews at the time of Jesus object to the notion that God the creator could become intimately present to his people by his own sovereign decision. This is after all a central theme of the book of Exodus. Their objection to St. Paul's preaching stemmed instead from the form this presence took, that of a crucified messiah. It was not the presence of God in history that scandalized. It was his weakness. In the book of Exodus the *mirabilia Dei* manifest that the God of Israel is omnipotent and unique. God overawes Egypt's Pharaoh, who is representative of the paganism of the nations. God destroys the Egyptian army in the Red Sea, sustains Israel in the wilderness, and eventually delivers them into the Promised Land. God incarnate in Christ employs his omnipotence in a different way. His triumph comes about through suffering and death.

The response to this Jewish sense of scandal is found, of course, in the physical resurrection of Christ. If Jesus is the Christ, why is he crucified? The Christian claim is not that God is uninterested in overcoming the powers of the world, but that he wants to overcome them in a more profound way than Israel had ever before deemed fathomable. The fulfillment of the promises to Israel comes about in Christ, but on an infinitely greater scale than was previously imagined. The death and resurrection of the crucified messiah are the definitive victory of God over the very worst that the human race is capable of, and are the gift of the greatest thing possible. God takes upon himself the consequences of human evil, suffering, and death so as to overcome them once and for all. In return he gives all human beings—"Jew and Greek alike"—the offers of grace, the forgiveness of sins, and participation in eternal life. To the Greeks, the Cross might seem too material and mired in finite reality and thus "foolishness." It may seem a story of failure and humiliation for Jews, and thus a "scandal." But as Paul says, in the resurrection Christ's death is revealed to be the "power of God and the wisdom of God."[15]

Skepticism and the Usefulness of Belief

Of course many of our contemporaries simply find this implausible. Human life is finite and we surrender to death in the end. The real world is comprised of practical calculations and the struggle for material success, not the lofty but ultimately unreal reflections of ancient sages. Christian beliefs about power, money, and sex are unrealistic. Aims of immortality are illusory. We should respond to suffering through scientific research, technological development, and sound political strategies. We can find happiness in this world through aims such as human love, sexual freedom, education, and the civic arts. In short, it is best to be reasonable, and avoid the temptations of religious metaphysics which distract us from realistic goals and our more modest but ultimately meaningful human tasks.

Thus modern secularism. Truth be told, it is not entirely novel, but has clear roots in ancient skepticism and Epicureanism. We cannot know very much about our human plight or its ultimate meaning (if there is one). Instead we should seek to manage our lives reasonably, seeking pleasure and avoiding pain. We find this criticism of Christianity articulated already by Celsus,

15. 1 Cor 1:24.

the third-century pagan philosopher. He argued that Christianity claims to know too much and aims for too much, or at least for what is outside the sphere of our limited rational knowledge. Only the uneducated can accept it uncritically. But its bold, unrealistic claims threaten to undermine our real possibilities for human happiness and civic reason. Religion has its uses, but it also has its place, and it needs to be modest if it is to be friendly to human well-being.

This viewpoint is unsatisfying, however, because it is based on resignation. Religious skepticism claims that it is the guardian of human happiness. But in fact it stems from the fear of making a mistake, and is based on its own form of spiritual paralysis and even despair. The human being is alive in seeking the truth and finding new and creative ways to love selflessly. Imprisoned in our own pleasures and limited sense of understanding, we grow old and self-referential. As Newman noted, reason without faith tends to obsess with objects that are inferior to man, that we dominate, but that at the same time make our intellectual pursuits complacent and less interesting.

Those who deliberately refuse to form a judgment upon the most momentous of all subjects; who are content to pass through life in ignorance, why it is given, or by whom, or to what it leads; and who bear to be without tests of truth and error in conduct, without rule and measure for the principles, persons, and events, which they encounter daily, — these men ... [should not] be granted the name of philosophers.[16]

16. John Henry Newman, University Sermon 14, "Wisdom, as Contrasted with Faith and with Bigotry," par. 27; see also par. 17: "those who, being used to nothing better than the divinity of what is historically known as the nonconformist school, — or, again, of the latitudinarian, — are introduced to the theology of the early Church, will often have a vivid sense of enlargement, and will feel they have gained something, as becoming aware of the existence of doctrines, opinions, trains of thought, principles, aims, to which hitherto they have been strangers." In *Fifteen Sermons Preached before the University of Oxford, between A.D. 1826 and 1843* (London: Longmans, Green, and Co., 1909).

Reasonable openness to God, then, is a source of spiritual youth in any person or culture. It maintains in us a sense of investigation, wonder, cumulative wisdom, and knowledge in the service of love. Refusal of the mystery of God makes us the unique masters of ourselves, but also imprisons us within the ascetical constraints of our own banal finitude. The privilege of the educated and wealthy is to be able to control their sense of wonder before the mystery of human existence, and to retreat into their own domain of competency and control. Often their inferiors do not have this luxury and are therefore more innately disposed to accept dependence upon God. Posing questions about God opens the human being up to new vulnerabilities, and therefore also to new forms of happiness that the artificial limitations of skepticism cannot foresee.

Augustine noted that deep-seated skepticism is a luxury item that the true intellectual cannot afford. He points out that belief—faith in what others tell us for our instruction—is fundamental for the intellectual life.[17] When we begin learning in any rigorous discipline (mathematics, observational sciences, philosophy, law) we have to leave behind the conventions of our presuppositions and entrust ourselves to those who instruct us. Concretely, human faith in authentic teachers is nearly always the basis for true growth in understanding, and not our own solitary intuitions or the presuppositions of the masses. Augustine then draws up a key set of distinctions. On one side, there is extreme skepticism, by which a person remains in a conventional posture, and risks nothing but also can gain nothing. On the other side, there is credulousness, a foolish form of faith by which we mistakenly entrust ourselves to a poor teacher, or even to a true teacher, but fail to understand the material for ourselves, remaining infantilized or rudimentary in our insight. Faith that "merely believes what it

---

17. Augustine, *On the Profit of Believing*, pars. 10–13, 22–27.

ought to believe" is "dead."[18] Between the two extremes is the middle way of "faith seeking understanding," one that is both human and Christian. We should accept instruction but also examine it critically and studiously, seeking to find the truth in what is said, to test it. Every body of knowledge has its own internal structure and laws, its insights, paths of reasoning, and genuine conclusions, that we must progressively make our own. There is a discipline to becoming a lawyer, learning constitutional principles and their applications from one's teachers. Likewise there is a discipline of the mind in becoming a Christian, learning the truth as revealed by God, and developing an intellectual understanding of God's mystery.

One can object, of course, that revelation presents us with a very different kind of subject matter than the other disciplines. Unlike law or mathematics, we cannot verify the truths of revelation independently from our own experience as we go along in our instruction, and must depend continuously upon the testimony of another. This is true. What should be kept in mind, however, is that even in ordinary experience, human beings tend to live "above" the merely empirical dimension of life. Behind the study of law we must confront the question of what true justice is, something we will never find through empirical measures. Behind mathematics, there is the question of perennial, unchanging truth, since the laws of mathematics apply always and everywhere that quantitative beings exist. Behind all such subjects is the question of God, who is the cause of all that exists. We cannot know what another human person wills or thinks except on the basis of voluntary trust in that person. So too with the transcendent God, we can learn from him personally only through faith.[19]

18. Thus Anselm, *Monologion*, par. 78, echoing Augustine; trans. J. Hopkins in *A New, Interpretive Translation of St. Anselm's Monologion and Proslogion* (Minneapolis, Minn.: Arthur J. Banning Press, 1986).

19. Augustine, *Concerning Faith of Things Not Seen*, par. 2.

What revelation gives, then, is the opportunity to be instructed not uniquely by our fellow human beings, but by God, who remains inaccessible in some way to all strivings of human philosophy and religion, yet who also reveals to us what we could never
discover by our own powers. To receive this instruction requires
supernatural faith, which is itself a grace. This grace, as Aquinas
notes, is received into the intellect, allowing us to judge that a
given teaching comes from God and is about God.[20] We can compare this to "ordinary" trust in a teacher by analogy. It is like the
difference between knowing that a physics professor exists and
studying his theories in books he has written, versus meeting him
personally and learning from him directly as a living source of
truth. As a disposition, supernatural faith is like natural trust in a
teacher, but it provides something more: direct access to the mystery of God who reveals himself to us and teaches us.

To seek to know God entails risk, undoubtedly, but it also
entails an irreplaceable possibility: that we could truly come to
know God personally, find friendship with God, and live with
him by grace. If this possibility is real, and not a mere myth or
human conjecture, then it is the greatest of possibilities, and one
that we should not dismiss through fear, resignation or complicity
with the conventions of our age. As Anselm writes:

> Indeed, for a rational nature to be rational is nothing other than for it
> to be able to discriminate what is just from what is not just, what is true
> from what is not true, what is good from what is not good .... The ratio-
> nal creature was made for this end: viz., to love above all other goods the
> Supreme Being, inasmuch as it is the Supreme Good .... Clearly, then,
> the rational creature ought to devote his entire ability and his entire will
> to ... understanding and loving the Supreme Good—to which he knows
> that he owes his existence.[21]

---

20. Aquinas, *Summa Theologiae* II-II, q. 1, a. 1; q. 2, a. 1 [hereafter "*ST*"]. All
translations of *ST* are taken from *Summa Theologica*, trans. English Dominican Province (New York: Benziger Brothers, 1947).

21. Anselm, *Monologion*, par. 68.

The real opposition, then, is not between faith and reason, but between a skeptical reason that is reductive, and a magnanimous, studious reason that engages in faith. Expansive desire for the truth breaks away from conventions, and awakens human beings to our true nobility, against temptations to self-diminishment. The Christian vocation of "faith seeking understanding" is both dynamic and restful. It gives us something greater than ourselves to ponder, and takes us out of ourselves toward God as our teacher. But it also allows us to know ourselves as rational beings, able truly to ask and even answer the deeper religious questions. Faith therefore creates a learning community. The Church is a place where human beings have the conviction to patiently seek the truth together, in a shared life of charity, one that is both cosmopolitan and personal, both reasonable and religious, both philosophical and theological. This communion in the truth is made possible, however, only because people have first accepted to be apprenticed to revelation through a common effort of learning the truth from another (i.e., God), who is the author of truth, and from one another.

Scripture

True teaching authority is based on the knowledge of the teacher, not the arbitrary use of power. The word *auctoritas* in Latin can mean "principle," "guide," or "one having warranted agency." So a legitimate teaching authority is an agent of the truth, one who enlightens others. Christ, however, is unique among teachers, because he does not only instruct externally through words (leading us progressively to see what he sees), but also enlightens us interiorly by grace. Christ, the eternal Wisdom of God, moves the mind and heart from within so that we can perceive intellectually the truths that he reveals. This, Thomas Aquinas argues, is one of the reasons it is fitting that Jesus did not write a book during his lifetime, but entrusted his teaching to others: so that we would not confuse the real presence of Christ among us with a text he wrote, but would instead learn of his presence through the teaching of the apostolic Church, a process that he assists and works through, by the presence of his grace acting in those who teach and in those who are instructed.[22]

Scripture is at the center of this process: the Old and New Testaments. The modern reader often feels daunted by the Bible. How does one begin to understand this collection of texts with its complex history? Who wrote the books? Are all of them supposed to be historical? If so, does that mean that a person who takes the Bible seriously must reject truths of modern science and archeological studies? Is the decision about "what is true" a matter of convention, adjusted continually by theologians to appease modern critics of Christianity? Perhaps most important: do we really know anything about the historical Jesus or are the texts all reconstructions of the early Christian community that fail to correspond to what Jesus really said or who he was? Why should we treat this ancient book as something essential today and why should we trust it? Is it possible for a text this ancient to be relevant to all times and places?

These are all reasonable questions. Answering them is an important and helpful part of the work of theologians and scripture scholars. However, they are also second-tier questions. The more fundamental one is: what is the essence of scripture? How is it intended to be used? And for this we should go back to what Aquinas says: scripture is primarily about discovering the presence of a person. Scripture reveals to us who Christ is, who God is personally. As an inspired book, it places us in living contact with the presence of God, enlightening us and strengthening the desires of our heart by grace. Scripture, then, is first and foremost a mystery that we live, and only secondarily a book that we subject to

22. Aquinas, *ST* III, q. 42, a. 4.

historical scrutiny. The latter is entirely warranted but if we begin only from that perspective, we lose sight of the essence.

Hans Urs von Balthasar speaks here of scripture safeguarding the "form of Christ," by which he means that it was written to reveal to us the determinate identity of the Son of God as a singular person who lived among us in Israel two thousand years ago. Jesus Christ is himself God, who took on our human form, who suffered, died, and was buried, who is resurrected from the dead physically, is glorified, and is now present to the Church.[23] Scripture brings human beings into living contact with this same Christ who speaks to the Church, with God who speaks to Israel. The Bible acts as a norm, then, by which we are confronted with revelation continually: divine teaching, not human convention, the challenging moral teachings of Christ, not our own half-enlightened moral intuitions—the real identity of God, not our own projections. If scripture is at the heart of our intellectual life, we are constantly challenged to question conventions and transcend our ordinary human expectations and presuppositions. Christ is the measure and guide of human experience, and not the inverse.

Believing this entails belief in historical truths of the Bible: there was an ancient people of Israel who was called into a covenant by God through Abraham and Moses. There were inspired prophets who followed in their wake. Christ, who was God made man, was crucified under Pontius Pilate and rose from the dead. He did appoint apostles, making Peter their head, and instituted sacraments of the New Law. In doing so he founded the Catholic Church.[24]

---

23. Hans Urs von Balthasar, *Does Jesus Know Us? Do We Know Him?*, trans. G. Harrison (San Francisco: Ignatius, 1983); *The Glory of the Lord, A Theological Aesthetics*, vol. 1: *Seeing the Form*, trans. E. Leiva-Merikakis (San Francisco: Ignatius, 1982).

24. See in this respect, the historical work of exegetes such as Marie-Joseph Lagrange, Roland de Vaux, Pierre Benoit, N. T. Wright, Larry Hurtado, and Richard Bauckham.

But here we should make two qualifying remarks: *first*, modern biblical scholarship, when done well, achieves modest results. Biblical scholarship can neither disprove nor prove the core tenets of Christian belief. One can demonstrate beyond reasonable doubt, for example, that there was an ancient nation of Israelites, that certain members of this group were believed to be prophets, that this people believed itself called into a covenant with God, that Jesus of Nazareth existed, that he made some fairly exalted claims about himself, that he was killed by Roman crucifixion, that some of his followers truly believed that they encountered him physically alive after he had been put to death, that the early Christian movement worshiped Jesus as God. None of this is trivial, but none of it proves that Christianity is true either. For that, supernatural faith is necessary because the subject matter of Christianity is a mystery that transcends natural human reason. Even people in Jesus' own day who saw or heard him needed grace to believe in him. As St. Paul says of himself before his conversion: "we once regarded Christ from a human point of view."[25]

Still, biblical scholarship is far from useless. On the contrary, it teaches us to understand the books of the Bible — their composition and the events that lie behind them — in a nuanced, historically sophisticated way. It does not tell us per se whether divine revelation is real, but if we accept the revelation, it can teach us how to believe in the Bible in a realistic, historically reasonable way.

This protects us against irrational notions of inspiration. These usually originate from some version of dictation theory, wherein a book is said to be composed immediately by God or an angel, without a human author. In this case, the language and concepts of the book inevitably are said to have no human historical origin or sociological context. Therefore, the text cannot be analyzed historically, if this means examining the human authorship and

25. 2 Cor 5:16.

25

cultural context. Such dictation theories are prevalent in both Islam and Mormonism, as well as certain forms of Christianity: they present us with a kind of fundamentalism that forbids rational study of the text on theological grounds, forbidding us to consider the human authors, the historical setting, or the literary genera. This kind of ahistoricism is unrealistic and leads quickly into ideological dead-ends. It sows confusion within a given religious tradition, and frequently gives rise to a counter-reaction: the intellectual rejection of religion. Fundamentalism taken as a form of religious purism ironically is often the cause of atheism.

The Bible is a divinely inspired book which has God as its origin, but is also a human book, and its humanity needs to be taken seriously. The Word has become flesh, in history and time, and this incarnational realism is reflected in the composition of the scriptures as well. The Holy Spirit is the principal author of scripture, but he works in and through genuinely human, historical authors.

Second, the Bible contains historical affirmations that are essential, but it contains many other forms of thought as well: metaphysical truths, ethical teachings and moral examples, symbolic discourse, love poetry, practical wisdom, theological doctrines. The first three chapters of Genesis, for example, teach us that God created the physical world, that the order of the world reflects the divine wisdom, that God is in no way the author of moral evil, that the human being is made in the image of God and has a spiritual soul, and that the human race was created in a state of grace but forfeited the privileges of this state through some kind of primeval act of disobedience.[26] These teachings are primarily metaphysical in kind. They have historical implications, and implicitly commit the Catholic Church to historical teachings of a

26. See on this subject, Joseph Ratzinger, *"In the Beginning": A Catholic Understanding of the Story of Creation and the Fall*, trans. B. Ramsey (Grand Rapids, Mich.: Eerdmans, 1995).

kind (such as the reality of a historical fall from grace), but it is an error to call this kind of narrative a "history" in the modern sense of the term. As Augustine pointed out in his disputes with Faustus the Manichaean, many people reject the Old Testament because they interpret it wrongly, failing to grasp its symbolic and spiritual senses. But when it is read according to the classical rules of the Church (which focus attention on the typological and metaphysical teachings of the Bible), then it is understood to be a deeply insightful, intellectually realistic book that can enrich human reflection over centuries.

The Catholic Church formulates the doctrine of scriptural inspiration in this way:

> Since everything asserted by the inspired authors or sacred writers must be held to be asserted by the Holy Spirit, it follows that the books of Scripture must be acknowledged as teaching solidly, faithfully and without error that truth which God wanted put into sacred writings for the sake of salvation. Therefore "all Scripture is divinely inspired and has its use for teaching the truth and refuting error, for reformation of manners and discipline in right living, so that the man who belongs to God may be efficient and equipped for good work of every kind" (2 Tim. 3:16–17). However, since God speaks in Sacred Scripture through men in human fashion, the interpreter of Sacred Scripture, in order to see clearly what God wanted to communicate to us, should carefully investigate what meaning the sacred writers really intended, and what God wanted to manifest by means of their words.[27]

The teaching here is that the scriptures are inspired by God in their entirety and teach infallibly all the truth that God has willed to reveal for our salvation. At the same time, God reveals himself through the medium of human authors, so we need to take seriously the diverse literary genres of the books of the Bible, and the discernible intentions of the sacred authors. Sacred truth is frequently communicated in highly symbolic fashion in the

27. Second Vatican Council, *Dei Verbum*, November 18, 1965, pars. 11–12; available at www.vatican.va.

first twelve chapters of Genesis (which contains archetypes like Noah or the tower of Babel). The legal writing of Deuteronomy in sixth-century B.C. is different from the Greco-Roman style of the Gospels in first-century A.D. The letters of Paul to local churches constitute a different form of writing from the apocalyptic narrative of John in the book of Revelation.

God speaks to the Church, however, in and through the whole of divine revelation. To understand scripture rightly, then, the Catholic Church insists on three theological criteria. The first is scriptural unity: the books of the Old Testament should be interpreted in light of the revelation of the New Testament, and each book of the Bible must be interpreted coherently in relation to the teaching of all the others. God speaks to us in a coherent, unified way through the manifold witness of all the sacred authors. The second is consonance with tradition: the Bible is received as the Word of God down through time in and through the tradition of the Catholic Church, and is rightly understood in the light of that tradition (a point I will return to below). The third is the "analogy of faith": the mysteries of faith need to be understood in the light of one another. The mystery of the Incarnation has to be understood in relation to God's election of the people of Israel (and vice versa). The mystery of the Eucharist has to be understood in relation to the mystery of the Incarnation. The mystery of the Church has to be understood in relation to the mystery of the Eucharist, and so on.

The Church also speaks traditionally about diverse "senses of scripture." The Bible has a literal sense and various spiritual senses, which are termed moral, typological, and anagogical.[28] The moral sense teaches us how we are to live. The typological sense refers to Christ as the fulfillment of the old covenant. The anagogical sense refers us to the end times, or to the last things, the final state of the world. Take as an example the Paschal Lamb

28. *Catechism of the Catholic Church*, pars. 117–18.

narrative from Exodus 12. The literal sense refers to an ancient liturgical practice (the sacrifice and ritual eating of a lamb) which the Israelites offered to God each year to commemorate their historical liberation from enslavement in Egypt. The moral sense denotes the divine obligation given to the ancient Hebrews to obey the terms of the covenant with God so that they might live in friendship with him, and be assured of his mercy. The typological sense refers to Christ, who is denoted in John's Gospel as the "Lamb of God, who takes away the sin of the world."[29] It is his Passover offering to the Father in the crucifixion that actively redeems humanity. His sacrifice recapitulates the Paschal Lamb symbolism and orders it toward a universal horizon. The anagogical sense is found in the book of Revelation, which depicts Christ in glory as the "Lamb who was slain," but who is now alive again, receiving the praise of the saints in heaven.[30] The final "Passover" is from our earthly state to the state of glory. These various senses of scripture teach us to read the Bible as a book concerned with our concrete salvation. The literal sense typically denotes the sacred events of salvation history. These events themselves point forward mysteriously to fulfillment in Christ and in the Church. The mystery of Christ and the Church in turn points forward to the life of the world to come. The moral sense, meanwhile, teaches us how we are to live spiritually in response to the grace of God, in the midst of our present world.

Why is the interpretation of the Bible so complicated, though? Shouldn't the religious truth we seek be simpler, more direct? Aren't Christians simply making excuses theologically for the all-too-human fragmentation or diversity of sources we find in this book? Not necessarily. After all, only an intellectually profound book is worthy of the sustained attention of every human culture and prolonged efforts of understanding. Simplicity is

29. Jn 1:29.
30. Rv 5:12.

dangerous in religious matters, except when it is conditioned by a strong dose of qualification. One can affirm simply that the New Testament teaches that Jesus is God, but this simple truth needs qualification. The four Gospels teach it in manifold and often only implicit ways. As Origen pointed out in the third century, the scriptures are complex from a literary, historical, and theological point of view precisely so that we are invited to think more deeply about their internal content.[31] This spurs on human thought, and makes Christianity the most intellectual of religions. God inspired a book because he wanted human co-operation in thinking about divine truth, not because he wanted anti-intellectualism and human abdication. This way of redeeming man makes him use his mind, not abandon it, which is the only real way religion could make any sense.

Likewise, we can say with Aquinas that "grace does not destroy nature, but perfects it."[32] The Bible is a book of human authors as well as of the Holy Spirit. Consequently, it is the product of a vast human religious culture with its internal traditions, external influences, occasional crises, and its moments of intellectual resolution. It is this richness of human experience that is inspired, not a magical world of authors removed from normal human life and

31. Origen, *On First Principles*, preface, and IV, 1–2; IV, 2, 8–9: "Although it is the Holy Spirit's purpose to enlighten holy souls, which have dedicated themselves to the service of the truth, concerning such matters and to others like them, He has in the second place an aim in regard to those who either cannot or will not give themselves to the effort and diligence by which they might deserve to be taught or to know matters so great and excellent.... His aim is to envelop and hide secret mysteries in ordinary words under the pretext of a narrative of some kind and of an account of visible things .... For this reason the divine wisdom has arranged for there to be certain stumbling blocks, or interruptions of the narrative meaning ... so that the very interruption of the narrative might oppose the reader, as it were, with certain obstacles thrown in the way. By them wisdom denies a way and an access to the common understanding ... so that by gaining a higher and loftier road through entering a narrow footpath it may open for us the immense breadth of divine knowledge." *Origen: An Exhortation to Martyrdom, Prayer, and Selected Works*, trans. R. Greer (New York: Paulist Press, 1979).

32. *ST* I, q. 1, a. 8.

its circumstances. As Austin Farrer once noted, the Bible is like a love-letter written by a soldier fighting in trenches on the battle-field. There is some blood and dirt on it and the paper is torn, but the message is beautiful and we can understand it.[33] The divine word speaks to us truly, but does so through the gritty reality of human historical life.

Teaching Authority:
Tradition and the Magisterium

Already in the second century, Irenaeus of Lyons pointed out the importance of Catholic tradition and magisterial authority during the controversy with Gnosticism. The gnostic Christ, he noted, is a caricature completely incompatible with the canonical portrait of Christ in the four Gospels. The texts of scripture can be rearranged just like the tiles in a visual mosaic of Christ, so that they no longer present an image of the God-man, but an image of a dog.[34] What prevents this misuse of the apostolic teaching is the living authority of the successors of the apostles. Among those, the one that is most prominent is the bishop of Rome, successor of both Peter and Paul.

33. "What is the Bible like? Like a letter that a soldier wrote to his wife about the disposition of his affairs and the care of his children in case he should chance to be killed. And the next day he was shot, and died, and the letter was torn and stained with his blood. Her friends said to the woman: the letter is of no binding force; it is not a legal will and it is so injured by the accidents of the writer's death you cannot even prove what it means. But she said: I know the man and I am satisfied I can see what he means. And I shall do it because it is what he wanted me to do, and because he died the next day." Austin Marsden Farrer, *Love's Redeeming Work: The Anglican Quest for Holiness*, ed. G. Rowell, K. Stevenson, and R. Williams (Oxford: Oxford University Press, 2004), 661.

34. Irenaeus, *Against Heresies* I, 8: "Their manner of acting is just as if one, when a beautiful image of a king has been constructed by some skillful artist out of precious jewels, should then take this likeness of the man all to pieces, should rearrange the gems, and so fit them together as to make them into the form of a dog or of a fox, and even that but poorly executed."

[We do this, I say,] by indicating that tradition derived from the apostles, of the very great, the very ancient, and universally known Church founded and organized at Rome by the two most glorious apostles, Peter and Paul; as also [by pointing out] the faith preached to men, which comes down to our time by means of the successions of the bishops. For it is a matter of necessity that every Church should agree with this Church, on account of its preeminent authority, that is, the faithful everywhere, inasmuch as the tradition has been preserved continuously by those [faithful men] who exist everywhere.[35]

Irenaeus goes on to list the bishops of Rome who have succeeded Peter and Paul down to his own day.[36] Here, then, we see already the normative teaching of the Church formulated theologically as early as 175 A.D.

35. Ibid., III, 3, 2.

36. Ibid., III, 3, 3: "The blessed apostles, then, having founded and built up the Church, committed into the hands of Linus the office of the episcopate. Of this Linus, Paul makes mention in the Epistles to Timothy. To him succeeded Anacletus; and after him, in the third place from the apostles, Clement was allotted the bishopric. This man, as he had seen the blessed apostles, and had been conversant with them, might be said to have the preaching of the apostles still echoing [in his ears], and their traditions before his eyes. Nor was he alone [in this], for there were many still remaining who had received instructions from the apostles. In the time of this Clement, no small dissension having occurred among the brethren at Corinth, the Church in Rome dispatched a most powerful letter to the Corinthians, exhorting them to peace, renewing their faith, and declaring the tradition which it had lately received from the apostles, proclaiming the one God, omnipotent, the Maker of heaven and earth, the Creator of man, who brought on the deluge, and called Abraham, who led the people from the land of Egypt, spoke with Moses, set forth the law, sent the prophets, and who has prepared fire for the devil and his angels. From this document, whosoever chooses to do so, may learn that He, the Father of our Lord Jesus Christ, was preached by the Churches, and may also understand the tradition of the Church, since this Epistle is of older date than these men who are now propagating falsehood, and who conjure into existence another god beyond the Creator and the Maker of all existing things. To this Clement there succeeded Evaristus. Alexander followed Evaristus; then, sixth from the apostles, Sixtus was appointed; after him, Telephorus, who was gloriously martyred; then Hyginus; after him, Pius; then after him, Anicetus. Soter having succeeded Anicetus, Eleutherius does now, in the twelfth place from the apostles, hold the inheritance of the episcopate. In this order, and by this succession, the ecclesiastical tradition from the apostles, and the preaching of the truth, have come down to us. And this is most abundant proof that there is one and the same vivifying faith, which has been preserved in the Church from the apostles until now, and handed down in truth."

But if scripture really is the word of God, why should the Church stand in need of tradition and a visible teaching authority? The reason is that scripture is an inspired book but is still "merely" a book. In the memorial words of Newman: "the Bible does not answer a purpose for which it was never intended," that is to say, it was not adequate on its own to "make a stand against the wild living intellect of man," and assure doctrinal continuity in the Church amidst the "anarchical world" of human history.[37] This is where tradition and the magisterial authority of the Catholic Church have an essential role to play.

Sacred tradition, as Yves Congar noted, is multilayered.[38] Certainly it entails the traditional dogmas and doctrines of the Catholic Church, which are employed to protect truth and promote true interpretations of scripture. But it also includes the teachings of great theologians, doctors of the Church, and saints which, while not necessarily infallible in all their details, act as tested resources for understanding more deeply the teachings of the faith. Tradition is not only about ideas. It also entails the sacred *practices* of the Church: her living celebration of the sacraments, the sacred liturgy, the moral virtues of the Church, her varied spiritual devotions and artistic customs, and commonsense wisdom found in her members, or embodied in ecclesiastical law. In all this complexity we find differing kinds of authority present, but also a beautiful and perennial spirit of unity across many ages and in varied cul-

37. John Henry Newman, *Apologia Pro Vita Sua* (New York: Penguin, 2004), 219: "The judgment, which experience passes whether on establishments or on education, as a means of maintaining religious truth in this anarchical world, must be extended even to Scripture, though Scripture be divine. Experience proves surely that the Bible does not answer a purpose for which it was never intended. It may be accidentally the means of the conversion of individuals; but a book, after all, cannot make a stand against the wild living intellect of man, and in this day it begins to testify, as regards its own structure and contents, to the power of that universal solvent, which is so successfully acting upon religious establishments."

38. See Yves Congar, *Tradition and Traditions: The Biblical, Historical, and Theological Evidence for Catholic Teaching on Tradition*, trans. M. Naseby and T. Rainborough (London: Burns and Oates, 1966).

tures. This constancy and universality of the Catholic tradition are features that no historian can fail to notice. They are striking testimonies to the enduring homogeneity and continuity of Catholic teaching, life, and practice across time. Moreover, Catholic tradition in no way undermines the true interpretation of scripture. On the contrary, precisely because of its vitality and essential identity maintained down through the ages, the tradition promotes the true knowledge of scripture in a uniquely exalted way that would be impossible in its absence.

Nor can critics of Catholic tradition avoid making use of some kind of tradition of their own. On a practical level, the rejection of tradition is not a realistic option for anyone who takes scripture seriously. For as soon as we begin to articulate what we think scripture means (or any other book for that matter), we inevitably set a precedent that can be accepted, denied, or qualified by another. In this way, every text that has a seminal role in human culture also acquires traditions of interpretation down through time, and these are embodied in turn in living communities that promote them or distort them, alter them creatively or develop them homogeneously, reject them or maintain them. This "context" of the text is the wild living mind of man referred to by Newman. To remain constant in any teaching down through time, any community that wishes to maintain its own unity must not only have principles, but also develop a commonality of vital intellectual teaching that is passed on to others across time and place.

This is why St. Francis de Sales, writing in Geneva in the wake of the Reformation, said that the Catholic Church does not dispute whether scripture is to be read within tradition or to be read outside of it, but whether it is to be read according to the human traditions of a John Calvin (some of whose key teachings function practically as a magisterium of reference for many over centuries) or through recourse to the Catholic tradition and established teachings of the Church.[39] The realistic question is not whether we will have a tradition, but which one are we to have. To expect each person to adjudicate for himself each and every possible Christian teaching within the course of a lifetime is absurd. Consequently, we do depend upon interpretations of others inevitably, and our own interpretations do contribute to those of a larger community. We are bound to receive the greater part of our understanding of revelation from a life in community with others.

Therefore, God has established in the Church from the beginning a living stream of apostolic tradition that is continuously maintained and safeguarded by divinely instituted authority. Had he not done so, a thousand incompatible interpretations of scripture on major issues would proliferate inevitably among Christian believers and splinter them into a disbanded set of divided communities. Furthermore, without such a unified tradition maintained down through time, no one person would ever be able to come to a comprehensive set of judgments about the truths of the faith, simply due to the sheer volume of enigmatic questions posed from theological controversies down through the ages.

The Church is not above scripture. She is only ever subordinate to it. But under the guidance of the Holy Spirit, the Advocate that was promised to her, she is able to resolve disputes about its interpretation progressively so as to build up a collective body of doctrines and practices.[40] These safeguard infallibly the truth of Christ revealed in scripture and in the earliest apostolic teachings. Therefore, "sacred tradition ... and sacred scripture of both the Old and New Testaments are like a mirror in which the pilgrim Church on earth looks at God, from whom she has received everything, until she is brought finally to see Him as He is, face

---

39. Francis de Sales, *The Catholic Controversy*, trans. H. Mackey (Charlotte, N.C.: TAN, 1989), a. 3, chap. 1 (112).

40. On the "advocate" ("Counselor" in the RSV), see Jn 14:16–17, 15:26, 16:7.

to face."[41] By her tradition, the Church remains united, and the Christian faithful are protected from error and can advance in the pathways of charity and holiness without deceit.

Evidently, all of this requires a concrete governmental process to be in place, one that stems from the time of Christ himself and his apostles. This is the office of the episcopacy centered around the bishop of Rome, the pope, who safeguards and promotes the unity of the Church. The episcopal magisterium (teaching office) of the Church existed long before there were councils or dogmas or official doctrines. It is this office of the bishops united with the pope that receives the teaching of the apostolic Church and safeguards it, maintaining the unity of the Church down through the ages.

Infallibility

But what about infallibility? Isn't that an exaggerated claim? To say that the Church's tradition is essential and that visible authorities have an irreplaceable role to play may seem sensible. But claims to infallibility can seem preposterous or pretentious. Can't human beings err, after all, and especially religious leaders? Won't they inevitably do so over a given period of time? Clearly human beings do err and popes and bishops, while sometimes quite holy or learned, can also live lives of impressive moral turpitude or harbor grave theological errors. Taken individually or collectively as human beings, they will err over time, often even in the short term!

But the claim to infallibility, while a bold one, is actually quite sensible in its own way. It is virtually a tautology, in fact, since it amounts to saying nothing more than this: if God has revealed himself, then what he has revealed is true, and the Church can come to know over time in a definitive way what God has re-

41. Second Vatican Council, *Dei Verbum*, no. 7.

vealed. These are not in themselves very astonishing claims. They rest on a more fundamental claim that is: God has revealed himself. But if that has occurred, why would it be so strange that God should assist the Church over time, in and through controversy and dispute, and *despite the terrible moral and intellectual limitations of her adherents*, to come to know the truth he has revealed? What would be stranger—in fact illogical in its own right—would be the claim that God has revealed himself most certainly but that we might just as certainly deny the capacity of the Church to identify his teaching with any certitude. If the Church cannot teach infallibly, then we are in fact required to say something absurd of just this kind. "God has revealed himself, but the Church can never say with assurance what God has revealed." In that case we might claim that there is an infallibly true revelation of God, but we must also admit that we cannot identify it, practically speaking, in any realistic way.

If God has revealed himself to the Church and the Church can identify his teaching infallibly (in however complex a process), we might still wish to deny that this should occur (ultimately) through the office of just one person (the bishop of Rome) as a kind of linchpin in the system. However, that would require us to expand the number of people who are linchpins: perhaps the five patriarchs of the most ancient Christian sees, perhaps all the members of the World Council of Churches, or perhaps all the pastors and theologians we find most intuitively amenable. But as the Dominican theologian John of St. Thomas rightly noted, if we claim that any of these configurations are able to denote for us (through whatever process we suggest) that there are infallible truths of revelation, then we are choosing to believe in a system more complex in some way than that of the Catholic Church and therefore at least as difficult to defend rationally, certainly no easier.[42] For to get five patriarchs, or the leadership council of the

42. On John of St. Thomas's theory of the papacy, see Charles Morerod, *Tra-*

World Council of Churches or a group of Protestant pastors all to teach the same thing definitively and to maintain this over time without error in and through a given tradition is no less difficult (miraculous even) when considered on a merely human level, than for God to inspire the office of the Roman papacy in collegiality with the bishops of the world to maintain the teachings of the apostolic faith homogeneously down through time, advancing truths in a developing but logically consistent way in response to the controversies of the day, or the needs of the age. And indeed, when we go out to consult the evidences of history, what do we see? That the Roman primacy has done just this for two thousand years, in the service of scripture and of Catholic tradition, in order to maintain the unity and holiness of the Catholic Church in a perennial way.

This does not mean that every time a pope speaks his mind or even composes a theological judgment that an instance of infallible teaching occurs. The papal office works toward many ends simultaneously: preserving the Church in the unity of charity, promoting genuine reconciliation among Christians, preaching and teaching the faith, consoling the afflicted, reaching out to the alienated, governing the Church in practical affairs, and giving prescriptions of discipline and asceticism. The office is basically conservative in function, in the sense that it promotes "conservation," much as in an ecological sense. The varied species of the Church's life and customs are preserved and promoted by the papal office, in communion with the bishops. This activity on their part does not replace theology. The popes and bishops may at times indeed be theologians of a very elevated sort, but they are not theologians *qua* bishops and popes. Their role in adjudicating the doctrine of the faith may make use of theological arguments, and they may consult theologians, but their determina-

dition et Unité des Chrétiens: Le dogme comme condition de possibilité de l'oecuménisme (Paris: Parole et Silence, 2005), 155–59.

tions stem from a charism that is given with their office. Indeed, in one sense, episcopal judgments about what pertains to the apostolic deposit of faith are what makes theology possible at all, because they clarify basic truths of the faith that are to be held by all. Theologians in turn can reflect on the meaning, coherence, and implications of the teaching of the Church. And since such judgments are ongoing, the work of theology can assist bishops in making their discernments and give reasons for or against a given development in Church teaching. Catholic theology, then, is both something less than and more than the teaching of the magisterium. It has less authority and exists only in dependence upon the apostolic teaching that the Church promotes. But it can examine this teaching and probe its inner meaning and depth, so as to explore the coherence, implications, and brilliant splendor of the teaching of Christ. Just as the tradition and authority of the Catholic Church are not opposed to the dignity of scripture but promote an authentic understanding of the latter, so they are not inimical to the authentic intellectual life of Catholic theology. On the contrary, they make the intellectual life of Catholic theologians a real possibility.

The Intellectual Form
of Faith: Theology

Theology is as natural as thinking. The first Christian theologians were not academics or research specialists, but ordinary believers trying to understand reality in light of the mystery of Christ. "Reality" includes everything and so it is not surprising that the early Church Fathers typically engaged with contemporary philosophies, as well as the naturalistic and cosmological claims of their age. Typically this stemmed from one of three motives: they sought to explain Christianity to newcomers; they wanted to defend it against its detractors; and/or they were responding to doctrinal controversies (heresies) that arose in the ancient Church. In this sense, theology began from practical necessity as well as a deeper interest in truth. On a most basic level, however, the early patristic writers were simply trying to make sense of things, to explain the "whole" of our lives with reference to Christ, allowing his light to be refracted in and through all the domains of creation and human learning. This vision of theology suggests that it is not a subject only for specialists who are a small minority of Christians, but is something natural to the intellectual life of any serious Christian.

Our intellectual engagement also affects who we become. The human being generally develops spiritually in two ways: through the intellect, and through the will. The intellect is what is most noble in the human being. Growth in understanding perfects the human being. We are duly impressed when people tell us they are physicists or philosophers, because these are subjects of serious difficulty. The will or love of the good is what makes the human person good, and completes or perfects the human being teleologically. We do not call people "good" simply because they are learned, but because they show compassion, empathy, virtue—because they are kind and are true friends. Human beings are made both to know the truth, and to become genuinely good through spiritual love. This is what makes them both noble and good. But these two developments depend upon each other in key ways: knowledge without love is sterile and cold, but love without knowledge lacks integrity, and is often superficial. Study of theological truth allows us to see the reasons for what we believe, deepens our convictions, and helps us to explain the integrity, coherence, and relevance of Christian belief. It also helps Christian love to take on a solidity and depth that are abiding.

Theology is a science in the sense that it has a proper object of study: the mystery of God made available in divine revelation.[43]

43. Thus Aquinas, *ST* I, q. 1.

This science differs from all others because its first principles are derived from God revealing himself in Christ, something that transcends the limitations of natural human reason. The perspective that theology gives us in turn allows us to understand all things in light of the God of revelation, since God is the source of all that exists. If we take this approach, then we can see right away that there can be no genuine conflict between theology and the sound conclusions of any other "science" (whether philosophical or modern scientific), because these sciences deal with truths about what exists, about what God has created. Their true conclusions can be understood "from on high" in light of a higher or deeper knowledge concerning the mystery of God. But if all that exists comes from the Holy Trinity, then nothing we discover in reality can stand in contradiction to the divinely revealed truth about God. Seemingly irresolvable conflicts of faith and reason, when rightly understood, are always in the end pseudo-problems.

What kinds of topics does theology treat, then? What problems does it solve? What questions could we possibly ask that it might profitably answer? The first answer is: it tells us who God is. Not as we could know God by our own natural powers, through philosophical speculation. On that level, we can come to know that God exists, but what God is in himself remains largely hidden from us, due to divine transcendence. Christian theology, however, considers who God is in himself, in his own inner life. The mystery of the Trinity is the primary mystery in Christianity, because it concerns who God is and the fact that God has willed to offer us knowledge of himself, and even participation in his own divine life by grace: "he has granted to us his precious and very great promises, that through these you may escape from the corruption that is in the world because of passion, and become partakers of the divine nature."[44]

From this first starting point, it is clear that theology also must

44. 2 Pt 1:3–4.

treat some other key topics. Can one really believe in the Trinity and still be a monotheist? How so? Does the New Testament really affirm unambiguously that Jesus is God the Son made man? If so, why did God become a human being? Is that an intelligible assertion? If God has become human, why is the world plagued with ongoing moral struggle and evil? What is a human being? Are we really capable of life with God or is that an illusory religious claim? If we are able to live life in the grace of Christ, what are we to make of our moral mediocrity and sin? How should we rightly understand the atonement of Christ, his redemptive death? Do we have to believe that God punished Christ, or is that an erroneous way of thinking? What use or real effects does the death of Christ have in our lives? How is it related to the sacraments and their effects on us? Is it intelligible to believe in transubstantiation? What is the proper effect of the grace of the Eucharist, when we take communion in a properly disposed state? And what about people who do not have any knowledge of Christ or the sacraments, or who are not Christian? Can we believe that they might still receive grace from God? How so? What are we to reasonably expect at the end of our lives? Is there life after death? Does the soul continue to exist after the demise of the body, and if so, how could this be a happy thing? Can we really believe in purgatory as a biblical notion, and if it is real, is it something we could reasonably desire? Perhaps most practically, if Christianity is true, then how should we live in this world? What does it mean to acquire virtues and avoid vices, and how can we be happy and reasonably productive in this life as Christians?

These are only some examples of basic theological questions. They are not reserved to theologians. Intellectually serious Catholics need to come to terms with them. Behind these examples, what is at stake is our knowledge and experience of divine love. We want to get right who God is, and what the mystery of Christ is, so that we can be in living contact with divine love. This knowledge is also essential so that we can speak to others about Christ and the Catholic faith in a coherent and serene way, but also as people who are intellectually happy. Theology is never reducible to the utilitarian function of apologetics. Theology is about happiness. Happiness is as much in the intellect as in the heart, and it stems from understanding the truth about ultimate things, and being headed in the right direction, being oriented existentially. We derive our moral stability in large part from having a perspective on the world that is realistic and profound. Happiness for Aristotle is unimpeded activity. The highest, most vivifying thing we can do is contemplate the truth. So understanding God deeply and rightly in light of revelation gives the intellect unimpeded activity and liveliness about what is most ultimate. It also gives us the stability of seeing things in perspective, and a peace that cannot be diminished even in the midst of the trials and travails of life. What grim stoicism and utilitarian efficacy cannot deliver, the work of theology can: the serenity of rest in God himself.

The idea of leaving our intellect behind to become spiritual is very strange and inhuman. However, it is a view that is very widespread, sometimes in conservative Christian circles, but more often in liberal Protestant and Catholic spheres. The vulgar commonplace form is the saying "I'm spiritual but not religious." The idea is that dogma constricts, and that religious practices blind us to the fact that God is larger than our conceptions and rituals. Spiritual people transcend the limits of dogma, creed, and regulation to live on a higher plane of spiritual awareness or a unity with God and others that is beyond all concepts. In fact, that is a very anti-intellectual viewpoint, marked by a latent despair of finding the truth about God.

But what about the counter-charge? Don't religious intellectuals simply seek to trap God within the constraint of their manmade systems? It is true that our conceptual knowledge is partial and that the mystery of God is not reducible to our partial knowledge of God's mystery. But we only aim rightly at God in and through our real knowledge of God, and this does entail language, concepts, thinking, and acting in ways that integrate us into the life of the Church. In other words, to live spiritually for God we need to make right use of dogma and theology. The early twentieth-century Catholic Modernist movement claimed that profound religious experience always transcends dogmas and relativizes them. This idea is based, however, on a superficial notion of mystery. Religious experience does not take place merely in our conceptions of the truth (as if holding to Church dogmas were somehow a sufficiently spiritual act), but it also does not take place by transcending conceptions either (as if giving up dogmas of faith were a super-spiritual act of mental asceticism). The goal, in fact, is to pass through the dogmas to the mystery that they signify, and to find God in and through the true teachings of scripture and tradition. Dogma is the guardian of mystery. It alerts us to its presence, and orients us toward God in constructive ways.

Some people see religious discipline as a constraint because it makes us engage in liturgical worship. Here again, however, the oppositional thinking is mistaken. The Church is liturgical not so as to limit our experience of Christ, but precisely so as to facilitate it. Human beings only ever express themselves meaningfully in language and gestures and depend upon them to live well with others. We pray better when we pray with our whole selves, body and soul, which entails using the senses, the body, visual art, music, and corporate worship. To deny this is to deny our animal nature and to fall into an unrealistic angelicism. The genius of Catholicism, like the Judaism from which it springs, is to be about the whole person, body and soul. The Word became flesh, and it is in our flesh that we return to God, in a corporate religious life in the Church. Our intellectual life needs to be grounded, then, in this reality, where we can become more realistic about the nature of our relationship with God, and so flourish. Otherwise, the danger is that we fall into a kind of pseudo-spiritual dilettantism that does not take seriously what it means to be a human being and a religious intellectual.

Prayer and asceticism, then, are part of the Catholic *intellectual* life. Disciplines of soul and disciplines of the mind go together. One of the most attractive things about the Catholic intellectual vocation is that it calls us to be people of a holistic integrity. Every facet of our life needs to come progressively into the light of Christ, not so that it may perish but so that we may live in a more truly human and divine way. When human beings are integrated morally, intellectually, and spiritually, their intellectual concerns and their moral pattern of life cohere. Their artistic sense and their capacity for self-giving are united. Their forms of recreation and rest are in harmony with their sense of worship and commitment. Their relationships of human love are deeply related to their aspiration to divine love.

This kind of integrity is rare in the world today, where we are constantly confronted with stories about morally divided lives, not only of people in positions of ecclesial responsibility but also among secular academics, political leaders, and increasingly so in the lives of ordinary people, especially in the tragic erosion of marriage in our society. De-Christianization leads to re-paganization. We begin to serve multiple gods and suffer the division of our selves. Without the grace of Christ, the "integration" of the human person is made more difficult, and even on many levels impossible.

The intellectual life of the human being needs to be coupled with an inner life: worship, prayer, the search for God's mercy, and the pursuit of Christian virtue. But we also need external forms of asceticism: the liturgy of the Church, regular sacramental practice including regular confession, prayer that makes use of the liturgy of the hours or devotional practices, commitment to the authorities of the Church and her forms of ordered common life. This is actually also all part of the intellectual life because it keeps us grounded: it ties us to others in ways that are corporate, that act as a check on our egoism but also open us up to a truth larger than ourselves and to a form of living that stimulates our reflection more deeply. The Church provides us with a storehouse of living wisdom, and it is in being connected to her life, and to fellow Christian thinkers, that we are likely to grow best intellectually.

This is also an important form of witness in our world today. Missionary spirit need not always be outward turned. Our own conversion to an integrity of life, especially an intellectual life of faith, is one that speaks to our contemporaries, who so often are bereft of orientation and who are on some level seeking a deeper meaning that only Christ can give them. To be a living member of the Church in our own times, then, is a witness to the world around us. For this, the pursuit of theological wisdom is essential.

Without genuine knowledge, no real love is possible. We cannot love what we do not know. And so, likewise loving God in the truth depends upon understanding God truly. The study of theology can detract from Christian love if it leads to the loss of faith, or becomes a formal academic exercise devoid of existential conviction. But as Aquinas notes, the study of theology can also be genuinely "meritorious": it can stem from charity, and can also intensify love, as we draw closer to what we know.[45] In fact, when we begin to love others, we seek to get to know them better, and even "study them in love" in a certain way. This is true not only in our natural experience, but also in the domain of supernatural life. Intellectual engagement with the Christian faith is essential to our personal relationship with Christ.

45. Aquinas, *ST* II-II, q. 2, a. 10.

2

GOD AND TRINITY

Who Is God?

The Nicene Creed teaches that God is the Holy Trinity: Father, Son, and Holy Spirit. Often, however, even Christians resist thinking about this belief. Sometimes we hear a person say, "it is simply a mystery to be believed." Many wonder if belief in the Trinity is even intelligible, edging toward a conclusion critics of Christianity often draw, which is that our faith is irrational and absurd. Do we believe *because* it's absurd? Obviously not.

This raises a key question, *the* key question: what is God? What does it mean to say that the three persons of the Trinity are the one true God, creator of heaven and earth? Does it imply that "the Son" is the physical offspring of God, as the Koran repeatedly states? Even if we reject that view as mistaken, we are still faced with a nagging uncertainty. The early Church's first councils were called to settle controversies about the nature of God. They were moments of intense debate and even open conflict. Why this passion about such a seemingly abstruse conception of God as Father, Son, and Holy Spirit? Is the doctrine of the Trinity based on the New Testament? Some modern biblical scholars say "no." Can one believe in the Trinity and be a true monotheist? For two thousand years, Jewish critics have said "no." And that answer seems only too plausible! Isn't the idea of a communion of three Trinitarian persons opposed to the affirmation of the existence of one God and creator? These are the kinds of questions that conspire in the minds of Christians to make any reflection on the God proclaimed by the universal Church a daunting prospect.

And yet any intellectually serious Christian must think about God. Our belief in the Trinity is *the* central feature of the Christian faith, even more fundamental than belief in grace, the precept to love others as Christ loves them, or the belief in the atonement of Christ. Moreover, this teaching about God as Father, Son, and Holy Spirit is *not* abstruse or remote. This mystery is *the single most practical truth* available to human beings. It tells us what is ultimately real. The light of the Trinity illuminates everything.

Affective and Theoretical Knowledge

We can think about the Trinity in two basic ways. First, we can start with our concrete, personal, affective relationship to God whom we encounter and know in the faith as Father, Son, and Holy Spirit. This is an interpersonal knowledge of "I and Thou." We might call this "intuitive second-person knowledge" of the mystery of God, as when we say to God: "You, Almighty Father, have revealed yourself to me in Christ." "Oh Holy Spirit of Christ, enlighten and sanctify us!" Second, we can focus on our speculative understanding of God as we consider the mystery theologically. How do we analyze the mystery of Father, Son, and Spirit as the one God?

These two pathways of affective knowledge and intellectual theory are distinct but not separable. In fact, they are deeply interrelated to one another. Consider an analogy to human relationships. It is one thing to come to know another person well in friendship, and another thing to reflect philosophically on the nature of human friendship. The relational, affective knowledge is primary because it is the lived experience of friendship which is irreplaceable, but our own theoretical understanding of friendship not only allows us to analyze what friendship really is, but also can help us live out friendship more perfectly. Heart and intelligence go together. So likewise with the Trinity, supernatural faith alerts us to the real presence of the Father, manifest in the Son made man, and to the gift of the Holy Spirit present in the Church, who dwells in our hearts by grace. This is a mystical reality that is primary, and is simply given to us to know by grace. We can become more and more aware of it over time through the deepening of our life of faith, interior prayer, and religious worship. However, knowing the Trinity personally, in the darkness of faith, we are also invited into the active consideration of the mystery, the intellectual reflection of theology.

The great works of reflection on the Trinity in the early Church—those of Irenaeus, Gregory of Nazianzus, Augustine, and others—are living meditations that spring from the inner life of faith, and from reflection on scripture and Church doctrine. They are profound intellectual works, but they are also grounded in a deeper mystical life and spiritual aspiration. Gregory and Augustine were trying to find union with God. The idea of study here is not a mere academic exercise. It allows us to grasp better who it is that we know in the faith and what we worship, to understand how this highest mystery of the faith illumines all other knowledge and understanding of the created world.

Hans Urs von Balthasar speaks here of doing theology on one's knees.[1] It is said of the great twentieth-century Swiss ecclesiologist Charles Journet that he stopped at regular intervals to pray before the tabernacle containing the Eucharist as he was compos-

---

1. See Hans Urs von Balthasar, "Theology and Sanctity," in *Explorations in Theology* I: *The Word Made Flesh*, trans. V. Littledale and A. Dru (San Francisco: Ignatius, 1989), 181–209.

ing his theological books. This idea of a "theology of union" or of a theology composed in and for the spiritual life of Christians is basically normative. For the Christian faith, knowledge cannot be separated from love and is always related to it integrally. As Aquinas says, "formed" faith is faith enlivened by charity, without which our faith (perhaps even very intellectually erudite and nuanced) is dead or lifeless.[2] At the same time, we have to insist that theology looks at questions of truth that have an integrity of their own, that are not reducible to the piety and emotional life of believers. Love without a transparent sense of responsibility to the truth usually degrades into sentiment, delusion, or cultural nostalgia. If theology is prayerful and spiritual, it is also probing, analytic, and rigorous in its own right. Theology has to be subject to real challenges and engagements with its external critics as well as with its own deepest internal intellectual struggles and enigmas. Thinking about the Trinity, then, is a spiritual exercise, but it is also a speculative one, and it is above all a search to find the fullness of the truth about God, unabated light free from all error. This search for the unalloyed truth is also itself a very profound element within the spiritual life. After all, Christ himself claims to be "the truth" who alone "will make you free."[3] The search for the God of Christianity is a search for the fullness of the truth. Otherwise it has no real purpose.

A Basic Statement of Trinitarian Faith

Before we treat the mystery of the Trinity theologically it is helpful to give a basic dogmatic statement of faith, so as to indicate an initial pathway, as it were, into the mystery. Here we should note four basic claims.

---

2. Aquinas, *ST* II-II, q. 4, aa. 3–4.
3. Jn 14:6, 8:32.

1. There exists one God who is the creator of all things, who has revealed himself first to the people of Israel, and finally most perfectly in the person of Jesus Christ. Christianity is therefore utterly monotheistic.

2. God has revealed in the New Testament that there is in his eternal life a communion of persons: Father, Son, and Holy Spirit. The persons are truly distinct, such that the Father is not the Son or the Spirit, the Son is not the Father or the Spirit, and the Spirit is not the Father or the Son. God is a trinity of persons.

3. Each of the persons is truly God. They each possess the plenitude of the divine nature and are one in being. Therefore, they have one will and one activity. When God creates or sanctifies, it is the Trinity that creates or sanctifies, and never simply one of the persons acting alone.

4. The Trinity is a mystery known to us only by divine revelation, but it does in turn cast light on all our other knowledge about the world. The doctrine manifests to us that there is in God a transcendent mystery of communion-in-love that is inexpressibly higher and more perfect than any human love. This divine love is the fundamental ground of all things, such that the Trinity created the world in light of the eternal love that the Father has for the Son in the Holy Spirit. Created persons were made in the image of God, and are meant to participate in the charity of God, the love that he has for us individually and collectively. For Christians, then, personhood is something primal to all reality. In the beginning there was personhood. God is a trinity of persons and he created the natural order in view of the communion of human persons with him, in the order of grace.

We can expand this set of claims by asking how it is that God is truly one in being and at the same time three persons who are truly distinct? Traditionally, the Church distinguishes here between one divine "nature" and three divine "persons." Consider an analogy to human persons. Three human persons each share a common human nature. That is to say, they are three persons who are the same *kind of thing* (a human being, a rational animal). In this case, there are three "whos" and only one "what," three persons who have one nature. However, there are three distinct beings, not one being. Three human persons do not have one individualized nature, but are three distinct individual human beings. So by analogy in God there are three "whos" (divine persons) who each partake fully of the divine nature, that is, they are each "what" God is: the eternal all-powerful creator. The difference, of course, is that while three human persons have one nature, they are also three distinct individual beings. God the Holy Trinity, however, is one being, who is three persons, each person being himself the one God, and having the fullness of the divine nature.

There is a complementary way of thinking about this mystery by comparison with the spiritual activities of a single human person, which is typically termed the "psychological analogy" for Trinitarian life. The eternal Father is the source of the eternal Son by way of generation. This generation is not physical but wholly spiritual. The Son is the eternally begotten "Word," or "reason," of God, in similarity to the way a concept proceeds forth from a human mind that gives rise to it. The Holy Spirit is the love that proceeds from the Father and the Son, just as human love proceeds forth from knowledge: when we know something we may come to love it. So the Father begetting the eternal Son and spirating the eternal Spirit is akin to the Father contemplating his eternal spiritual Word and loving the Word in his eternal Spirit who is love.

We should note that this second analogy works in an almost inverse fashion to the first. In the first comparison to three human persons, we noted that God is a communion of three persons who share the same nature, but corrected this analogy by noting that the three persons in God are so deeply united as to be one in being. In this second analogy from human knowledge and love, we considered God as one person who has a fullness of knowledge and love, but we must also correct this analogy by noting that *in God* the Word that the Father begets in his act of knowing (i.e., the Son) is a person distinct from the Father, and the Spirit who proceeds from the Father and the Word as love is a person distinct from the Father and the Son. The first analogy "breaks down" due to unity: God is a unity of persons in a way that three human persons are not. The second "breaks down" due to the real distinction of persons: in human beings, the inner life of knowledge and love is proper to one person alone. (I alone experience personally from within my own knowledge and love.) In God the inner life of knowledge and love consists of a distinction of persons in communion. Each analogy is a corrective to the other, because God is truly one in being, like a single activity of knowledge and love, and God is truly a communion of persons having one nature, like three human persons.

Each of these comparisons allows us to think about how God the Holy Trinity invites human beings to sanctification in the grace of Christ. The psychological analogy from knowledge and love suggests that the Trinitarian God wishes to sanctify us each individually, in our knowledge and love, by raising us up to contemplate his eternal Word, Jesus Christ, and by uniting our hearts with the charity of the Holy Spirit. As we grow in the knowledge of God, we become more like the Trinity. Our minds and hearts are conformed inwardly to the mystery of the Trinity, and we begin to know ourselves more deeply and acquire a healthy self-love and interior sense of autonomy. The analogy from distinct human persons suggests that God wishes to sanctify us collectively. The grace of the Holy Trinity draws human beings into a profound communion with one another in the knowledge of Christ and in the love of the Spirit, and makes us more relational. In their mutual love for one another, human beings who follow Christ begin to resemble, however imperfectly, the communion of persons in the Trinity. The Catholic Church is before all else a communion of persons.

This brief statement of Trinitarian faith does not of course prove that the doctrine is true. In fact, it may give rise to greater puzzlement or skepticism. Intellectual puzzlement about God is not strange. Paradoxically, it signals opportunity. The mind moves forward into God by actively seeking understanding of him. We should return, then, to the most basic theological claim of all: the affirmation that God exists. From here we can move forward to consider the principles of Trinitarian faith in greater depth.

The One God

Traditionally Christian theologians begin with unity. There is only one God. This is one of the first statements in the Nicene Creed. "I believe in one God, the Father Almighty, Maker of heaven and earth, and of all things visible and invisible." The one God being referred to is the Trinity, to be sure. This is why the Father is named, just as the Son and Spirit are mentioned a few lines later. But the presupposition from the beginning is of the unity of God. Monotheism is a first presupposition of Trinitarian theology, not a conclusion. It is a starting point based on which we understand the rest, not a hypothesis that is up for grabs.

The reasons for this are multiple. One is the Old Testament, which teaches in many and varied ways that there is only one God, who is the creator of all things, and that the unity of the creation (the harmony of all the elements in the created order) is a reflection of the divine wisdom of God, who is one. This monotheism was central to the identity of the ancient Israelites. Based on this core conviction they incessantly criticized the irrationality of polytheism and struggled internally against compromising forms of religious syncretism. However, this idea was also carried over into the New Testament, as early Christians from the beginning worshiped Jesus Christ as "Lord," that is to say as "YHWH," the name of God revealed to Moses at the burning bush.[4] In this way, the earliest Jewish Christians, who were monotheistic, were demarcating the fact that Jesus is identical with the God of Israel. The early Christians did not do away with Jewish monotheism, then, but understood it more radically in light of what they took to be the revelation of Jesus Christ, and of the Holy Spirit. The one God of Israel is the Father, Son, and Holy Spirit. Accordingly, the early Christians were steadfastly critical of the polytheism of the surrounding culture and refused to sacrifice to the gods on behalf of the emperor. They were willing to suffer persecution and face death in order to confess the truth about the God of Israel over against what they took to be the irrationalities of the cultic worship of the Greco-Romans.

In addition, however, reflection on the unity of God is essential for thinking about the Trinity in itself. The premise of the claim that there is a distinction of persons in God is that there is one God and thus that each of the three persons is God. What do we mean to denote then when we say "God"? What is the one divine nature (i.e., the unique divine essence or "godliness of the one God") that is common to the Father, Son, and Holy Spirit? If we cannot think about the divine nature that each person possesses, then we cannot really think about the Trinity at all. This point will become clearer as we proceed, but at the moment we can say that if we want to understand how Jesus Christ and the Father are one in being, or how the Holy Spirit is eternally God just as the Father and the Son are eternally God, then we need to be able to think about what God is, in his unity, wisdom, and divine power, so as to be able to say something clear about what it is that the Father, Son, and Holy Spirit all share in identically.

4. Ex 3:14–15.

Traditionally, Catholic theology makes use of a fair amount of philosophy when thinking about what God is. In the previous chapter we argued that biblical revelation is not irrational and that it does not do violence to natural human reason. Here we can make a related claim that is different and stronger: biblical revelation not only respects natural human reason. It also invites us to make use of natural human reason in the service of the revealed truth.

This is clear enough if we simply think about the idea of God in the Old Testament. There is one transcendent God who is the creator of all else that exists, which depends upon him for its very existence in every instant. God is therefore present to the created world in the very depths of its being but God is not identical with the world. God is in some mysterious way personal, characterized by incomprehensible wisdom and divine goodness or love. This is the traditional monotheistic claim. However, we might immediately ask a series of good philosophical questions, based on our ordinary experience of reality. Do we see signs, for example, in the ordinary realities around us (including ourselves) that things as we know them *really are dependent* for their existence upon another? Does the order of the world, as far as we can make it out, tend to suggest *at least the possibility* of an origin in divine wisdom? Does the physical world seem self-explanatory or could there be good reasons to think that the existence of the material world implies the necessary existence of something transcending matter? These are not unreasonable questions, and in fact, the claim that revelation is compatible with natural reason requires at least that there is some kind of possible rational harmony between what we think about the world philosophically based on ordinary experience of the world and what we find being taught in the revelation of the Catholic faith.

Understood in this light, the traditional Catholic insistence on the "proofs for the existence of God" are not first and foremost about trying to gain universal consensus regarding the philosophical question of the existence of God. They are not even first and foremost about trying to show that it is rational to believe that God exists (though this is true and sometimes the arguments help agnostic people see this). The central aim of them, instead, is to show that there is a way of human thinking about God that can reach up toward God even as (or after!) the revelation of God reaches down to human reason, so that the two cooperate "under grace" or in grace. The point is that grace does not destroy human nature but heals and elevates it to work within faith in a more integral way. Thinking about the one God philosophically is meant, in Catholic theology, to be a form of humble acceptance of biblical revelation. How can we see the world realistically, philosophically, in light of the revelation of the God of Israel? This Catholic approach eschews then two contrary extremes: a *fideism* that would seek to know God only by means of Christian revelation (with no contribution of natural human reasoning about God), and a *rationalism* that would seek to know God only or primarily by philosophical argument, to the exclusion of the mystery of the revelation of God.[5] Faith and reason are meant to work together in this domain, not stand opposed.

The Illative Sense

Standard undergraduate introductions to the "proofs for the existence of God" tend to focus predominantly on the demonstrative character of these arguments. Do they begin from sound premises? Do they attain valid conclusions? Can we pose objections or obstacles to their logical resolution?

There is nothing wrong with this kind of probing of logical

5. See here the classic Catholic statement on faith and reason in the document of the First Vatican Council, *Dei Filius,* April 24, 1870, and the *Catechism of the Catholic Church,* pars. 27–43.

rigor, but by focusing predominantly on this aspect, one often misses the point. The traditional Catholic arguments for the existence of God are not geometrical proofs derived from self-evident axioms, but are something more elevated and deal with a subject matter that is more elusive. They function primarily as intellectual discernments about the nature of reality as we perceive it all the time. They begin from things around us so as to perceive the necessity of a transcendent origin, God the creator, who remains hidden and hence not immediately subject to the constraints of our "clear and distinct ideas." That is to say, thinking about God is realistic and philosophical, but it also seeks to acknowledge the numinous character of our existence and the ways that our limited, finite being points toward something transcendent, necessary, and eternal, which is the cause of our existence. Thinking about God in this sense is difficult for the human mind, not because theology is soft-headed, but simply because the subject matter is so elevated and not intrinsically capturable in the way mathematical or empirical topics are.

There are many ways of approaching the question of God philosophically, and the Catholic tradition has given rise (and continues to give rise) to a multitude of rational arguments, some of which are incompatible with one another (such that intense philosophical dispute occurs continually within the Catholic faith, a sign of its respect for the autonomous development of philosophical reason). There are arguments from the metaphysical structure of reality (the being of the world), arguments from beauty, from the very idea of God as perfect (Anselm's famous ontological argument), from the order of the world, from the moral drama of human existence, from the desire of man for an infinite good, and others as well. Aquinas is often said to have given five demonstrations of the existence of God, but in fact he gives between fifteen and twenty arguments in various locations in his work.[6] Many of

6. On Aquinas's varied arguments for the existence of God, see John Wippel,

these have their roots in previous thinkers, particularly Plato, Aristotle, Avicenna, and a host of patristic authors.

It is important to note that more than one argument or philosophical way of thinking about God can be true simultaneously. There are various routes up the mountain, so to speak. This is because the world around us is complex and so the complexity of the world can "bespeak" or indicate God in different ways. It is one thing, for example, to note that the existence of interdependent physical realities requires a transcendent, non-physical cause. It is another thing to note that the human being is marked inwardly by a dramatic struggle between moral good and moral evil. These two truths can be indirect indications of the mystery of God distinctly, but also in a *simultaneous and convergent* fashion. Various truths we come to about the world *converge* to suggest a larger overarching truth.

This is the case not only for arguments for the existence of God, but also for our larger perspective on religious and cosmic questions more generally. Atheists, for example, often inhabit intellectual traditions of argument that attempt to explain a variety of truths from within a diverse but convergent set of unified theories: "The Bible is a purely human book." "There are no good philosophical arguments for the existence of God." "The problem of evil mitigates against claims to the contrary." "All that exists is in some way purely material." "Human origins are explicable by recourse to a materialist account of the theory of evolution." "Whatever moral or aesthetic truths there are within human existence are best safeguarded by secular political systems." These are all very different claims but they are held by many people as a set of convergent, interrelated ideas about reality, and the more one holds to a greater number of them, the more the others may seem plausible or reasonable. This is something like what John Henry

---

The Metaphysical Thought of Thomas Aquinas (Washington, D.C.: The Catholic University of America Press, 2000), 379–500.

Newman referred to as the "illative sense" of rational assent to the truth.[7] We tend to see things in sets or groups of collected truths. Meanwhile, such complex deliberations touch upon the cords of our heart. We are affected by what we want to be true, or what we want not to be true, by our unconditional desire to find the truth or our fears of inconvenient truths. Otherwise said, the heart is both affected by and *affects* our thinking about major questions like atheism or the existence of God, because there are implications for other aspects of our life and our overall take on reality in a broad sweep of domains.

This is why thinking about the one God is often, for each of us, deeply interrelated to (even if logically distinguishable from) a whole host of other issues. Has God revealed himself in the Old and New Testaments? Does belief in God mitigate against confidence in the modern sciences or are the two deeply compatible? Can we argue that there are absolute moral principles and if so how is this related to belief in God? Does the human longing for meaning suggest that human beings have a religious destiny or purpose? Can moral good and evil, and the human conscience, be understood ultimately without some kind of eventual reference to God?

Straightforward philosophical reflection about God, then, has its own integrity as a form of argument, or reasoning, but it is also embedded within a web of existential concerns and reflection on a wide array of issues pertaining to reality. The plausibility of believing one thing, especially a truth about God, is connected to the plausibility of believing a great deal of other things.

7. John Henry Newman, *An Essay in Aid of a Grammar of Assent*, chap. 9.

Rational Arguments for
the Existence of God

Without entering into a technical discussion, we can sketch out some traditional ways of thinking about what God is, approaches that stand up to the test of time, and that have as much meaning after the scientific revolution as they did prior to it. Unsurprisingly, we have chosen here to state briefly three arguments derived from Aquinas.[8] A first form of argument has to do with *existence and essence* in all the realities we experience.[9] By essence, we mean the given natures of realities around us: human beings, kangaroos, oak trees, stars, stones, atoms, quarks, and whatever else. Reality is made up of various "kinds" of things or natures, and accordingly we group things realistically by using such categories. (This grouping process, incidentally, is the basis of modern scientific realism and the formulation of scientific laws.) But if we consider two members of a given kind (two human beings, for example) they clearly have distinct existences. If another person perishes, you or I do not cease to exist, nor does the whole human race cease to exist. What this shows more fundamentally is that in any given kind of thing we experience in the world, existence is not identical with essence. To be a given kind of thing (a tree, a water molecule, a kangaroo, or a star) does not entail that this thing exists by necessity. Why is this important? Because it allows us to see that everything we experience *receives* its existence or is *given* being. It participates in existence, but it is not the cause of its own existence. On the contrary, all that we experience can be or not be, and the "gift" of being depends at each moment on a host of external causes or agents, as when a human being who can exist or not exist depends upon other factors, like oxygen, heat from

8. For a helpful restatement of Aquinas's "Five Ways." see Edward Feser, *Aquinas: A Beginner's Guide* (Oxford: Oneworld, 2009), 62–120.
9. See Aquinas, *On Being and Essence*, chap. 4.

the sun, and a host of other cosmic factors, all of which in turn *exist* in dependence upon others.

So existence is a kind of philosophical mystery. Everything that we experience exists, and being or existing is not reducible to one kind of being alone (like human existence or the existence of oak trees). Nor is anything we experience the cause of its own existence. Instead, the individual things we experience are all dependent in the order of being, and can be or not be. They receive their existence from others. But if each thing that exists is caused, or depends upon others for its very existence at each given moment, then there is no ultimate sufficient reason why there is anything in existence at all. It does no good simply to push back the question to another caused reality and then another. Something must be first that exists necessarily and that gives being to all the rest. We can ask (due to the capacity of things to exist or not exist) why there is something and not anything, but we cannot really answer this question in a satisfying way unless there is something that exists necessarily, something that exists by nature, or whose essence it is to exist. Therefore, to make sense of a world of perishable, contingent beings, we need to posit something that always is, and cannot not be, which is the cause of everything else. And this is one way of speaking indirectly and imperfectly about God: God is "He Who Is." God is himself subsistent being, the transcendent cause of all that exists, from whom we receive the gift of being.

A second way of thinking about God can be derived from the consideration of *change in material realities*.[10] Every physical being, no matter how small or how great, is intrinsically subject to the capacity or "potency" for change or alteration. Physical things are constantly being subject to changes by other physical things: changes of place (like our constant rotation around the sun), changes of size or shape or weight (quantitative changes),

10. Aquinas, *ST* I, q. 2, a. 3: this is the so-called first way.

changes of quality (like moving in or out of sunlight so as to become warm or cold), and changes of coming to be or passing away
(as when a physical body is produced, like a puddle of rain, or ex-
tinguished, like wood burned in a fire). A world of physical beings is a world of wall-to-wall *interdependency*. All that is physical
is being changed or altered continuously by other things and so
depends for its manner of being upon a constant constellation of
external causes. This means that no physical being can be what it
is without continual reference to other realities acting upon it or
that it in turn acts upon. There are Eastern religious traditions,
such as Madhyamaka Buddhism, that conclude from this fact
that everything that exists is impermanent and changing, and
that nothing is stable and enduring. The world is in a process of
flux from beginning to end. Can we simply posit an infinite number of mutable realities and leave it at that? Many people want to
ask this question *chronologically* and argue for a first cause *before*
the Big Bang, where we need something to kick start the cosmos
into being. Others want to argue against this position that the
world can be chronologically infinite, with successive Big Bangs
of expansion followed by collapse. Aquinas eschews both these
forms of argument (for and against belief in God), because when
it comes to chronological claims about the origins of the universe
we lack sufficient evidence to make any final assertions.[11] We
were not there to confirm if the universe had a physical beginning
or how it did. Scientific speculations are probable rather than certain, and do not lead directly to knowledge of God, who cannot
be grasped by scientific theories. (The latter are limited to the
quantitative domain, and if God exists he is not a subject of mathematical study or scientific experiment.)

Instead we should think not in chronological terms but in

---

11. See Aquinas, *On the Eternity of the World*, and William E. Carroll, "Creation,
Evolution and Thomas Aquinas," *Revue des Questions Scientifiques* 171, no. 4 (2000):
319–47.

actual terms: is it adequate to claim that all that exists *right now* or *at any given present moment in the universe* is a collection of interdependent material beings? In our given moment of time, each thing that exists in the physical world depends upon other material things for its existence. So can there only be a sum total of material things *now*? This is an inadequate theory, because no material, physical thing can completely account for its own existence-in-dependence upon others. Multiplying an indefinite number of such dependent material things does nothing to alleviate the problem. If there is a great chain, or web, of actually dependent material things, we need to explain this by reference to a cause that is immaterial, and that is not changed by others or dependent upon others. In contrast to the theories of Madhyamaka Buddhism, we should say that the *existence* of a physical universe in flux is the sign of a transcendent source of the material world, one who is immaterial, not subject to alteration and dependency upon others, and who is the author of all the others (i.e., God).

Last, we can consider the argument from the order of the world.[12] This is not the argument of William Paley, the argument that the world shows signs of being a great artifact, like a watch, that is made by an intelligent mind. An artifact has its order imposed upon it from without, as the artist shapes the matter into the form he likes. The argument from order found in Aquinas is of a different kind. It is based on the *intrinsic* order within things, not the *lack of intrinsic order* that Paley's argument presupposes. This intrinsic order has to do with the typical, natural behaviors of things. We find in the material cosmos certain predictable outcomes: if we throw a stone into a lake it sinks; fire consumes combustible substances; water crystallizes into ice at a given temperature. So too in living things: the living cell reproduces and replicates its DNA, the plant nourishes itself through photosynthesis, dolphins travel in schools and have signals for play and

12. Aquinas, *On the Eternity of the World*. This is Aquinas's so-called fifth way.

for danger; human beings not only sense and feel but also think and make reflective decisions. We see patterns of order in things themselves that make manifest their internal natures and predictable actions or behaviors. The things we experience are not themselves the self-determinate source of the order we experience in them, meaning that they do not author or stimulate their own internal order. They develop according to ordered patterns but do not choose these patterns for themselves, nor are we the authors of them.

We might argue that such ordered patterns in nature are simply the fruit of earlier ancient historical processes, such as hundreds of millions of years of evolution and billions of years of cosmic expansion and alteration. But this simply pushes the question back a step, since those sweeping alterations occurred due to ordered processes present within the cosmos and within the vast history of living forms, and certainly (undeniably) the vast history in question gave rise progressively to the ordered world we see today (which is still changing and may yet be reordered on a massive scale). The dispute is not about the *history* of order in things (wherein for the sake of argument one might accept everything found in the modern scientific perspective). Indeed, the development of order across a vast spectrum of cosmic development and evolution of species *is itself* clearly a form of order in the world we can delineate with the help of modern scientific theories. Otherwise, there would be no intelligibility in the modern sciences. But since there is such order in the vast world of things we see around us, and we did not author it, we must posit that the intellectual ordering of realities in the world does not originate from anything within the world, nor from something that is itself ordered by another. In effect, a thing that tends toward action or perfection in a given order is not the cause of the kind of thing that it is, but must depend upon others. It would do no good simply to push the explanation of the order of the world back by recourse to an infinite series of dependent orderers who are themselves dependent in turn on others. We can come then to the reasonable conclusion of a transcendent wisdom, that we call God, that is the source of the deeper ordering inscribed within the realities themselves that we experience. Whatever God is, God must have his purpose or end in himself, in being himself, knowing himself, and in loving himself, for he cannot be dependent upon another for his fulfillment or realization.

So we have noted above a few ways of thinking about the mystery of God philosophically: God is the necessary being who is the cause of all else that exists. God is not material or physical but is the author of the physical world. God does not depend upon others to attain his perfection or internal order but is the transcendent wisdom that is the cause of the dynamic order we find in the world. Truth be told, to say all this about God is not to say very much. It is to note primarily *that* God is, but does not allow us to say very much about *what* God is in himself. In fact, traditional Christian theology notes that our knowledge of God in himself is primarily *apophatic* or negative: we can say more about what God is *not* than what God is.[13]

The Divine Names

It is important to keep this in mind when thinking about the divine attributes or the traditional "divine names" employed to speak of the divine essence. They are in great part human ways of speaking carefully about what God is not, as well as what God is. We can consider here a few traditional examples.

The Church Fathers and the great medieval scholastics insist upon the *simplicity* of God as one of the primary attributes we should employ when thinking of the divine nature. When we speak of the divine simplicity we mean to say that God is not a

---

13. Aquinas, *ST* I, q. 3, pref.

composite reality of the kind we experience in the physical world or in the created order. Most evidently, God is not a physical body. Therefore, the divine nature cannot be represented visually or corporeally. God is not subject to material change or development. Also, God is not an individual within a larger species, like a *kind of god*, the way human beings are a kind of animal. There are not many gods, as there are many human beings. God is entirely unique and is the only author of all the various created kinds of things. He is not one of them. While no human being can say, "I am man," God can indeed say, "I alone am God" or "I am deity."

Again, God is not subject to the possibility of being or not being, but he is one who exists by virtue of his very nature or essence. The divine nature is subsistent being, or as Aquinas says, God is "existence itself ... an infinite ocean of substance."[14] Accordingly, Christians and Jews alike traditionally have interpreted the divine name revealed to Moses at the burning bush to be "I am He who is."[15] Finally, when speaking of divine simplicity, we must note that God's properties, such as his goodness or wisdom, are not distinguishable from his essence. No human being can say "I am wisdom" or "I am goodness" but in the case of God, we *must* say that God *is* wisdom and *is* goodness, and that therefore what we denote by these various terms of perfection is somehow *one in God*. God simply is his being, wisdom, and goodness, and in such a way that they all are identical in God, but also in a way that is beyond our immediate experience or comprehension.

We may also say that the divine nature is *infinitely perfect*. The perfection of God is related to the fact that God is not causally dependent upon others but is the cause of all others. Accordingly, he does not receive the perfections of his nature from others but causes all perfections in others. To say that God is "infinite" is to say that he is "not finite." Certain finite perfections we see in cre-

14. Aquinas, *ST* I, q. 13, a. 11.
15. Ex 3:14.

ated nature, like being, goodness, truth, and beauty, are capable of existing in an infinite way, without imperfection. We cannot reasonably conceive of an "infinite stone" or "infinite physical eyesight" but we can conceive of the possibility of infinite goodness or infinite wisdom. The divine nature has no imperfection or capacity for improvement, because either of these would imply God's dependency on another, as if God could be subject to improvement based on his engagements with creatures. But God is the cause of all else that exists, the author of all perfections in creatures. He does not receive his perfections from them. So, we must say that if God exists and is the author of a world in which there are various perfections in the order of being, then God possesses these same perfections in an infinitely higher way that we do not immediately comprehend or experience directly. God's infinite perfection is mysterious and marks him off as utterly transcendent of his creation.

If God is infinite, he is also eternal. Boethius defines eternity as the perfect possession of the plenitude of life.[16] What he means by this is that God is so perfectly alive that he does not undergo any progressive development toward perfection. Progress implies a kind of temporality, as things pass from their capacities to their improvement or "from potency to act." But God is pure act or the pure actuality of being, so that he does not undergo any progressive realization of his perfections. The created world is subject to constant change and alteration and this is the source of temporality. Time, after all, is basically a measure of change: the earth turns on its axis according to a given rhythm and moves around the sun according to a predictable pattern, just as plants grow over time and human beings grow in predictable ratios measured by years (of the earth moving around the sun). God is not subject to various kinds of physical, emotional, or spiritual change. He simply *is*, eternally.

16. Boethius, *The Consolation of Philosophy* V, 6.

God is also *good*, or as we said above, the divine nature is *subsistent goodness*. Goodness is the property of something that has reached its perfection or its goal. We say that someone is a good swimmer when he can swim vigorously, with speed or duration. A good apartment is one that meets human needs, in terms of size, location, or cost. A good person typically is taken to be a person who is capable of virtuous moral actions, of justice, charity, mercy, and kindness toward others. In created realities, goodness is typically achieved, or perfected. A seedling grows into the perfection of being a vast tree, a "good tree" according to its species. A human being becomes progressively more ethical (or fails to do so). But God is pure actuality and so the divine nature, which is the cause of all goodness in created things, is perfectly good. God is his goodness and cannot be subject to any diminishment in the infinite goodness of his nature. This means also that God is in some mysterious way "personal," in that God is not physical and is an eternal act of goodness and knowledge. God must know himself and in knowing his own eternal infinite goodness, must love himself without any shred of egoism. We might say that God just is a subsistent act of spiritual love and joy, because God possesses eternally the knowledge and love of his own infinite goodness.

Finally, we say that God is *infinite wisdom*. Wisdom is a form of intelligence or understanding that orders all things. We say someone is wise when he can explain to us important matters or guide us in crucial decisions. To be wise is to understand the deeper nature of what things are and how things work, and to govern or guide others in light of this understanding. Human wisdom is acquired slowly over the course of a lifetime, but God is the intelligent author of all that is. Consequently, we must say that in God there is infinite knowledge: the knowledge that God has of himself and of his creation. God knows all things perfectly, in the depths of his creative wisdom, and he governs all things in light of this wisdom.

Of course in saying this we are confronted immediately with the problem of evil, of why it is that God allows such tremendous defects in the things he creates, especially suffering in the lives of human beings, and of why God permits so many real and terrible moral evils in human history. We will return to this subject in the next chapter, but it suffices to say here that there is nothing very irrational in saying that God the creator is infinitely good and wise, but that his creation is finite and therefore subject to various limits and defects. It is the *intensity and gravity of human suffering and moral evil* that particularly causes us scandal, and this is deeply interrelated with the issue of human sinfulness, and the shape that redemption takes in Christ in his crucifixion and resurrection. In this mystery we perceive the "deeper goodness and wisdom" of God at work remaking the world in the wake of human sin, through God's own suffering on our behalf.

We are trying to understand the divine nature and so far we have said that God truly exists, and is simple, infinitely perfect, eternal, good, and wise. We do not perfectly grasp what it means to attribute these terms to God, because we do not perceive God in himself or know him immediately. We know that God is, and can say a great deal about what God is not (how he is unlike creatures). Accordingly, we have tried to say some true things about what God is in himself, but we also say these things by *analogy*. That is to say, if God is simple, good, wise, and the like, he is so in ways that are utterly different from creatures. In 1215, the Fourth Lateran Council said that for every similitude we posit between creatures and God, there is "an even greater dissimilitude." To speak of the divine nature, then, is to stand with Moses on Mount Sinai, peering into the darkness of the mystery of God.

Simply by considering God as he who is simple, perfect, eternal, good, and wise, we can immediately perceive a certain kind of "creation mysticism" that arises from thinking about the creator. As the cause of all that exists, God is he who sustains all things in being, and so he is immanently present to all that exists, or is "omnipresent." In the words of Dionysius the Areopagite, "God is all things insofar as he is the cause of all things," and in the words of Augustine, "God is closer to us than we are to ourselves."[17] At the most intimate interior level of all that exists, God is hidden but utterly present as he who gives existence to all that is.

This also means that realities that spring from God, and that are more manifest to us, are a kind of visible expression or natural "sacrament" (sign and instrument) of the presence of God. The beauty and complexity of nature, its immense, intricate order and vast history, are visible expressions of the infinite hidden wisdom of God. His divine eternity and wisdom are manifest in the unfolding effects of time and creaturely history. The creation is the written tableau on which God expresses his being outwardly.

So too, the human soul is the special expression of the mystery of God, because the human being possesses intellectual understanding and moral freedom. Whereas God is infinitely wise and good, the human soul is capable of becoming progressively wiser and better. The soul is an image of God, then, a created reality that reflects in a special way the hidden presence of the omnipresent God who creates the spiritual soul and upholds it in being. God sustains us in being and is present in the most intimate depths of our soul, beckoning to us as rational creatures by the natural attraction of his uncreated truth and goodness. We are naturally able to think about God and search for him, he who is hidden in the very depths of our being.

Understanding this *natural presence* of God the creator is very helpful for thinking about non-Christian religions. The Islamic insistence on the transcendence of God underscores a profound

17. Dionysius, *The Divine Names* V, 4 (PG 3:817). My translation is based on Aquinas's Latin rendering of the phrase in *ST* I, q. 4, a. 2: "omnia est, ut omnium causa." Augustine, *Confessions* III, 6, 11: "interior intimo meo et superior summo meo" (more interior to my innermost and higher than my highest self); translation by the author.

truth: that there is only one creator, that polytheism is unreasonable, that God is not identical with the creation, and that immediate knowledge of his divine identity remains *naturally* inaccessible to the creature. We have no *natural* gift of friendship with God. However, on the other extreme, one can understand the Hindu Vedantic mystical traditions that seek to find God present in the heart of created realities and that emphasize God's immanent presence in the soul, even if these traditions sometimes tend to equate God with the innermost being of the soul itself.[18] A similar vision can be found in a modern idiom in Transcendentalists such as Henry David Thoreau, who sought to find contact with God in and through contemplation of the creation. A more balanced perspective is found in various Christian mystics such as Meister Eckhart or Jonathan Edwards, who emphasized at times quite brilliantly a sense of the metaphysical presence of God the creator in all things, and particularly his presence in the human soul, calling it homeward toward himself.

Knowing the Trinity

The one God who created heaven and earth is also the Most Holy Trinity, the eternal procession of the Word or Son who proceeds from the Father and the eternal spiration of the Holy Spirit who comes forth from the Father and the Word. Why should anyone believe that God is triune or that the Trinity is the deepest mystery of God's identity?

There are a number of reasons, all of which stem from the life and teachings of Jesus of Nazareth, and from the framework of apostolic teaching in the New Testament. First there is the fact

18. Non-Christian religious rituals, problematic as they may be at times due to associations with polytheism, ancestor worship, or superstitious practices, nevertheless manifest a human desire that the cosmos reveal God, or the sacred, so as to mediate a direct encounter with the divine. Here we see a natural human longing for contact with the creator, distorted though it may sometimes be.

of what Jesus did and taught during his historical life. The New Testament does not depict Christ merely as an ethical teacher, an eschatological preacher, a religious genius, a wandering sage, or even merely as a miracle worker (all of which are various modern liberal Protestant views of Christ). In the Gospels Jesus claims to perform miracles by his own will and power.[19] He forgives sins, and claims to have authority to interpret definitively and abrogate aspects of the Mosaic law, actions normally reserved only to the God of Israel.[20] More astonishingly, Christ claims to be one with God: "I and the Father are one."[21] He makes multiple statements suggesting that he personally pre-existed the creation of the world, that he has been sent into the world so as to be the unique savior of humanity.[22] It is difficult to understand anything about the historical life of Jesus of Nazareth and the shock he gave to both his disciples and to fellow Jews at the time if one removes from the four canonical Gospels all of these very high claims of Christ. It is simpler, from a merely rational, historical point of view, to believe that Jesus gave offense to others precisely through making these sorts of claims.

Second, there is Christ's death and resurrection, which the early Christians claimed *revealed* his true identity as the eternal Son of God. It was especially after the resurrection of Christ from the dead that his followers claimed to understand by the enlightenment of grace that Christ, the man who had lived and died among them, was himself truly God, one with the Father.[23]

Third, there is the testimony of the apostolic Church. The earliest Christians not only worshiped Jesus (whom they took to be

19. Mt 8:3; Jn 9:1–6, 31–32.

20. On the authority and power to forgive sins, see Mk 2:5–7; Lk 7:48–50, 23:43; Jn 8:1–11. On abrogating the Mosaic law, see Mt 5:17–48, Mk 2:27–28, Jn 5:1–23.

21. Jn 10:30.

22. On pre-existing the world, see Jn 8:58, 17:5, 18:37. On being sent into the world, see Jn 8:42, Lk 19:10, Mk 10:45.

23. Rom 1:4, Acts 2:36, Jn 20:28.

the God of Israel become man) but also believed that he personally "pre-existed" prior to his Incarnation.[24] That is to say, that
he was the Son of God who is the eternal wisdom through whom
God created the world. John writes in his prologue "in the beginning was the Word, and the Word was with God and the Word
was God ... All things were made through him ... and the Word
became flesh and dwelt among us."[25] The early Church took the
apostles to be making these claims not due to human conjecture
but in light of a divinely revealed insight or understanding. The
apostolic Church claimed to grasp the true identity of Christ because of the sending of the Holy Spirit upon the Church to enlighten the followers of Christ as to God's own identity.

Finally, having mentioned Jesus, we can say analogous things
about the divinity of the Holy Spirit. Just as the New Testament
teaches that Jesus, the Son, is God but also distinct personally
from the Father, so also it affirms that the Holy Spirit is personally distinct from the Father and the Son. As Jesus himself says:
"When the Counselor comes, whom I shall send to you from the
Father, even the Spirit of truth, who proceeds from the Father,
he will bear witness to me."[26] Here the Holy Spirit is promised to
the Church, after the death and resurrection of Christ, and is depicted as a personal agent who is distinct from the Father and the
Son.

We can reasonably ask whether the New Testament is inspired,
and whether a revelation took place at all in the life of Jesus of
Nazareth and in the early Christian movement. But if such a
revelation did take place it is definitely Trinitarian in form. The
earliest Christians believed the Father, Jesus, and the Holy Spirit
each to be God, and also believed that there is only one God.

We can add a qualification here. If what we are saying is true,

24. Phil 2:6–11, Heb 1:1–4, Col 1:15–20.
25. Jn 1:1, 1:3, 1:14.
26. Jn 15:26.

why did it take three hundred years for the Church to formulate an official doctrinal account of the mystery of the Trinity in dogmatic language? The reason is that the apostles and early Christians had primarily a vibrant personal, concrete, and intuitive knowledge of this mystery, which they expressed clearly in the scriptures, in unambiguous ways. However, it took time to draw out the implications of this teaching in more conceptually developed formulas. The two forms of knowledge are not opposed. We have deep, clear intuitions all the time that we then draw out into more developed reflective forms. I may know that striking an innocent person is unjust, and feel it deeply and say so, but working out the rationale for this intuition and articulating it in philosophical form may take time. The developed rationale is no substitute for the more fundamental intuitive understanding, but it helps us see all the implications of the intuition. In fact, a single intuition can carry in itself the seeds of a multiplicity of arguments. Likewise, it is one thing to know Jesus personally and to know that he is God, one with the Father and the Holy Spirit, and another thing to reflect on all that this entails about our belief in God. We can reflect for a lifetime on the plenitude of cognitive riches latent in the New Testament. The dogmatic reflection of the Church is not a betrayal of the fundamental mystery, nor is it an improvement on the knowledge of God that was possessed by the apostles. Rather, it is a study of their teaching that helps us better to grasp what the apostles themselves knew more profoundly than we do, albeit in a more implicit, intuitive way.

The Trinity and Christian Mysticism

Furthermore, the intellectual study of the Holy Trinity is important but secondary when compared to our spiritual life of communion with the Trinity. Faith gives us a living participation in this mystery, not merely a conceptual knowledge of it. The Father may be known personally in the darkness of faith, which is both obscure and luminous. Jesus Christ the Son of God and the Word of the Father may be known personally, and loved and adored. The Holy Spirit may be implored and prayed to personally, as the inner director of our spiritual life. By grace, the Holy Trinity comes to inhabit the soul of the believer, not so as to be fused with the creature, but so as to elevate and enlighten both mind and heart, leading each human being into deeper intimacy with God through knowledge and through love.

The inner life of the human being is structured by acts of knowledge and love, and so there is a kind of image of the Trinity in each person, as St. Augustine in particular emphasized. The inner "reason" or *logos* in us corresponds however faintly by analogy to the inner Logos and Word of God, the eternal procession of Wisdom who proceeds from the Father. The inner movement of spiritual love in us, our restlessness of heart, corresponds by analogy to the eternal Love who is the Holy Spirit, a love that proceeds from the Father and the Word. In other words, there are eternal processions of personal truth and personal love in the very life of God. The order is similar to what we find in ourselves, who are made in the image of the Trinity. Just as in us love proceeds from knowledge or is born of knowledge, so in God, the Father in knowing himself generates the eternal Word, and in loving himself, spirates the Holy Spirit in and from the Word. The Son is the eternal Wisdom of the Father. The Spirit is the eternal Love of the Father and the Son.

For the Christian mystic this is not a merely abstract truth. Union with God need not entail extraordinary experiences. It can happen in a seemingly ordinary, day-to-day way, under the veil of faith, and in the presence of the Blessed Sacrament of the Most Holy Eucharist. We are all invited to come to know the mystery of the Trinity personally, and to contemplate the Son and Word in the darkness of faith, thus lifting up our reason to the Reason of God. We are all invited to love God above all things, with the supernatural gift of charity, so as to have our hearts conformed inwardly to the indwelling love of the Holy Spirit. The interior life of the Christian thus takes on a "Trinitarian form," as the heart and mind of the human person are elevated into friendship with God, the Most Holy Trinity. Nothing could be less abstract. In fact, this is the most concrete reality that there is: the union of the soul with God by grace.

The fourteenth-century Dominican mystic Catherine of Siena expresses this very beautifully in her letters. In writing to her Dominican confessor Bartholomeo Dominici in 1375, she exhorts him to accept the gift of friendship with God:

I am inviting you, in this blazing charity, to plunge into a peaceful sea, a deep sea. I have just rediscovered the sea—not that the sea is new, but it is new to me in the way my soul experiences it—in the words, "God is love." And just as the sun shines its light on the earth and a mirror reflects a person's face, so these words echo within me that everything that is done is simply love, because everything is made entirely of love. This is why he says, "I am God, Love." This sheds light on the priceless mystery of the incarnate Word, who, out of sheer love, was given in such humility that it confounds my pride. It teaches us to look not just at what he did, but at the blazing love this Word has given us. It says that we should do as a loving person does when a friend comes with a gift, not looking at the friend's hands to see what the gift is, but looking with the eyes of love at the friend's loving heart. And this is what God's supreme, eternal, more tender than tender goodness wants us to do when he visits our soul.[27]

As this quotation suggests, union with the Trinity is intimately bound up with spiritual union with Christ in his historical Incarnation, passion, and resurrection. To contemplate the Trinity is to seek union with the person of Christ and to seek to live in him, in charitable love for all other human beings. To seek to live

27. *The Letters of St. Catherine of Siena*, trans. S. Noffke (Tempe: Arizona Center for Medieval and Renaissance Studies, 1998), 1:96.

in Christ is to seek union with the Trinity. Teresa of Avila, the sixteenth-century Carmelite mystic, warns against the temptation of seeking to find God or the Trinity "beyond" the sacred humanity of Christ, as if we would go to God apart from the Incarnation and passion of Jesus. Her advice to her sisters "never to abandon the sacred humanity of Jesus" is rich with theological implications.[28] The study of the Trinity is meant to help us understand more deeply the mystery of the *life of Jesus itself*, to see his unity with the Father and the Holy Spirit, in his actions of healing, forgiving sins, and bearing witness to the truth, but also in the mystery of the crucifixion, death, and resurrection of Christ. The paschal mystery of Jesus reveals to us the identity of Christ as the Son of God, but also the wisdom and power of the Father, who raised Jesus from the dead, and the gift of love that is the Holy Spirit, poured out upon the Church from the Cross.

Thinking about the Trinity

Having laid the groundwork, then, we can consider the mystery of God as Trinity more formally. Speaking by way of initiation, we can say there are three principles for thinking clearly about the mystery: (1) procession of persons, (2) identity of essence, and (3) unity of operation.[29]

The basic claim that there is a *procession of persons* in the Trinity stems directly from the New Testament itself. The Son of God is said to be the eternal Logos or Word of the Father, who proceeds from the Father and through whom the Father creates all things.[30] The Holy Spirit is said to come forth from the Father and the Son, or from the Father through the Son, and to be sent

28. Teresa of Avila, *The Interior Castle*, Sixth Mansion, chap. VII.

29. For more on these principles, see the classic Trinitarian work of Gregory of Nazianzus, *Five Theological Orations*, as well as the *Catechism of the Catholic Church*, pars. 232–60.

30. Jn 1:1–3, 8:42, 16:28.

by God the Father and by Christ upon the Church.[31] As theologians have noted from early on, this implies that there are real relations in the communion of the three persons. The Father is the eternal origin or principle of the Son who is his Word. The Father and the Word spirate the Holy Spirit who proceeds forth from them. It is traditional to say then that the persons are distinguished by their relations of origin. The Son is the one eternally generated from the Father as the begotten wisdom of the Father, and the Spirit is eternally spirated from the Father and the Son, as the love who is shared by the Father and the Son.

Evidently when we speak of an eternal "generation" of the Son and an eternal "spiration" of the Spirit we are speaking analogically, using ordinary human language to describe a mystery. We should not understand these notions anthropomorphically, in terms of our ordinary experience as physical beings. There is no physical generation in God. The begetting in question is wholly spiritual. The Son proceeds from the Father as his Word or spiritual wisdom, analogous to the way human knowledge proceeds from the human knower. The spiration of the Spirit is not a psychological act of love as we find it in a human being (a love that can come and go), but is the eternal procession of the person who is subsistent love, and who comes forth from and is present within the Father and the Son. Thus the mystery of the Holy Trinity is a mystery of communion of persons, in the eternal truth and love of God.

The three persons are also *identical in essence*. This is the second principle. The Son is not lesser in being than the Father, nor is the Spirit lesser in being than the Father and the Son. There are no gradations of being in the Trinity. The three persons are all equal in dignity because each of them possesses the plenitude of the divine nature. Here we should bring together all that was said above

---

31. On the procession of the Spirit, see Jn 15:26; on his being sent from the Father and the Son, see Acts 1:4, 5:32; 1 Thes 4:8; Gal 4:6; Rom 8:9–11.

about the one God: God is simple, infinitely perfect, good, eternal, and wise. To ascribe the divine nature to the Father entails that we ascribe all these attributes to the Father. The Father is simple, perfect, eternal, and the like. But this means that the Son and the Spirit are each equally simple, perfect, eternal, and the like.

The reason for this is that the eternal generation of the Son and the eternal spiration of the Holy Spirit entail the communication of the divine nature to the person who proceeds from another. The Father generates the Son as his eternal wisdom and in so doing communicates to him the plenitude of the divine nature that he possesses as God. The Father and the Son spirate the Holy Spirit as the eternal love they share and in doing so communicate to him the plenitude of the divine nature. This is why we say that the Son is "God from God, light from light" in the Nicene Creed. He is "begotten not made" because his "being-from" the Father does not entail any inequality or diminishment. The Son is not a creature but is God. The same is true of the Holy Spirit, who the Creed says "is worshiped with the Father and the Son" as God.

This equality of the three persons entails more than the fact that they share the same divine nature, because in God nature and being are one. As we noted above, in God there is no difference of nature and the singular individual. No human being can say, "I am humanity," but God can say, "I am deity." So likewise the three persons in their eternity can each say, "I am the one God." The Father is the one God. The Son is the one God. The Holy Spirit is the one God.

How can this be, if there are truly three persons? The answer is to be found in the notion of the processions and the relations of origin we have just mentioned. The Son is eternally begotten of the Father and receives from the Father all that he is as Son, but this means that he also receives from the Father all that the Father is or possesses as God. Just as the Father is simple, infinitely perfect, good, eternal, and wise in himself, so he gives the Son to possess eternally his own same divine nature that is simple, perfect, good, and the like. The Son is eternally begotten as he who is entirely one in being with the Father. The same is true of the Holy Spirit as the procession of love, who receives in himself all that is in the Father and the Son. At the heart of all things, then, is the mystery of an eternal gift of love, in which the Father always gives all that he is to the Son without in any way being diminished in his own plenitude, and he and the Son with him give all that they are to the Spirit, in a communion of eternal love. The Son possesses in himself as God all that is in the Father and the Spirit. The Spirit possesses in himself all that is in the Father and the Son. The Father who is the eternal principle or origin of the other two persons possesses in himself all that is in the Son and the Spirit.

The third principle has to do with the *unity of operation* of the three persons. Here we are referring to all that God does "outside" of himself: the work of creation and the work of redemption. The creation is all that God has made and that he actually sustains in being. This is a work of the three persons of the Holy Trinity. The Father never acts as Father outside of the Wisdom who is his Son, and the Love who is his Spirit. Consequently, when the Father creates all reality and upholds it in being, he does so *through* the Son who is his Word or Reason, and *in* his Spirit who is his love. It is the Trinity who creates. So likewise in the mystery of human redemption: the gift of grace that comes forth from God and is poured out into our human minds and hearts comes forth from the Holy Trinity. God the Father illumines our minds by faith. He does so, however, through his eternal Word and in the eternal Spirit. The love that God pours out into our hearts by grace is poured out through the Word incarnate, who is the eternal truth made man, and in the Holy Spirit who is himself uncreated divine charity.

The traditional saying here is that "all works of the Trinity *ad extra* (outside of God himself) are works of all three persons." We can never ascribe the divine work of creation, the governance of divine providence, or any event of grace and salvation only to one person. It is untrue to say that "only the Father creates" or that "only the Son reconciles" or that "only the Holy Spirit sanctifies." If the Father creates, he does so through the Son and in the Spirit. If the Son reconciles, he does so as one sent from the Father and does so in the Holy Spirit whom he in turn sends into the world. If the Holy Spirit sanctifies he does so as one sent from the Father and the Son, who acts always with the Father and the Son.

All of this can seem to many like a complex conceptual game. This is particularly true if we think about it detached from a living concrete faith in the persons of the Holy Trinity. Here we should keep in mind the advice of Teresa of Avila: never leave behind the sacred humanity of Christ. Thinking about the Trinity in this more theoretical way is admittedly demanding, but allows us to return to the biblical portrait of Jesus at a deeper level and to engage with his mystery more profoundly. Jesus of Nazareth is one with the Father not only because he is a man of great holiness, but because he is the eternal Son who proceeds from the eternal Father. He is God made man. When Jesus promises to send the Holy Spirit upon his disciples and the Church, he does so not only as a man, but as God, who is one with the Father in the sending of the Spirit. When Jesus Christ is crucified, it is God who is crucified. Jesus is the eternal Word of the Father who speaks from the Cross, revealing to us that he is one with the Father. "I and the Father are one .... When you have lifted up the Son of man, then you will know that I am he."[32] The Word that God speaks from the Cross is a *verbum spirans amorem*, a "Word spirating Love."[33] From the Cross, Christ crucified who comes forth from the eternal Father sends the Holy Spirit who is love upon the world.

32. Jn 10:30, 8:28.
33. Aquinas, *ST* I, q. 43, a. 5, ad 2.

All this being said, St. Paul is right to emphasize that in this life "our knowledge is imperfect," and that "now we see in a mirror dimly" but later "face to face."[34] That is to say, in this life we behold the mystery of the Trinity only under the veil of faith, in the darkness of faith. We may attempt to think of God more profoundly and in doing so to love God more deeply. However, we also do so *in via* or "on pilgrimage" toward the final term of faith: the beatific vision of God. That is to say, what we profess about God in this life by faith we hope in the life to come to see clearly. The spiritual exercise of thinking about the Trinity in love is meant to deepen our union with God in this life in view of the perfecting of this union in the next. The final goal of the Christian life is to perceive God face to face.[35] In the beatific vision (which is what is really meant by the colloquial term "heaven"), the intellect of the human being is filled with the radiant presence of the eternal Word who is the wisdom of God. The will of the human being is set on fire by the presence of the Spirit who is divine love. The soul enters into its final homeland by peering upon the eternal mystery of the Father in his goodness and wisdom. All of this will seem like folly to the unbeliever or the skeptic, who is not enlightened by living faith. But it is the most fundamental of realities and the most real destiny to which the human being is called. It is also the sacred goal of human existence that alone can truly fulfill the human mind and heart of each person, and make us truly happy.

Is Trinitarian Faith Monotheistic?

Finally, we should consider a well-known objection. Is it really true that the Trinitarian faith of Christians is a genuine form of monotheism? Can one really believe that God the creator is eter-

34. 1 Cor 13:9, 13:12.
35. 1 Jn 3:2, Rv 22:5.

nally one in being but that God is also this communion of three persons? Does the Catholic faith not amount to a contradiction in terms?

The first thing to say is that there is a distinction between things we can come to know by natural reason and things we can come to know only by supernatural faith in divine revelation. The mystery of the Holy Trinity is a truth of divine revelation, not a truth of natural reason. Working by its own resources, philosophical reason can never prove or disprove the mystery of the Trinity.

The reason for this is the following: our natural knowledge of God is indirect and inferential. We can know that God exists based on the *effects* of God that are his creatures, and which show a definite *trace* of God as their transcendent cause. From this we can come to the certitude that God exists, that he is one, and that he is the creator of all that is. Monotheism, then, is a rational truth, however difficult it may be for many of our contemporaries to perceive this.

At the same time, however, God transcends his created effects infinitely and we have no direct natural knowledge of what God is in himself. As Aquinas says, we can know *that* God is, and primarily *what God is not*.[36] This means that naturally speaking the inner identity or personal mystery of God remains a profound and insoluble philosophical enigma. Yes, it is true that the Christian can say with certitude that God the Holy Trinity is the author of the creation, because God has genuinely revealed himself in Christ. However, the effects of the creation as known by mere reason are effects resulting from the Trinity acting as one in the sense we have underscored above. The Father, Son, and Holy Spirit are one in their action of creating and sustaining all things in being. Consequently, if we approach things simply in terms of natural reason, we may come to think rightly that God exists, but

36. Aquinas, *ST* I, q. 3, pref.

we cannot demonstrate from philosophical premises the truth of the mystery of God as Trinity. For that knowledge, God must take the initiative to step across the brink and reveal himself to us personally, by grace.

Second, then, we can see that this is quite fitting in a way. Christianity tells us that the most ultimate knowledge that we can obtain about God does not arise as a mere natural possibility and is not a native right, but is a sheer gift, rather like the gift of friendship by which we come to know another person who reveals to us who he is. God can choose to give us the grace of intimate knowledge and love of his own mystery, and has even created us in such a way that we are naturally capable of receiving this gift, as spiritual creatures, unlike the other animals who do not have rational capabilities of the same kind. But the gratuity or sheer givenness of the gift remains always present as a structural feature of our knowledge of God the Holy Trinity: "By grace you have been saved."[37] The faith is intellectually enticing precisely because it elevates us *beyond* our natural knowledge but also in accord with our own deepest natural desires and possibilities: the natural desire to know God personally and to experience somehow what God is in himself. Grace speaks to our desire for the absolute. It is not an accident, then, that Catholicism has insisted far more than Islam or even Judaism on the hope of the beatific vision, the "face to face" encounter with God. This hope is intimately related to the belief in the Incarnation. God has become human so that we might look upon God in human form, and aspire to the spiritual vision of the Holy Trinity in the grace of heaven.

Third, we can say this to the most typical objection: no, there is nothing intrinsically logically inconsistent in saying that God the creator is absolutely simple or one in being, and in saying that God is a communion of three persons. Belief in the Trinity never

37. Eph 2:8.

has been and never can be logically incoherent, for reasons that are implicit in what we explained above. The belief in the processions of the persons (of the Word and the Spirit) is based on relations of origin, but this belief simultaneously emphasizes that the persons who proceed (the Son and the Spirit) both possess the plenitude of the divine nature. That is to say, each person is a subsistent relation. The Son is utterly relational by being from the Father by virtue of his eternal generation. But the Son is also the subsistent being of God. He is God from God, who has in himself all that is in the Father and the Spirit. The Father likewise is entirely relational, as the paternal origin of the Son and Spirit, and has in himself the plenitude of the deity, and thus possesses all that is in the Son and the Spirit. The Spirit is entirely relative to the Father and the Son from whom he proceeds as love, but he has in himself the plenitude of the divine essence, and thus all that is in the Father and the Son.

From the standpoint of natural reason alone, then, it is not possible to determine whether this mystery of the Holy Trinity is real or not. But the idea is not logically incoherent or inconceivable, even if it does represent a mystery different from anything in our ordinary experience of creatures. Theologically we can see the fittingness of belief in the Trinity because it does help us make sense of a core aspect of reality: our capacity to relate to other human beings in love and in relations of shared truth and responsibility. The communion of human persons is like a faint image, one that is very different from the mystery of communion in God, a mystery that *is* God. But if God is the mystery of communion in truth and love that is the Father, Son, and Holy Spirit, this does help us understand why the human community is created to become a society of love, a communion of persons bound together by grace who participate in their own way in the life of charity that emanates forth from God.

Ultimately our decision to believe in the mystery of the Trinity is deeply related to how we understand the person of Jesus Christ. If Jesus Christ is the Son of God, if he is truly resurrected from the dead, if the New Testament teaching of the apostles is genuinely inspired, then the mystery of the Trinity is real. If Christ is real, the Trinity is the deepest mystery of God. We cannot believe in Christ without belief in this mystery, nor can we believe in this mystery without believing in Christ. The Trinitarian faith is not a secondary aspect of Christianity, but is the summit and source of all the rest. This truth casts perspective on everything else, and allows us to "interpret" reality from a most ultimate vantage point. This claim will become increasingly evident in the chapters to come in which we consider other elements of Catholicism in light of the mystery of God.

3

CREATION AND THE
HUMAN PERSON

Creation *ex Nihilo*

In Plato's dialogue *Timaeus* he portrays God as a demiurge, an artist who fashions the world out of pre-existent matter. God shapes the world like a kind of primal clay, but in doing so he also coexists with the clay. Matter and God are first coexistent principles. We may think that this vision is very primitive or crude, but it is similar to one most people hold today when they think of "creation." In the beginning God gave the universe a push, by means of the Big Bang or some other primordial event. Then he helped to "shape" the universe by guiding its cosmic development and the evolution of living beings. When people argue from the modern sciences that God exists, they often argue from this kind of premise: it seems most probable that the world as we know it today could not have been fashioned without a guiding intelligence. Unfortunately, such lines of argumentation frequently ignore the fact that it is primarily the *existence* of the world that requires an explanation, and not its historical development. Unsurprisingly, atheists form their views by reacting against this notion: we do not need God in order to explain the history of the universe. The laws of science tell us all there is to know about "how things began" or came to be.

None of this has much to do with the traditional Catholic understanding of creation *ex nihilo*, or "creation from nothing." When Aquinas defines this term he makes clear that it simply denotes the creation of all that exists by God without any instrument or pre-existing matter.[1] The idea is not only that God once made all that there is but that God *continually* creates and sustains in being all that exists at any and every moment. Here we are considering creation at a deeper level than anything that happened in the early stages of the cosmos (just after the supposed Big Bang) or at any juncture along the way. The point is that God gives being to all things that ever exist, at no matter what juncture we envisage in the history of the cosmos. Evidently, this means that God is the origin of the material world, and of all living things, with all their laws, development, and internal evolution of forms. Even if there were nothing particularly interesting about the history of the cosmos and its internal development, God would still by necessity be the creator of all that exists.

If we begin from this "deeper" metaphysical definition of creation, it follows that the modern sciences cannot ever prove or disprove that the world is created. Why so? These sciences examine quantitative and measurable (empirical) features of reality that are available to the senses. They operate only through dependence upon measurable phenomena, mathematical models, and theories of material causation. Meanwhile, the created character of all that exists—its very dependence in the order of being—is much more fundamental than anything we can quantify or study by mathematics and the observational sciences. It is something we can perceive not with our senses, but rationally and philosophically. All that exists can be or not be, and is held in existence by the causality of God. Thus the belief in creation is not only a

1. Aquinas, *ST* I, q. 45, a. 5.

truth of faith, but also something that we can come to perceive intellectually or metaphysically.

This also means that the doctrine of creation can never be understood accurately as a rival to modern scientific truth or historical study. If the cosmos does have a very ancient history beginning from the initial "Big Bang" 13.8 billion years ago, and if there is a history of the evolution of living forms, beginning with single-cell bacteria on earth 3.8 billion years ago, this presents no argument for or against a doctrine of creation. It simply means that what God gives being to or maintains in existence is itself subject to change and development. God gives being to things that are themselves causes of events in history. That the world of creatures is a world of causes is so obvious that we do not even think about it, but what we should realize is that we and other creatures can only be true causes of events in the world because God himself causes us to be and sustains us in being. Seen from this perspective, the history of cosmic change through causality is itself metaphysical evidence of the reality of the creator.

To some people such reflections may seem like so much metaphysical mumbo-jumbo, incautious speculations derived from a bygone medieval age. However, the trace of our created origin is something that is difficult for any person to evade intellectually for very long. After all, the trace of our potential nothingness is something we are all aware of. There was a time when each one of us did not exist, and there is a time when each of us will not exist anymore (at least not as we exist now). It is not uncommon to hear someone speculate that "existence is pointless" or "absurd." If a person says "I wish that I had never existed," or "human existence has to be endured stoically," we may find his perspective despairing or shortsighted but we do not find it unintelligible or irrational. There is something fundamentally gratuitous about our existence, and this is true not only of human persons, but of every material reality we encounter, since it is by essence an ontologically contingent reality: something that can be or not be. What the notion of creation adds to this observation is that something that exists, but that is also contingent, does not explain sufficiently its own being. The universe of contingent material things is a universe derived from another, a universe *given* being by God the creator. This truth is not wishful thinking or even one derived uniquely from supernatural religious faith. It is based on the bedrock of human reason, and is one of the most fundamental philosophical insights.

Two significant consequences follow from the vision of creation we have just sketched out briefly. The first is that there is never any rivalry between the primary cause of being—which is God the creator alone who produces all that exists—and the "secondary causes" that we find in the created order. The physical world is full of realities that impact or act upon one another, and this gives rise to a vast cosmic history. So too, the world of living things—vegetative and animal—has its own intelligibility as a world of living beings that act upon others just as they are acted upon. Consequently, there is also a vast history of living beings. Similarly, we can recognize the distinctiveness of rational agents, human beings who think, reflect, and act with free deliberation. Accordingly, there is a vast history of human interactions, cultures and civilizations that derive from human ideas and decisions. At each of these "levels" of being (which we will return to below) we find diverse, very real forms of genuine action and causation. To admit this is not to negate that God causes all these things to be. The inverse is the case. This diverse arrangement of created causes *exists* due to the fact that God creates it and sustains it in being. There is no opposition, then, between belief in God and the affirmation that creatures themselves give rise to complex intricate histories: the history of the cosmos, that of evolving, living forms and that special history of free, rational human agents. But the histories in question only come to pass, or only exist at all, because God gives being to all created agents which are themselves in turn true causes.

Second, and finally, it is important to distinguish among created causes between those that act by natural necessity versus those that act by free contingent decision-making.[2] "Necessary" created causes are those that act in predictable ways determined by their natures. Water freezes at a given temperature. Acorns grow into oak trees. Horses eat oats and reproduce their like kind. It is this stability of natural causes that allows us to understand the structure of reality and make accurate predictions about outcomes. "Contingently free" created causes can be understood here as those that act in and through deliberate, free decisions. Angels and human beings, as we shall have occasion to talk about further below, are free creatures. They make choices based on intellectual knowledge and free will. Thus they are truly created causes (dependent upon God for their very existence, even as they undertake free actions) and yet they are also truly free, contingent causes. The freedom of creatures and the creative power of God are not rivals to one another. On the contrary, angels and human beings are truly free to will this or that, to love and choose this or that, because they are created and sustained in being by God's loving freedom. Our created freedom is a participation in the freedom of God, one that becomes more perfect the more God's creative power is present, not one that is eclipsed or destroyed by the presence of the action of God. Free actions are not entirely ours *or* entirely God's. They stem entirely from God *and* entirely from us simultaneously, as God gives us to exist as the free and autonomous creatures that we are.

2. Aquinas, *ST* I, q. 19, a. 8.

A Hierarchy of Natures

The created world is complex. This complexity is obviously numeric: there is an immense multitude of things in the universe. But the complexity also has to do with *kinds* of things present in the universe. There are nonliving physical beings, living things that are vegetative in kind, animals (who are differentiated from plants because they have sense-knowledge), and rational animals that are distinguished from other animals by the presence in them of rational intelligence and deliberative free will. The Catholic faith also holds, based on the revelation of scripture, that angels exist. Angels are pure spirits, intellectual creatures that have free will but that are without physical bodies or sensate life.

We can note that this multiplicity of kinds of beings can be thought of in hierarchical terms.[3] The distinct powers of a given kind of thing—its abilities—are revealed through its actions. Living things, for example, differ from nonliving things because they have internal capacities for self-organization, self-movement, nutrition, growth, and reproduction. We see this even in single-cell organisms. Nonliving things, by contrast, are passive in nature. They are moved by physical forces by which they act upon one another. There is in them no struggle for survival, based upon the need for nutrients, self-protection, or reproduction. Sensate living things, meanwhile, are different from plants because they not only nourish themselves, grow and reproduce, as plants do. They also have sense-knowledge, perception of the world around them, the most basic form of which is the sense of touch. All sensate creatures have the sense of touch, by which they can perceive something of reality by contact with the world around them. More complex animals have more than one sensation (sight, hearing, smell, taste). They also have internal sense powers like sense-memory (higher animals have memories and can learn cer-

3. As noted by Aristotle, *De Anima* II, c. 3.

tain things from experience), and even imagination (in the case of complex mammals like dolphins or apes), by which they can show some degree of creative adaptation to new circumstances. Animals thus exhibit powers and properties not found in plants or in nonliving things.[4]

The human being is distinguished from other animals by reason and free will. These intellectual powers are not simply a higher development of sense powers found in other animals. They are fundamentally different in kind. This assertion is not derived from conjecture or religious willfulness, but is philosophically reasonable. It is based, for example, on the consideration of the human capacity to form universal concepts, and to identify universal causes. We make use of universal concepts regularly, every time we speak, and so language is something that makes us fundamentally different from other animals. They may cry or signal, but our sounds (which are employed according to the conventions of various language traditions) always carry within them a universal signification. The word "man" does not designate only a particular sensate experience of human beings, whether black or white, male or female. It signifies the nature whereby a human being is what it is, as distinct from any other sort of thing. The word "triangle" does not signify only particular sensate images we have of triangles (which are only ever *either* isosceles, scalene, or equilateral triangles). Rather, the conceptual definition of a triangle (as having three sides of straight lines, with angles that add up to 180 degrees) is universal in form. It applies to any and every such triangle that ever has been or could possibly be.[5]

These universal concepts like "human being" and "triangle" are at the basis of all our knowledge and permit the flourishing of the sciences. Once we begin to think about "what a thing is" we can examine its causes and begin to analyze its stable properties.

4. See the analysis of sense perception and imagination in Aristotle, *De Anima* II, c. 5–III, c. 3.
5. Aquinas, *ST* I, q. 76, aa. 1, 2, and 5.

This allows us in turn to transform or alter our environment by applying our knowledge and by undertaking the construction of complex tools, artifacts, and technology. This is why we human beings can conceptually order and organize our living environment and the other animals in a way no other animal can.

The capacity to identify the natures and properties in realities around us, and to form universal concepts based on them, is not something that stems from our sense powers. The sense powers (like sight or hearing and the sensate memories and imaginations they permit) are always specified by a particular sense image or sound. They are drawn from singular material instances of sensation and repeat or refer back to these. A sense memory of a song refers us back to that particular melody. The imagination of a particular person refers us back to his or her sensible features. Our rational knowledge, by contrast, is non-sensible in kind. It is universal precisely because it abstracts from any particular material example, and can refer to each and every material case. To be able to produce this kind of abstract universal knowledge, our intellect must be of a different order than our sensations and internal sense memory. It must be able to produce concepts that are universal and immaterial, that is, not bound to an individual material item, and that grasp the natural forms or essences of things distinct from this or that particular material instance.[6]

This spiritual character of our rational action is also manifest in our free decision-making. Human beings are not moved uniquely by sensible instincts or their bodily emotions like fear or sensate pleasure. They are motivated by the search for what is good, understood intellectually and universally. This means they can distinguish goods from one another rationally and deliberate about what to choose based on ethical convictions and not merely due to instincts or animal appetites.

6. For more on this line of argument regarding the spiritual soul, see Feser, *Aquinas*, 132–62.

This is apparent first and foremost in our capacity to choose freely goods that transcend our senses. Human beings can pray to God and worship God, and can devote themselves to higher pursuits of learning not immediately concerned with temporal or physical concerns. They can be driven by a deep sense of justice or mercy that takes account of the human dignity of others, independently of whether this advances their physical condition or that of others. Likewise, human beings can freely choose to pursue various goods over and against certain of our physical and animal instincts. This is especially manifest in marital fidelity, self-giving friendships that transcend rivalry, and cases where we might fear death (as in warfare), but can freely give our lives for the sake of the good of others. Religious consecration to God, in poverty, chastity and obedience, is a central example of this "primacy" of the spiritual life, in which human beings offer themselves more radically to God in virtue of the human understanding and desire that is proper to them as *spiritual* animals.

Angels, meanwhile, are not animals with bodies, but immaterial spirits, creatures made by God with intellect and free will. They are naturally directed toward God by their innate spiritual desires for truth and love, but they are also created mutable and free, and can turn away from the mystery of God.[7] Angels are unlike human beings in that they are not animals. They are not born of other angels and cannot reproduce corporeally. They

---

7. *Catechism of the Catholic Church*, pars. 328–30: "The existence of the spiritual, non-corporeal beings that Sacred Scripture usually calls 'angels' is a truth of faith. The witness of Scripture is as clear as the unanimity of Tradition. St. Augustine says: "'Angel' is the name of their office, not of their nature. If you seek the name of their nature, it is "spirit"; if you seek the name of their office, it is "angel": from what they are, "spirit," from what they do, "angel"' (*En. in Ps.* 103,1,15: PL 37,1348). With their whole beings the angels are servants and messengers of God. Because they 'always behold the face of my Father who is in heaven' (Matt. 18:10) they are the 'mighty ones who do his word, hearkening to the voice of his word' (Ps 103:20). As purely *spiritual* creatures angels have intelligence and will: they are personal and immortal creatures, surpassing in perfection all visible creatures, as the splendor of their glory bears witness."

do not have physical sensations and emotions and are not subject to physical danger or death. In essence, they are pure contemplatives, creatures made to know and love God, who are able to be in communion with him and with one another by grace. Much or all of what we know about the angelic world (and its counterpart, the demonic) we know from revelation.[8] Angels may be beings in many ways spiritually superior to the human race, but they are also somewhat numinous and inaccessible. Most of our understanding of them comes not from the angels themselves, but from God, who reveals a great deal about them to us in a distinctly human way: in the human words of scripture and in the human life of Christ.[9]

8. *Catechism of the Catholic Church*, pars. 331–33: "Christ is the center of the angelic world. They are *his* angels: 'When the Son of man comes in his glory, and all the angels with him' (Matt. 25:31). They belong to him because they were created *through* and *for* him: 'for in him all things were created in heaven and on earth, visible and invisible, whether thrones or dominions or principalities or authorities — all things were created through him and for him' (Col. 1:16). They belong to him still more because he has made them messengers of his saving plan: 'Are they not all ministering spirits sent forth to serve, for the sake of those who are to obtain salvation?' (Heb. 1:14). Angels have been present since creation and throughout the history of salvation, announcing this salvation from afar or near and serving the accomplishment of the divine plan: they closed the earthly paradise; protected Lot; saved Hagar and her child; stayed Abraham's hand; communicated the law by their ministry; led the People of God; announced births and callings; and assisted the prophets, just to cite a few examples. (Cf. Job 38:7 [where angels are called 'sons of God']; Gen 3:24; 19; 21:17; 22:11; Acts 7:53; Exod. 23:20–23; Judg. 13; 6:11–24; Isa. 6:6; 1 Kings 19:5.) Finally, the angel Gabriel announced the birth of the Precursor and that of Jesus himself (Luke 1:11, 26). From the Incarnation to the Ascension, the life of the Word incarnate is surrounded by the adoration and service of angels. When God 'brings the firstborn into the world, he says: "Let all God's angels worship him"' (Heb 1:6). Their song of praise at the birth of Christ has not ceased resounding in the Church's praise: 'Glory to God in the highest!' (Luke 2:14). They protect Jesus in his infancy, serve him in the desert, strengthen him in his agony in the garden, when he could have been saved by them from the hands of his enemies as Israel had been. (Cf. Matt. 1:20; 2:13,19; 4:11; 26:53 Mark 1:13; Luke 22:43; 2 Macc. 10:29–30; 11:8.) Again, it is the angels who 'evangelize' by proclaiming the Good News of Christ's Incarnation and Resurrection (Luke 2:8–14; Mark 16:5–7). They will be present at Christ's return, which they will announce, to serve at his judgement. (Cf. Acts 1:10–11; Matt. 13:41; 24:31; Luke 12:8–9.)"

9. For a very helpful treatment of the theology of angels see Serge-Thomas

Based on what we have sketched out above, one can perceive in creation a hierarchy of forms, running from the "lowest" grade of being to the "highest." At the base of this hierarchy is the vast world of material, nonliving things, the cosmos in which life first emerges. Living things then emerge in a distinctive hierarchy, from purely vegetative beings, to sensate animals, with the progressive emergence of rational animals, which are both spiritual and physical. Finally, there are the angels, pure spirits that may commune with human beings, but which do not emerge from the physical world at all. From purely material creatures to purely spiritual creatures, the universe has a certain unity to it that is manifest in and through the vast "diversity of kinds" that constitutes the cosmos.

Natural Sciences and the Book of Genesis

What we have presented thus far is a short summary of the teaching of scripture as interpreted in the Catholic tradition. Is such a viewpoint compatible with the modern sciences and what they themselves tell us about the beginnings of the universe, as well as the evolution of living species?

First we should note that Genesis is primarily a revelation of *metaphysical* truths about the world, not a modern scientific treatise. Consider, for example, Genesis 1. There the creation of the world is depicted over against the irrationalities of ancient Babylonian religion.[10] For the Torah, there is only one God, and God is not a physical body. God is neither male nor female, but is transcendent of the physical world. His deity is immeasurable and hidden, but his activity of creation is characterized by divine

Bonino, *Angels and Demons: A Catholic Introduction*, trans. M. Miller (Washington, D.C.: The Catholic University of America Press, 2016).

10. See Ratzinger, *'In the Beginning...'.*

wisdom. He creates all things through his word or reason. And all that God has created is good. The universe is an ordered, intelligible totality created by God and is not something divine. It should not be worshiped and is not to be confused with the first principle from which all things originate. The universe is composed of a multiplicity of visible beings that are also arranged hierarchically, in which man stands at the summit. The human person is made in God's image as male and female, and is the most noble reality in the visible creation. Due to his powers of created reason and freedom, the human person is capable of friendship and communion with God. Human marriage and the transmission of life form an intimate part of God's plan for the creation from the beginning. Genesis 2–3 goes on to show that God is not the author of moral evil, but that evil has entered the world through the transgression of rational creatures. Note that none of these teachings is trivial: each of them can be pondered for the duration of a human lifetime. And yet they are all communicated in a brief passage, beautiful to human reason, in a language that is at once simple, accessible, and utterly profound.

This does not mean there are no historical consequences to the teaching found in Genesis. On the contrary, we can sketch out at least six major teachings there that concern the structure of reality as we know it. These are not modern scientific claims, but they do necessarily have historical implications. (I will return to several of these at further length below.)

1. God gives being to all that exists, but in such a way that there is a first temporal beginning to creation. The teaching that the universe has a finite history is an article of the Catholic faith.

2. God is not only the author of all that exists, but also the universal governor of the order of the world. The hierarchy of forms discussed in the previous section is something that

has its origin in God's eternal knowledge, and which reflects his wisdom and will.

3. The human being is at the summit of visible creatures because it is made in the image and likeness of God. This is due to the fact that the human being has an immaterial soul with spiritual powers of intellect and will. This soul is the form of the human body: that which gives it its inmost definition and identity. The human being, in other words, is not two things, a body and a soul, but is one thing, one being, that is a union of material body and immaterial soul.[11]

4. The human being was created in original justice: that is to say, in grace and in friendship with God. It was a privilege of this initial state that the human person might be preserved from natural death by the power of God, and progressively sanctified in view of eternal life. Physical death is natural to all animals, and in a way is natural to human beings, considered from the point of view of their physical bodies. But the human being is a spiritual animal, created from the beginning with a spiritual soul and in a state of grace. Had our first parents not sinned, they would have graduated to a higher form of life promised to them, on the condition of their cooperation with the grace of God.

5. The human being fell from the grace of God, historically through an actual sin that took place in the beginnings of human history. Our first parents thus lost the grace of sus-

11. *Catechism of the Catholic Church*, pars. 365–66: "The unity of soul and body is so profound that one has to consider the soul to be the 'form' of the body: i.e., it is because of its spiritual soul that the body made of matter becomes a living, human body; spirit and matter, in man, are not two natures united, but rather their union forms a single nature. The Church teaches that every spiritual soul is created immediately by God — it is not 'produced' by the parents — and also that it is immortal: it does not perish when it separates from the body at death, and it will be reunited with the body at the final Resurrection (Pius XII, *Humani Generis*: DS 3896; Paul VI, *CPG* § 8; Lateran Council V [1513]: DS 1440)."

tained friendship with God, and the mysterious preservation from death that they possessed in that state.

6. The human beings who sinned in the beginning then transmitted human life to their descendants deprived of the original gift of grace. This is the state known as being "born in original sin": each human being has a body from its parents, and a spiritual soul created immediately by God. Both are good in themselves. However, in the absence of "original grace" human beings are now naturally subject to death and marked interiorly by various forms of disharmony between our spiritual powers of reason and our animal inclinations toward aggression and sensuality. The result is that human beings tend toward an exaggerated spiritual selfishness, alienation from God and religious truth, and easy enslavement to various forms of ambition, greed, and lust.

Is any or all of this compatible with the most advanced views of modern natural science? Some religionists and some atheists say that it is not. However, Catholicism affirms that the findings of modern science and the traditional dogmas of the faith are entirely compatible, rationally and serenely so. Mainstream modern science postulates that the universe as we know it today first emerged from a high-density energy state, one that was initially very small and that expanded massively. Based on the gradual expansion rates of the universe and its size, this event can be posited to have occurred approximately 13.8–14.5 billion years ago. The expanding cosmos and its internal physical forces gradually produced conditions of sufficient status and complexity that organic life could emerge and survive within the physical world. The first organic life forms were probably single-cell bacteria that emerged on earth approximately 3.8–3.6 billion years ago (prokaryotes). Progressively these life forms evolved through genetic mutation and the persistent survival of superior forms. Eventually more complex living species emerged, with internal organic parts and systematic organization capacities for nourishment and reproduction. The first simple animals may have emerged 600 million years ago, with a progressive development of forms, from fish to amphibians to reptiles to mammals. Great ape forms emerged in the past 20 million years, while hominids who were ancestors to modern humans began to develop 2.5 million years ago. Anatomically modern humans (or living forms anatomically like human beings) emerged sometime in the past 200,000 years. Paleontology detects the presence of distinctly human culture (archaeological signs of art, language, complex tools, and clothing) by at least 50,000 years ago.

None of these affirmations is opposed fundamentally to the religious and philosophical views we have presented above. On the contrary, there are many points of basic harmony or compatibility. However the universe initially began, it is likely that the cosmos as we know it today was first constituted only by nonliving beings. It was a gradual expansion and formation of these beings that has produced a world in which living things can come to be. Living forms, meanwhile, may have emerged gradually from nonliving things (a view that both Augustine and Aquinas are open to), or they may have come about through a "special creation" of God initiating something new in the first cellular organisms.[12] In either case, there is a kind of historical continuity between nonliving things and living things, but also a differentiation and progression from one kind of reality to another, up the scale of perfection. Living forms are more perfect ontologically because they are self-organizing and can self-reproduce. Furthermore, they have evolved and developed over time, so that some have achieved higher degrees of perfection and complexity than others. This is

12. See Augustine, *The Literal Meaning of Genesis*, trans. J. Taylor (New York: Newman Press, 1982), V, 8; VIII, 3; and Aquinas, *ST* I, q. 69, a. 2; q. 71, a. 1, ad 1; q. 73, a. 1, ad 3; q. 118, a. 1, s.c.

manifest in living things that have developed new adaptive capacities, better methods of survival, and higher forms of sensate knowledge. Of particular importance are the sense functions of mammals: our hominid ancestors had highly developed sensate memories, complex vocal skills, and limbs that allowed for subtle forms of toolmaking. All of this served historically as a kind of preparation or foundation for the emergence in human beings of specifically rational, spiritual activities of language and complex technology.

At a given time, then, we can postulate that due to a new initiative of God, animals were elevated to a higher level. God began to create spiritual souls in human animals, and so the human adventure began. There was a passage from the "merely animal" world of *homo sapiens* to the specifically spiritual world of the human person. This is the passage where God initiated the new project of humanity, by creating the spiritual soul, and infusing it as the "form of the body" in what constituted the first human beings. (We might hypothesize that this took place around 50,000 years ago, given the evidence of human culture provided by paleontology.)

Here one should note that the question of the presence or absence of a spiritual soul in the human person cannot be resolved by the modern sciences, which study only the biological, chemical, and physical features of the human person and which by their very methodology cannot attain to the immaterial and spiritual features of the human being. The sciences cannot say, therefore, whether we need to postulate the special creation of a human soul in order to fully understand the "human animal." In truth, the modern sciences cannot even study in an immediate way the psychological and sensate dimensions of human experience (our internal first-person experience of the senses). They do not grasp what it is to be an experiential subject as such. Even less, however, can they tell us what universal knowledge is, why an action is good or evil, what human freedom is, what existence is, or why we are able to consider philosophically the natures and properties of realities. They can say nothing about spiritual reality: the soul, angels, or God. Consequently, if we can learn a great deal about human origins from the modern sciences (particularly regarding the origin of our human, animal bodies), we nevertheless can learn very little from them about the specifically rational character of the human spiritual soul and its immateriality. Even less can we understand from the sciences what the mystery of grace is, and what it would mean for us to be created in a state of grace, or for us to lose that state so as to be subject to an internal disorder or disharmony of body and spiritual powers. The moral drama and the religious mystery of human existence escape the knowledge of the modern scientist insofar as he operates only within the limitations of his discipline. However, the sciences do have a great deal to contribute to our knowledge of the created order, and should not be feared or resented. Just as the religionist has much to learn from the sciences, so too the scientist as a human being is able to transcend the constraints of his or her "merely" scientific understanding of reality, and can also consider the philosophical and revealed knowledge of God and of the human person that is made available to us by other means than mathematical, empirical studies.

Why the Human Person?
The Meeting Point of the
Spiritual and Physical

Based on what we have argued here, we can now note a connection that exists between this Catholic vision of creation and the understanding of God as the Holy Trinity that was presented in the previous chapter. We said there that God in his inmost identity is a mystery of relational persons, the communion of love of the Father, Son, and Holy Spirit. Thus the ultimate foundation of all reality is both *personal* and *interrelational*. If this is the primary truth that is behind all other truths, then it casts a theological light upon all else that exists. We can see in light of the Holy Trinity that the physical cosmos ultimately exists for *spiritual persons* and for *relational love*. The human community is a community of persons, of personal, spiritual animals, who can choose to live in the truth and to love one another authentically, or to live in falsehood and selfishness. This "calling to truth and love" that is proper to the human person is inscribed in our very being as spiritual persons. It is also meant to be lived out or enacted in our bodies, as the bodies of persons. Here then we can see a fundamental truth of the cosmos: there is a relational character to the hierarchy of being. The nonliving things exist for or are relative to the living things. The living things that are nonhuman (plants and animals) have their own integrity and should be respected and preserved from destruction, but they are also relative to the human being and exist to sustain and preserve human life. Human beings are the bridge, then, between the physical world and the spiritual world. They can be in communion with the physical cosmos and the other animals, through the respect of their environment. They can also be in communion with God and with the angelic community of persons through grace. They can live in communion with one another through spiritual and corporeal lives of truth and love.

The human being is the "bridge" between the spiritual and the physical world in a twofold way. In the ascendant direction, the physical world mounts up toward God, or "returns" to God through human actions of knowledge and love. This is especially true in corporate worship, or liturgy, in which the human visible world is made wholly relative and turned toward God in adoration. In the descending direction, man is the "place" that the spiritual world is made visible or manifest in the cosmos. The human community is a kind of icon or image of spiritual life manifesting itself in bodily, visible form. When human beings are turned toward the truth of God, this icon can become a sign of the transcendent mystery of God, a visible church. But when the human being turns in on itself in pride and rejection of God, it can also become a spiritually empty image covered over by spiritual melancholy, lust, violent frustration, and self-destruction. Ultimately, then, the human being is meant to be a special "location" of grace in the cosmos, where the spiritual gifts of God descend through human reason and human freedom into the preservation and construction of a beautiful physical world: a human common life based upon truth, moral goodness, and beauty. The human body can serve the spirit of man so as to acknowledge God in and through human actions. In the bodily life of the human being, the physical cosmos can glorify God.

Imago Dei

Based on the teaching of Genesis, Christianity affirms that the human person is created in the "image" and "likeness" of God or *toward* the image and likeness.[13] The next verse of scripture specifies that "male and female he created them." The Catholic tradition draws out a number of conclusions from these premises. First, the human being is made in the image of God in a stable way due to his or her nature, as a rational person, having a spiritual soul with incorporeal powers of intelligence and free will. There is a dignity to every human person by virtue of our nature, one that is inalienable and that is the basis for unequivocal moral respect of persons and their basic human rights, from the time of conception until natural death.

Second, the human being is one substance or one concrete being composed of both body and spiritual soul. The human ani-

13. Gn 1:26.

106

mal is not two things: a spiritual substance of soul and an animal body, related to one another. There is one composite person who is both body and soul, a spiritual animal, a corporeal person. Death, then, represents the rupture of the human body and the immaterial spiritual soul, a rupture that destroys the integrity and unity of the human person, even if the human spiritual soul survives death.

Third, men and women are equally made in the image of God. They are identically human as to their species or essential nature. Both men and women are rational animals, persons created in the image of God. They are not essentially differentiated (as if they were different species!) but differentiated by very fundamental properties of the human body, those pertaining to sexuality and physical generation. These differences deeply affect the biological, hormonal, psychological, and emotional life of the person, so that it is realistic to speak of various real differences between men and women that result from their sexual differentiation. Human beings are naturally gendered physiologically as male and female in view of sexual complementarity, male-female friendship, marriage, human reproduction, and shared male-female parenthood.

Finally, the human being is created *toward* or *unto* the image of God because this image is not only static but ultimately dynamic. The human person is particularly capable of becoming like God through *activities* of knowledge and love. There is a movement from merely having a human nature and spiritual capacities to activity and dynamic perfection in activity. The other physical creatures in the cosmos (nonliving things, plants, and animals) all bear within themselves some vestige or trace of the uncreated Logos and Wisdom of God. They reflect the creator each in significant ways and are deserving of respect and preservation from destruction by man. But the human being remains the summit of the visible creation and can become more profoundly so only if he develops a more dynamic, perfect relationship toward God.

Here we should note a close parallel between what we said about God in the previous chapter and what we are saying here regarding the *imago Dei*.[14] God in his very being and simplicity is active knowing and loving. He eternally knows and loves his own eternal perfection and goodness and creates all things freely in light of his own infinite perfection and goodness. The human being becomes more perfect by the active knowledge and love of God, and in this way imitates God in his own knowledge and love of himself. Furthermore, this image of God in man is Trinitarian in kind. God is an eternal procession of Wisdom, the Son who is generated from the Father, and an eternal procession of Love, the Spirit who proceeds from the Father and the Son. So likewise, analogously, the human person is a creature that is animated from within by the dynamic desire for the truth and the desire for love. These dynamic capacities in us are only ultimately fulfilled in the life of grace, when we come to know who God is as the eternal Father through the contemplation of the eternal wisdom of Christ and the Holy Spirit, who is love.

Like the persons of the Holy Trinity, then, the human being was created "in the beginning" to be relational in its own way. The human person is made first and foremost to be in relational communion with God, and to be in relational communion with other persons and with nonrational creatures in light of his relationship with God. It is for this reason that Aquinas, following the Church Fathers, argued that political life—that is, organized life in community—is natural to the human person and is not a result of the Fall. From the beginning, the human community was meant to be one of interdependency, implying degrees of perfection, education, and governance. At the heart of the human community is the natural institution of family life, which is created by God directly and not by human government or arbitrary

14. For more on this subject see Augustine, *The Trinity*, trans. E. Hill (New York: New City Press, 2012), esp. chap. XIII.

cultural conventions. Other natural institutions would include human learning, intellectual and manual work, artistic creativity, and the cultivation and care of physical creation.

The human being, in this vision of things, is not merely a highly evolved animal, like other animals (even if there is a clear basis in modern scientific discovery for the affirmation of evolution). Rather, there is something higher and new that is present in the human community. Human persons are capable of spiritualizing and sanctifying their environment through moral and intellectual works of political life: learning, education, governance, family life, and the arts. To deny these distinctively human dimensions of existence is to fall into a morbid materialism that is reductionist and unrealistic. The human being is ontologically complex—both spiritual and corporeal—and any ideological attempt to reduce the human being to something less (as one finds both in twentieth-century Marxism and in twenty-first-century scientific positivism) is both irrational and dangerous, because it ignores the inherent spiritual dignity of the human person.

Creation in Grace: Original Justice

In light of the grace of Christ, Catholic theology "looks back" on the original state of the human being as one that entailed a gift of original grace. This was lost by the original sin of our first parents. St. Paul's letter to the Ephesians refers obliquely to this mystery of original justice, while his letter to the Romans refers to the mystery of original sin, an act of disobedience committed by the first human beings, which resulted in the loss of grace, and the inheritance of natural death, as well as wounds of sin in every human being.[15]

The first thing to say about original justice is that it is a state of "justice" analogically speaking. That is to say, the justice in ques-

15. Eph 5:31–32; Rom 5:12, 7:21–25.

tion is not primarily moral or legal (a state of moral righteousness before God). Rather, it is a state of "health" or "integrity" in which the spiritual soul is subject to God (through faith in God and love for God), and the human body is subject to the soul (due to the presence of the grace of God). We might call it a kind of original harmony between the human being and God, and within the human being itself, as well as between human beings.

Second, we should note that original justice implies the presence of grace in the human being from the beginning. The Catholic Church, on the basis of scripture, teaches that the human being was created in a state of grace.[16] That is to say, the human person made in the image of God was "originally graced" with the theological virtues: the infused virtues of faith, hope, and charity. These gifts allowed the first human beings to live in communion with God the Holy Trinity, and to know and love God in a life of communion that was both visible and invisible. Human society was created originally to be an *ecclesial society*. Natural human virtues such as prudence, justice, fortitude, and temperance were meant to be elevated toward God within the life of grace.

---

16. Second Vatican Council, *Lumen Gentium*, November 21, 1964, no. 2; *Gaudium et Spes*, December 7, 1965, 12–13 (both documents are available at www.vatican. va); *Catechism of the Catholic Church*, pars. 374–76: "The first man was not only created good, but was also established in friendship with his Creator and in harmony with himself and with the creation around him, in a state that would be surpassed only by the glory of the new creation in Christ. The Church, interpreting the symbolism of biblical language in an authentic way, in the light of the New Testament and Tradition, teaches that our first parents, Adam and Eve, were constituted in an original state of holiness and justice. This grace of original holiness was to share in divine life. By the radiance of this grace all dimensions of man's life were confirmed. As long as he remained in the divine intimacy, man would not have to suffer or die. The inner harmony of the human person, the harmony between man and woman, and finally the harmony between the first couple and all creation, comprised the state called 'original justice.'" Some medieval and modern theologians have held that the first couple was created first in a state of pure nature and then elevated soon thereafter into a state of grace. This position is permissible in Catholic doctrine. However, one should note that even in this case, the creation of the human person clearly takes place in view of the life of grace and friendship with God.

The human community was meant to be indwelt by the presence of the Holy Spirit and aided by his interior gifts of inspiration and enlightenment.

Along with this gift of human communion with God by grace, the scriptures posit that the original human beings received certain interior graces that established profound harmony between the sensate powers of the soul and the spiritual powers of the soul. This harmony came as a gift of grace, not a pure inheritance of nature. Naturally speaking, there can be tensions between our sensate animal appetites and our natural spiritual desires for truth, goodness, and moral nobility. The first human couple were devoid of this tension due to a mysterious grace of preservation that was given to them, and that we see present since only in the cases of Jesus Christ and the Virgin Mary, the new Adam and the new Eve, who are free from the disharmony of self that is an effect of original sin.

Finally, scripture teaches unequivocally that the first human persons were given the grace (at least in promise) of preservation from natural death. This point should be considered carefully. It is natural for physical bodies to undergo eventual corruption and for animals to die. This is no less true for human beings for whom death is natural. However, scripture reveals that the eternal project of God was to elevate animals into the world of spiritual life— to create the first human persons as spiritual and animal—in order to spiritualize matter. The human being was created in grace so as eventually to become a place of "divinization"—where God would spiritualize the cosmos and the human body, making it a manifestation of his spiritual wisdom, goodness, and power. This was to take place progressively through the cooperation of the human community with God by obedience to the grace of God in faith, hope, and charity, not due to the power of human nature working alone.

The goal of the physical creation from the beginning, then,

was the creation of the human person. The goal of the creation of the human person was to establish an ecclesial communion with God effected by grace. The goal of this life of grace was to permit human beings to live in stable friendship with God in view of the grace of the beatific vision, the deifying vision of the blessed Trinity. This beatifying vision given to the human *soul* of the human person would in turn affect the human *body*, and indirectly the whole physical cosmos. In the words of St. Irenaeus, "For the glory of God is the human being fully alive; and the life of man consists in beholding God."[17] Human beings were meant to become the spiritual monstrance of God, wherein the glory of God would break out into the whole creation, shining like a radiant spiritual light in the midst of the physical world.

Two interesting claims follow from those we have just made. The first is that the original graces of human existence were meant to be preserved and communicated by the first human parents of humanity in and through a social life of marriage, procreation, and education. Had the first human couple not sinned, each human being would have been "conceived without sin" and in a state of grace. Marriage as a kind of original sacrament would have symbolized the life of grace that unites us to God, but also communicated it effectively to offspring through the transmission of human life *within* the life of grace. The life of the Church would have been more essentially wed, then, to the natural life of the human family and to the political life of the larger human community. It might not even have entailed an institution entirely distinguishable from those of the family and human city. In a fallen world, this is obviously something now unimaginable for us in many respects, a possibility that was forfeited. Our conjectures about life before the Fall should not be confused with the concrete Christian economy of grace that we now inhabit, and which has developed quite differently.

17. Irenaeus, *Against Heresies* IV, 20, 7 (translation slightly modified).

Second, it follows that human nature is meant to exist in a state of grace, and that without such grace, the human person is terribly impoverished in his very being and activities. The acts that make us resemble God most, acts of knowledge and love, are perfected in this life in particular through the infused graces of faith, hope, and charity. The greatest saints who are closest to God are those who know God most intensely and mystically within faith, and who hope in and love God most profoundly. Even after the loss of grace the human person remains in the image of God and retains a spiritual nature, but that nature is severely truncated and incomplete without a right orientation toward its true homeland and a genuine knowledge of God.

The Fall

If what we have said is true, then the human being is precariously located between the visible and invisible worlds and has in himself a delicate internal balance of the rational and the sensible, the spiritual and the corporeal. According to scripture, this balance or harmony was maintained from the first through the presence of grace, orienting the person toward the heights of the spiritual life. It was lost, however, by what Newman calls the "aboriginal calamity" of original sin.[18] The original sin is defined by St. Paul as one of primal disobedience, a movement in the heart of the first parents of humanity whereby they turned away from God as the giver of grace, rejecting the inner movements of infused faith, hope, and love.[19] In this way, they forfeited the state of original justice or integrity and willed to live instead in reference to their own constructions of good and evil, apart from God and over against the mystery of God.

This primal event is presented in scripture in highly symbolic

18. Newman, *Apologia*, 217.
19. Rom 5:12–19.

terms, but its historical reality is not difficult to believe in. The human condition is deeply marked by the effects of evil, moral ignorance, and human weakness. According to traditional Catholic theology the primary effect of original sin in the first parents of humanity was their loss of grace, and thus the loss of their friendship with God. However, two other effects ensued. First, a disharmony of internal powers: the life of reason and free will is easily compromised by the "animal" in us, particularly through the passions of sensate desire (i.e., the excessive love of sense pleasures) and irascibility (i.e., excessive anger or laziness). The human being is all too often less than reasonable due to excessive emotional influences and bodily addictions. Second, the human being is subject to death, a natural characteristic of human life, but one we are no longer protected against by the gift of God. Consequently, the body and the soul live in a certain tension with one another. While the soul at its deepest level is made for enduring truth and the fulfillment of personal love, the body is bound by weakness, sickness, and death. There is a kind of duality running through the human being that is hard to understand without the help of divine revelation.

The internal disharmony that resulted from original sin is transmitted to all the descendants of our first human parents. Original sin is not "something" that is transmitted, like a biological disorder. That idea is irrational. Rather it is best understood as an effect of the "real absence" of grace. We continue to receive a nature composed of body and soul, which are both good in themselves: the body comes from our parents and the soul directly from God the creator. What is now missing, however, is the original grace that kept this unity of body and soul harmonized and unified morally. As a consequence, the nature we inherit lacks the integrity it once possessed in the state of original justice, and is instead characterized by four kinds of "wounds." The first is *ignorance*, which affects our intellect: we are unable to grasp who God is personally, and live in a kind of spiritual orphanhood regarding the knowledge of our creator. The second is *malice* or *egoism* in the human will. This is a self-referentiality of the human heart that tends to desire its own good above that of others and even in preference to the goodness of God. This wound of sin causes in us a fundamental distrust of God and an affective antipathy to religious truths. Third is *weakness* that affects our emotional life of fortitude, so that it is more difficult for us to struggle to obtain difficult goods. We are typically slothful or indifferent in the face of serious moral demands. Finally, there is *concupiscence*, an exaggerated desire for sensate pleasures of food, drink, and sex, wherein human beings seek rest or even personal transcendence primarily in the pleasures of the senses, rather than in the goods of the spiritual life. It is not only all individuals who are marked by these wounds as enduring characteristics. It is also all human cultures, which are marked by various "social structures of sin": collective habits or characteristics that incline people to acts of moral ignorance, selfishness, complicit weakness, and lust.

Due to the "inheritance" of original sin, the human community lives under the inevitable shadow of various forms of existential turmoil. Consider, for example, our moral misery. On the one hand, human beings sense that we are driven by noble desires for greatness, love, self-giving, and of seeking after the absolute. On the other hand, we discover continuously our reasons for moral wretchedness, guilt, or shame. Those who claim there are not objective moral standards are also those who often become the most morally imperialistic and self-righteous, or those who suffer the most internally from the sense of disorientation and error. Pascal describes man's simultaneous "greatness and wretchedness," his inextinguishable spiritual desire to live a life of ethical beauty and the torment of his sense of banality and boredom, if not to say ugliness and spiritual poverty.[20]

20. Blaise Pascal, *Pensées* (Oxford University Press, 2008), chaps. III and VI.

Likewise, we are subject to the enigma of physical death, even while we can aspire actively to find eternal life. Here Pascal famously describes the human person as a "thinking reed": we are physically frail, tiny beings adrift in a vast cosmos, and at the same time, we have a capacity to reason even beyond the physical constraints of the cosmos.[21] There is an unstable union in us of spiritual and corporeal, or the personal and animal, even as we are bound by the inevitability of death. Man is not precisely a "being towards annihilation," because the soul does not cease to exist at death. However, the human person is truly, as Heidegger stated, a "being towards death": mortality is a boundary that sets a question to everything else the human person does in this life.[22]

This boundary creates a deep question for all human beings. What does the human condition ultimately consist of? Are we destined to become purely spiritual in the end, a mere soul separated from the body? Are we material alone, such that we cease to be at death? In the face of the mystery, it is understandable that many who have not received divine revelation—particularly the revelation of the resurrection of the dead—have posited other alternative theories. Some give in to the despair of materialism, and attempt to deny that human life has any transcendent meaning, a view that obliges one to minimize the meaning of existence. Others, like the Gnostics, have claimed that the body is evil and that true personhood is spiritual alone. Death is a deliverance from a world of bodily suffering and temporal illusions. This view ignores the fact that the body is good and is an integral part of the human person. Still others have posited the problematic theory of reincarnation, in which the souls of those who die are transferred into new living bodies. One advantage of this view is that it maintains some hope of body-soul reunification. The problem is

---

21. *Pensées*, VI, 113.
22. Martin Heidegger, *Being and Time*, trans. J. Macquarrie and E. Robinson (New York: Harper and Row, 1962), 279–311.

that there is no personal continuity between subjects across time as souls reincarnate, so that personhood is seen as something accidental or unnecessary to the soul. But the spiritual soul really is personal through and through, because it is inherently characterized by the intellect and the will, faculties that are the seat of our personality. A developed personality cannot be eradicated and reformatted anew.[23] Furthermore, the soul is the formal principle of a human body. I am the composite of my soul and body, not my soul alone. And so, I cannot be the same person if my soul begins to inhabit the body of another. If the soul survives after death, and if the soul is meant to be embodied (which it is), then the soul needs to be eventually embodied in such a way as to *reconstitute* the original person.[24]

In opposition to theories of materialism, Gnosticism, and reincarnation, Christianity posits that the "answer" to the human condition is found ultimately in the resurrection from the dead. Our spiritual soul is meant to be reunited to a material body, but this can only be the case in the long run if God "re-creates" the world by raising the dead in glorified human bodies. If Christ is truly raised physically from the dead in a glorified body that will die no more, then there is a promise of general resurrection for the human race. Not only can we hope to encounter God spiri-

---

23. In this sense, Eastern religious traditions that affirm the illusion and transience of personhood, and the successive reincarnation of the soul without a continuity of personal characteristics, fail to grasp the individual and personal destiny of each human soul, just as they fail to grasp the personal nature of the absolute principle, God the creator. Aquinas offers convincing philosophical arguments for the personal characteristics of the human spiritual soul even after death and the metaphysical impossibility of reincarnation in *Summa Contra Gentiles* II, cc. 79–87, esp. c. 83.

24. In *Summa Contra Gentiles* IV, cc. 79–81, Aquinas argues that the resurrection of the body is rationally fitting, given the immateriality of the spiritual soul, and the fact that the human soul is meant to be embodied. His argument from fittingness is not meant to demonstrate philosophically the necessity of the resurrection, which is a mystery of faith, but to show the harmony of this Christian mystery with the reasonable hopes of our philosophical understanding.

tually after death as personal immaterial souls, but we may also hope eschatologically ("in the end times") for the union of body and soul anew in the life of the world to come. Seen in this ultimate light, the mystery of original sin is "good news" because it confronts us with the enigma of death, and this enigma in turn points us toward the answer of Christ.

The Non-Christian
Search for God: Natural Law
and Grace

The Catholic Church permits theologians to hold a diverse range of views on the consequences of original sin in the human race and on the state of the fallen human being. However, there are two extremes that must be avoided. Responding to what traditionally has been considered an excessive pessimism, the Council of Trent rejected the view of the Reformers that fallen human nature is in a state of "total depravity." This is the view that the human person in the fallen state has either entirely forfeited being in the image of God, or is wholly incapable of any act of moral goodness. Trent underscored that even in the fallen state, and marked by selfishness and godlessness, the human being is capable of some natural and moral good.[25] On the other extreme of exaggerated optimism the Council Fathers noted that the fallen human being, no matter how great or good its nature, can in no way merit the salvation and the forgiveness of sins that comes about uniquely through the grace of Christ. Salvation is through grace alone.[26]

When Aquinas considers the fallen state of man he makes an important set of distinctions.[27] First there is the good of our na-

---

25. See the Council of Trent, "Decree on Justification," cc. 5, 7, and 25; *Catechism of the Catholic Church*, pars. 1701–9.

26. The Council of Trent, "Decree on Justification," chap. 1–6.

27. Aquinas, *ST* I-II, q. 85, a. 1.

ture as rational animals, which remains unchanged even by sin. A human being does not change its species due to sin, and thus remains fundamentally good, as one made in the image of God. Second, there are our inclinations toward basic human goods. These are weakened or wounded by sin but not destroyed. We remain fundamentally inclined toward basic goods like happiness, friendship, virtue, and even the knowledge and love of God. But alongside these good inclinations we have contrary inclinations toward vice, in the form of ignorance, selfishness, and shallowness. Third, there is the perfection of our nature in the order of grace, which was given to us in original justice, and which is forfeited by the effects of original sin. No matter how good or well-intentioned the fallen person is, his natural powers are incapable of attaining this higher gift of grace that alone truly completes and fulfills the human person.

This vision of fallen human beings is certainly sober but also leaves us with the sense that there are noble natural aspirations that remain inscribed in the heart of man, even in the fallen world. This is important theologically since, as we will consider below, God can and does work with our natural aspirations when he gives human beings grace. It is this fundamental set of inclinations inscribed in our rational nature that Catholic theology traditionally names "natural law." Natural law is not first and foremost a set of propositions or self-evident axioms, and even less is it a set of positive laws drawn up by society. It is something much deeper and more fundamental: the tendency in the human being that draws him into the moral life and into the practical task of discerning wrong and right, and of choosing good and rejecting evil.

The first principle of the natural law is happiness. Traditional Catholic moral theology insists rightly that every human being is inexorably drawn toward happiness. Everyone wishes in some way to be happy and strives to do so in every act he makes, however indirectly. Behind all our acts of freedom and all our rational decisions (conscientious or not) is the aim of happiness.[28] In addition, this inclination toward happiness is not entirely nebulous. There are precise goods or ends that alone fulfill the human being.[29] Among the most basic tendencies we have are the rational desire to exist and to preserve ourselves in being, the desire to couple and marry so as to reproduce and raise children in community, and the rational desire to live in friendship with others in a just society. We also have a natural desire for the truth, including a desire to know the first principle and cause of all reality (God). This natural desire for the truth grounds our innate capacity for religious behavior.

Our natural tendencies incline us toward various goods: family life, work, political society, education, moral responsibility, religious behavior, moderate rest, and relaxation. Desires for these goods are inscribed in us as rational, sentient beings and are ineradicable, even when we choose not to act upon them. When we do act on them (and all of us do in various ways), we begin to have to negotiate the prudent arrangement and hierarchical ordering of goods. Do we pursue our work chiefly in view of our personal fulfillment, or the good of our families, or of our larger society, or do we do it for God? If the answer is "all of the above," then how are these diverse goods interrelated? Are some more important than others? How do our personal choices regarding other human beings relate to the ultimate truth (concerning God and religion)? How does our treatment of other human beings correspond to our own legitimate desire to love ourselves and to be loved?

It is in developing answers to these questions that we begin to see the necessity of the four *cardinal virtues*. *Prudence* is the virtue of practical intelligence, by which we make rational, ethical

28. Aquinas, *ST* I-II, qq. 1–2.
29. See Aquinas, *ST* I-II, q. 94, a. 2.

decisions to order our lives well and to prioritize our pursuit of goods so as to order all things ultimately toward God. *Justice* is the virtue that gives to each one his due, recognizing the dignity, responsibility, and rights of each human being. Justice qualifies our free human actions so that our decisions reflect a true respect for the capabilities and limitations of each person. Justice always has to be applied with a concern for equality and fairness but also mercy and prudence regarding particular situations. *Fortitude* is the virtue that qualifies our pursuit of difficult goods. The struggle to withstand trials or to obtain hard-won goals tests our mettle as persons and can wear on our emotions, as we undergo bouts of audacity or fear, hope or despair, anger or resignation. Fortitude is the virtue of fighters, that allows us to maintain patience and courage so as to persevere even in the face of difficulties. *Temperance* is the virtue that moderates our enjoyment of emotional and sensate pleasures. The senses are good and our emotional passions are good in themselves. But pleasures of food, drink, and sexuality, among others, risk to dominate human freedom and make us act unreasonably, selfishly, or irresponsibly. The virtue of temperance is a guardian of sane action, and guides the human being to enjoy sensate goods in a charitable, self-giving, spiritual way rather than a gluttonous or animalistic way. Intemperance, especially in matters of sex, seems to have an almost immediately numbing effect on a person's relationship with God. It also undermines a person's sense of genuine self-worth, increases isolation and immaturity, and inclines a person toward manipulation or objectification of others.

The virtue of religion is a kind of crown of the other natural virtues. Aquinas argues that religion is a dimension or "potential part" of the virtue of justice.[30] If justice is the virtue of rendering each his due in general, religion is the virtue of rendering God what is due to God in particular. That is to say, acts of religion

---

30. Aquinas, *ST* II-II, q. 81.

are acts of prayer and devotion by which we raise our minds and hearts to God to acknowledge our created dependency upon God, to invoke his divine providence, and to place ourselves under the natural attraction of his sovereign goodness and love. It pertains to the natural law—to the deepest natural inclinations and instincts of the human being—to be religious and to acknowledge God in religious contemplation and adoration.

If all this is the case—if human beings really tend toward happiness through the pursuit of genuine goods, by way of the cardinal virtues and religious activity—then why is humanity so confused and divided on so many issues pertaining to morality and religion? Here we should return to what was said above: as a result of original sin (our original gracelessness), our basic moral inclinations are *weakened* and we suffer *contrary inclinations*. In opposition to temperance, all human beings tend to various degrees and in various ways toward sensuality and the accompanying dullness of spirit that it engenders. In opposition to fortitude, they tend toward moral weakness and cowardice. In opposition to justice, human cultures are rife with a plurality of injustices, unfair inequalities, and arbitrary privileges. In opposition to prudence, human beings are often marked by moral ignorance and existential disorientation. They frequently make foolish, unenlightened, and self-destructive choices, or fall into the rut of mediocre compromise.

The theatre of human action, then, is one marked by a dramatic struggle between good and evil, virtue and vice, light and darkness. No matter how dull our moral lives may seem at times, the deeper turmoil of human decision-making abides and remains irrevocably serious. Our human freedom provides us with daily opportunity for great moral responsibility but also remains a heavy burden that has to be endured and accepted.

At the center of this drama is the human conscience. Conscience springs fundamentally, as St. Augustine saw, from *syn-*

deresis: the first moral intuitions of human reason.[31] We know instinctively that certain actions are good and others evil, even before we work out a prolonged rationale to justify them. It is wrong to take innocent human life and right to protect and provide for it. It is wrong to deceive and tell untruths, while living in the truth is a more noble way of being. However, as Aquinas noted, the conscience can be obscured from perception of the true good, either due to the difficulty of cases involved ("is it always wrong to steal *in every case*?"), or from cultural mis-education, or due to our fallen inclinations and personal sins, which obscure our capacity to perceive the good.[32] To commit adultery is always wrong, according to the teaching of scripture, no matter how understandable its motivations in complex human situations. But we are able frequently to rationalize even obvious sins, from those of adultery or abortion to smaller "venial" sins of slight detraction of another person's reputation, to the telling of white lies. Because our hearts are often divided between light and darkness, human beings are riddled with moral complexity, and so our consciences are often opaque.

Human religious behavior is not exempt from this rule, and provides perhaps its greatest illustration. True knowledge and love of God are what are most difficult for human beings, naturally speaking, due to their elevated character. These highest but most difficult goods are deeply affected by the contrary inclinations of human selfishness, ignorance, and sensuality. The religious history of humanity is therefore fraught with ambiguity. While human beings remain naturally religious, at least in mere capacity, they can also be deeply superstitious or fanatical, worshiping the wrong thing or seeking to serve the divine (or the gods) in the wrong way (such as by human sacrifice, or suicidal bombing). Even when human beings participate in a true religion, they can use religious

---

31. Augustine, *On the Trinity* XII, 2, 5, and 8; Aquinas, *ST* I, q. 79, a. 12.
32. Aquinas, *ST* I-II, q. 94, a. 6.

authority for the sake of illicit gain, profane the sacred, or abuse power in selfish and manipulative ways. In doing so they become a counter-witness to the truth of the Gospel. Non-religious persons also frequently perpetuate religious injustices. They can cultivate a studied indifference to religious matters, one that is either philosophically sophisticated or culturally crude, so as to numb themselves and their children to any sensitivity to the transcendent. In doing so they show ingratitude to God, and suppress within themselves a core dimension of the human spirit. If they seek to eradicate the presence of all religion from academic culture, political discussion, or the larger life of human society, they inadvertently set themselves up against God.

Despite the dark murkiness that mars all human history and culture, human nature does remain fundamentally inclined toward the truth and moral goodness, as well as a religious relationship to the absolute. Furthermore, the Catholic Church, following scripture, teaches that even from the beginning, after the Fall, God has offered grace throughout history in various and diverse forms, to all peoples in all times and places. "For, since Christ died for all men, and since the ultimate vocation of man is in fact one, and divine, we ought to believe that the Holy Spirit in a manner known to God offers to every man the possibility of being associated with this paschal mystery."[33] The field of battle that is human history, then, is not only marked by a struggle between good and evil in human nature, but also by the presence of God's grace and the possibility of its effective acceptance or its rejection and refusal.

As Pope John Paul II noted, this universal action of divine grace in history takes place principally in the human mind and heart, especially the moral conscience:

The Church knows that the issue of morality is one which deeply touches every person; it involves all people, even those who do not know

33. Second Vatican Council, *Gaudium et Spes*, no. 22.

Christ and his Gospel or God himself .... [It] is precisely *on the path of the moral life that the way of salvation is open to all.* The Second Vatican Council clearly recalled this when it stated that "those who without any fault do not know anything about Christ or his Church, yet who search for God with a sincere heart and under the influence of grace, try to put into effect the will of God as known to them through the dictate of conscience ... can obtain eternal salvation .... Nor does divine Providence deny the helps that are necessary for salvation to those who, through no fault of their own, have not yet attained to the express recognition of God, yet who strive, not without divine grace, to lead an upright life. For whatever goodness and truth is found in them is considered by the Church as a preparation for the Gospel and bestowed by him who enlightens everyone that they may in the end have life."[34]

Human religious traditions are marked both by sin and ignorance as well as by true philosophical or moral teachings. The latter can be indications of the work of grace.

Other religions found everywhere try to counter the restlessness of the human heart, each in its own manner, by proposing "ways," comprising teachings, rules of life, and sacred rites. The Catholic Church rejects nothing that is true and holy in these religions. She regards with sincere reverence those ways of conduct and of life, those precepts and teachings which, though differing in many aspects from the ones she holds and sets forth, nonetheless often reflect a ray of that Truth which enlightens all men. Indeed, she proclaims, and ever must proclaim Christ "the way, the truth, and the life" (John 14:6), in whom men may find the fullness of religious life, in whom God has reconciled all things to Himself.[35]

In summary, then, the human person is never saved by his or her natural powers, or by simply acting in accord with the natural law, even if the latter is deeply inscribed in the human mind and heart. It is the grace of God active in human history in view of the merits of Jesus Christ that makes eternal salvation possible.

34. John Paul II, *Veritatis Splendor*, Encyclical Letter, August 6, 1993, par. 3, quoting the Second Vatican Council, *Lumen Gentium*, no. 16.
35. Second Vatican Council, *Nostra Aetate*, October 28, 1965, no. 2.

Despite their ambiguities and even their serious manifest errors, non-Christian religious traditions serve as a testimony to man's search for God in the shadows of this world. They can be places, sometimes despite themselves, in which the grace of the Holy Spirit is active and through which Christ is progressively made manifest. Irenaeus of Lyons described the world *prior* to the coming of Christ as the age of the Holy Spirit in which human beings were seeking God, often under the hidden influences of grace, but had not yet found God in his manifest, revealed form, by means of the Incarnation. This era of seeking prepared gentile humanity to receive the higher, perfect revelation of God that would come forth from the people of Israel.[36]

Salvation Is from the Jews:
Prophecy and Judaism

The mystery of Israel is a mystery of election. God chose a particular people from out of all the peoples of the world. He revealed himself to them personally and formed a covenant with them by means of the Mosaic law, the rites of the Old Testament, and the teachings of the prophets. In one sense Israelite religion is the fulfillment of the universal human search for God. In Israel, humanity has found God. However, it is crucial to note that in the Torah, the discovery of God is a gift. God descends to humanity by way of revelation. Outside of this gift, we find only the "ascent" of the human being striving to find God, riddled with confusion, and tempted to despair. In Israel, humanity discovers the grace and hope of having a true, stable life with God.

"That is all very well," one can object, "but the covenant with Israel was exclusive and restricted to one people, not universal in kind." Here we confront what theologians typically term the "scandal of particularity": God has chosen to work in a unique

36. Irenaeus, *Against Heresies* IV, 20, 1–8.

way through one people alone. There are intelligible reasons for this: God's choice of Israel reveals to us the mystery of God's preferential love, his jealousy. The contrast between Israel and the nations also serves to instruct all human beings. It demonstrates the contrast between the truth of the divine revelation and the lingering confusion and idolatry of the nations. The political and cultural insignificance of ancient Israel in the midst of greater nations also demonstrates the gratuity of divine election. God works through human beings even in the midst of their seeming powerlessness. Finally, the singularity of Israel among the nations is prefigurative of the singularity of Christ among all human beings. God chose a particular people as his own. He also became one particular human being, an Israelite who would die for all others. From the singularity of Israel and Christ God brings forth the universal offer of salvation and the Church.

Despite indisputable biblical teaching regarding the election of Israel, mistaken Christian rejection of the Old Testament as divine revelation has a very ancient pedigree. In the second century A.D., the heretical innovator Marcion asserted that the Old Testament portrays God in terms that are cruel and anthropomorphic, and argued that the revelation of Jesus Christ could not truly be based in the prior teachings of Judaism. He proceeded to eradicate all Old Testament references from the New Testament. The fourth-century Manichaean sect followed suit arguing that the physical world is evil and that the god of the physical world depicted in the Old Testament must be the author of evil. They illustrated this claim by invoking the great number and austere severity of the laws of the Torah, and the fact that the god of the Old Testament engages in holy war.

This ancient form of anti-Judaism may seem alien to us today, but the claims it makes are typically repeated in modern secular culture. The Old Testament claims the physical world is good, but "anyone can see that it is a world filled with violence and evil." The

Old Testament is filled with supposedly irrational prohibitions (especially regarding sexual libertinism!). Old Testament morality is the construction of ancient Jewish priests, seeking to create an "ethics of the weak" based on mercy, rather than an ethics of strength and nobility (Nietzsche).[37] Finally, the Old Testament is the source of the notion of holy war, which is a principal source of fanatical violence conducted ideologically in the name of religion.

If Christianity is true, however, then the Old Testament is divine revelation and has an irreplaceable role in human culture. How, then, should we meet these objections? The first thing that should be said is that divine inspiration occurs within a given human culture and historical period. God condescends to inspire human prophets. He does not ignore or destroy their humanity. The Old Testament, then, beginning with the early Mosaic movement in thirteenth-century B.C., is a document composed in an ancient, archaic Near-Middle Eastern context. It was given in view of the religious evolution of humanity, and was meant to culminate in Christ. Therefore, the revelation given in the Old Testament is shaped by the context in which it was originally given and the people whom it was meant to instruct (a people set apart for worship of the one God). Many of the rites, laws, and customs present in the Torah, then, are idiosyncratic primarily because they were meant to form a religiously distinct people—not a universal Church—and because they were meant to sharpen a sense of unconditional allegiance to the one God in a world in which genuine polytheism predominated. There is thus a certain level of militancy in the message of the Torah as well as skepticism about non-Israelite forms of religion, even if this is not the deepest or most predominant theme.

At the same time, the Old Testament is marked at its core by

37. See the assessment of ancient Judaism of Friedrich Nietzsche in *On the Genealogy of Morality*, trans. C. Diethe (Cambridge: Cambridge University Press, 2008), and in *The Anti-Christ*, trans. J. Norman in *The Anti-Christ, Ecce Homo, Twilight of the Idols and Other Writings* (Cambridge: Cambridge University Press, 2015).

profound universal truths that are meant to enlighten all of humanity: religiously, philosophically, and ethically. Central to the revelation is the mystery of God's goodness and mercy toward all humanity and of his justice for those who are most downtrodden, the victims of human history. Here then we should note briefly five universal factors that are at the heart of Judaism and that carry over into Christianity and its central tenets.

First, *monotheism*. Considered simply from the point of natural reason, the Old Testament historically effectuated a profound historical purification upon human reason, often marked by religious superstition and irrationality. The heart of the Mosaic law is centered on the reality of monotheism. There is only one God, the transcendent creator and source of all being, who has made heaven and earth. Because God is the primary source of all material realities and the intelligible order that is found in them, there is nothing in the material world that should be divinized or worshiped. On the contrary, the entire visible world is subject to human knowledge and scientific study. Just as revelation seeks to make the human being relative to God by knowledge and love, so also it makes the visible creation relative to human reason and human freedom. Man is made in the image of God. He has a certain hierarchical primacy within the visible world.

Second, *the elevated morality of the ten commandments*. At the heart of the Mosaic law are the ten precepts found both in Exodus and Deuteronomy.[38] According to the Christian tradition, these embody the natural law that is inscribed in the heart of every man. Positively, they manifest the virtues we should cultivate in order to love others truthfully and achieve authentic happiness. Negatively, they underscore actions or vices that are intrinsically evil. "You shall not commit murder" designates negatively that it is always wrong to take innocent life, and even (implicitly) that it is wrong to hate one's neighbor or cultivate antipathies toward others. Posi-

38. Ex 20 and Dt 5.

tively, the precept denotes that every human being is deserving of respect, just treatment, and a certain appropriate form of love. "You shall not commit adultery" designates negatively that the human person should not engage in unchaste actions (adultery, fornication, inappropriate sexual fantasies). Positively, it denotes that the human person should cultivate the virtue of chastity: the integration of human sexuality into authentic personal love, whether by abstinence (outside of marriage) or faithful, conjugal love (within marriage). "You shall have no other gods before me" negatively prohibits idolatry, religious indifference, and atheism. Positively, it enjoins the human being to seek to know God and to love God above all things through authentic religious worship.

These commandments are very demanding. They offer us a portrait of the moral beauty of the human soul, one made possible by God's grace. Their universal character is not a subject of debate. By way of Christianity they have been commented upon through the ages and have had an effect on every human culture, including in the development of modern democratic politics and law. Western moral thinking from antiquity to the Renaissance to modernity (including the modern conception of human rights) has its original basis in this tradition of thought. Nor is it clear how one might coherently maintain any reference to the universality of the moral law and of human rights first inculcated by Judaism without reference to man being made in the image of God, and to God the creator, who is revealed in the Old Testament. God is the first foundation of the universal moral law.

Third, *expectant universalism*. Judaism is often accused of being sectarian, but at its heart the Old Testament is clearly universalist. The revelation given to Abraham is intended for all peoples. "By your descendants shall all the nations of the earth bless themselves, because you have obeyed my voice."[39] The prophet Isaiah promises Israel that the gentile "nations shall come to your light, and kings

39. Gn 22:18.

to the brightness of your rising."[40] This notion is important because it is implicitly Catholic in its implications. The Church that is to come forth from Israel and from Christ, is meant to bring the revelation of God to all human beings. All of humanity, then, will be addressed by the revelation of God. It is important to see that the mission of Christ and the sending of the apostles to "all nations" has its fundamental roots in the revelation given to Israel.[41] Without this background, the New Testament makes no sense.

Fourth, *messianism and the notion of historical progress*. The Old Testament breaks with religions that posit a merely cyclical or static conception of nature and history by positing that God is doing new things in historical time and that history has a progressive direction. The modern notion of political and social progress is in many ways problematic. It is frequently wed to the idea that the only meaning to existence is found in our present life and that human beings can save themselves morally by their own efforts alone. In this way it ignores crucial truths about the perduring effects of original and personal sin, and our constant need for the grace of God, and for a culture and practice of mercy and forgiveness. Nevertheless, human beings can progress in many domains over time, both personally and culturally, especially with the help of God's grace and the "leaven" of divine revelation. The Old Testament is the key place from which we derive this notion, historically speaking.

Furthermore, the Old Testament alludes in many and varied ways to a mysterious messianic figure who is to come, a descendant of David who will deliver the people of Israel, vindicate her cause against the gentile nations, and usher in a time of perfect grace and knowledge of God.[42] This messianic ideal unites two of the previous elements listed above: the promise of a revelation

40. Is 60:3.
41. Mt 28:19.
42. See, e.g., Gn 49:10–11, Dt 18:15–19, 2 Sm 7:12–16, Ps 110:1–2, Is 53–56, Dn 7:2–20.

that is universal, and the aspiration to perfect spiritual progress that animates human history. Christ stands at the center of this dynamic as one who brings the deepest truths of Judaism to perfection and who opens the revelation up to all humanity.

Finally, *eschatological hope in the face of injustice, human suffering, and death.* The Old Testament does not ignore the deepest evils that beset human beings but confronts them directly. The covenant with Moses has its beginning in response to Pharaoh's genocide of the Hebrew people.[43] Genesis portrays death as a fundamental threat to human well-being and to the meaning of the whole creation. Job acknowledges the terrible mystery of the suffering of the innocent. Lamentations considers the horror of violent military conquest, with the resultant loss of life or political exile. The two books of the Maccabees explore the realities of martyrdom as a result of religious fidelity and the consequent question of what happens to those who die out of fidelity to the covenant with God. In all of this, the Bible proposes sound points of human and religious orientation. God is sovereignly good. In him there is no shadow of darkness, and so we should rightly seek our refuge in his protection and goodness above all. Suffering and illness can have a purifying effect upon us in this world, but we cannot always account readily for the suffering of the just or the innocent, and should be wary of trying to account for suffering too easily with facile theological explanations. Both in life and in death we are in the hands of God, who guards the souls of the just and who can raise the dead to life.[44] Ultimately, then, human history is not morally meaningless. God will vindicate the righteous and have mercy on the weak, but will judge the actions of the wicked and those who refused to show mercy or to confide in the providence of God.[45]

43. Ex 1–2.
44. Wis 3:1 and Dn 12:2–4.
45. 2 Mc 7.

In short, we can say that on the topic of suffering and death, the Old Testament stands out as a *book of hope*, one that is pregnant with the expectation that God will save humanity and deliver us from the power of evil and death, in the end times. This "eschatological orientation" of the Old Testament gives us the sound knowledge that the goal of history lies *beyond history* in our union with God himself. It finds its culmination in the message of the resurrection of Jesus Christ from the dead, which is the ultimate key in revelation to understanding the mystery of suffering and death. Jesus resurrected from the dead is God's ultimate response to the mystery of human suffering.

Based on the five features we noted above, one can say that Friedrich Nietzsche is right in saying that Judaism provides the fundamental metanarrative of Christian and indeed all monotheistic cultures. "Salvation is from the Jews."[46] Nietzsche saw this as a nefarious influence that needed to be rejected and purged. Belief in the God of the Old Testament must be overthrown by a "revaluation of all values," so that human action can be based not on the primacy of moral law and mercy for the weakest, but on aesthetic beauty and the political triumph of the most noble and the spiritually strongest.[47] Whatever the merits of Nietzsche's considerations, the Old Testament remains forever fundamentally pertinent. It provides the true perspective on God as creator, the universal character of moral norms, the rightness of the universal human desire for revealed knowledge of God, the confidence in providence as we work toward human progress, and the vitality of hope in the face of suffering and death. Rightly considered in its deepest themes, the Torah is not a morbid or violent book. It is a book about the liberation of slaves from Egypt who gain their freedom by serving what is in fact the real absolute: the truth of

---

46. Jn 4:22.

47. For characteristic examples of this viewpoint, see Friedrich Nietzsche, *On the Genealogy of Morality* I, 7; *The Anti-Christ*, 25–27.

God and his ethical imperatives. This message is not one of superstition, but of genuine rationality and authentic freedom. In it we see the human quest for God fulfilled and surpassed. What begins in Judaism reaches its highest achievement in the mystery of Christ and of the Church.

4

INCARNATION AND
ATONEMENT

Why Did God Become Human?

In the previous chapter it was stated that the human being is a kind of bridge between the physical world and the spiritual world. Created in the image of God, man can tend upward—ordering all things toward the creator—or downward into the exclusive pursuit and domination of visible, created things. This tension inscribed within humans marks us with a deep spiritual restlessness and instability, since we cannot live rightly either as angels or mere nonrational animals. Human beings are marked simultaneously both by immortal longings and by the certainty of death. They form a crossroads between God and the whole material creation, standing at the heart of the created order. This is one reason the devil, in his revolt against the wisdom of God, seeks to wrestle humanity away from God so as to make a caricature of the creation of God and to mark the world of men with clear signs of moral capitulation and spiritual failure.

Christianity claims that God's central response to human sin, however, has been to become human. Why? If the human situation is marked by opaque meaning, residual moral frailty, and physical mortality, then why should God embrace our situation?

If God is real, ought he not simply to have chosen to remake the human condition from scratch, by divine fiat? Why should he unite himself to us in our very imperfect situation? The answer is divine love. God manifests his mysterious wisdom and power not by destroying or instantly resolving our situation, but by offering us his divine mercy, grace, and friendship, and by offering all this to us in the midst of our suffering and moral fragility. Divine love has its own customs which are infinitely wise, but which are not those of men. God sees fit to "rehabilitate" the human race after sin not by destroying it, but by entering into it via incarnation, in the vulnerability of being a human child and of death by crucifixion, so as to invite the human race to discipleship and to resurrection from the dead.

In the ancient Church, there were two great traditional answers to the question "why did God become human?" One was from St. Athanasius and the other from St. Anselm of Canterbury. Athanasius answers that God became human so that human beings might "become God," that is to say, that they might be united to God by grace.[1] The premise to this argument is that human beings stand in need of salvation from death and nothingness. In effect, then, salvation for the human person consists in union with God, who is eternal and undying. But in that case, nothing can save us short of God himself. No mere creature can unite another creature to the creator. Consequently, Christ can only save us if he is truly God made man. It is God himself who has united the human race to God by becoming human, and has thus made it possible for us to have eternal life through union with Christ.

St. Anselm offers a different argument, one that is complementary.[2] He begins with the reality of our sinfulness and alienation

---

1. See Athanasius, *On the Incarnation*, translated by a Religious of CSMV (Crestwood, N.Y.: St. Vladimir's Seminary Press, 1993).

2. Anselm of Canterbury, *Why God Became Man*, in *Major Works*, ed. B. Davies and G. R. Evans (Oxford: Oxford University Press, 1998).

from God. The truth is that as human beings we are caught up in webs of moral complicity and existential disorientation. "If we say we have no sin, we deceive ourselves, and the truth is not in us."[3] There is a chasm between ourselves and God that we cannot cross by our own powers. The dignity and righteousness of God are infinite, while humanity has unjustly placed itself in a state of rupture with God. While this starting point may seem pessimistic or moralizing, Anselm's point is not to motivate us by way of guilt, but to give us unshakable hope and spiritual consolation. We need a way back to God that comes from us (wherein a human being reconciles us to God) but one that is also infinite in value (wherein God unites us to his infinite righteousness). God became human, then, so as to redeem our situation from within, as he who is the most human of all, and simultaneously as he who is infinitely holy. Christ atones for human sin by being himself humanly loving and obedient in our stead, as our sinless representative before God. Because Christ is God, his self-offering on our behalf is one of infinite holiness, reconciling us with God's absolute righteousness. His atonement acts as a compensation for human sin that is more than sufficient for all the sins of the human race. Consequently, even in the face of our own sinfulness we should not live in alienation from God, but in confidence and friendship with God by faith.

The first of these classical explanations portrays salvation primarily in terms of *divinization*; the second portrays it primarily as *atonement*. In fact, they are deeply interrelated. If man is the bridge between the visible and invisible worlds, then Christ became human to repair that bridge. In classical language, Christ is the "one mediator between God and men."[4] By atoning for our human faults before God, Christ makes possible the hope and expectation of divine mercy, grace, and friendship with God. He

3. 1 Jn 1:8.
4. 1 Tm 2:5.

thus opens the doors of heaven, so that the human being—even in his frailty and mortality—can aspire to union with God. We can hope to be "divinized" or made children of God by grace not despite but even in the midst of our suffering and mortality, because Christ has opened up a way toward the Father even in the midst of the very real limitations that each human being encounters in this world. St. Catherine of Siena says that Christ is the bridge, or "pontiff," between heaven and earth that God has undertaken to build, so as to offer human beings a way back toward God.[5] In effect, even after each of us has wandered in darkness or sinned, God does not annihilate us or eradicate our human freedom. Rather, he himself steps into our human drama, shares our history, and invites us to be remade freely from within by the grace of his love. Christ is a new creation born out of the old, and we are remade by being united to him. God became human and subjected himself to a human death like ours so that even through death we might be united to God, in the mystery of the resurrection. The cross is a passage for every human being back to the absolute.

The Divinity of Christ

It may seem that we have gotten ahead of ourselves. After all, why ought we to presume that Christ is God? And even if one were to affirm this, what would it mean? Can God become human without ceasing to be God?

The New Testament teaches unambiguously that Christ is God. There have always been those who denied this. In the fourth century the Arian heresy held that Christ is the *creature* whom God made first, God's pre-existent Wisdom who preceded the rest of creation, and through whom God created all else that is. (A similar view is still found today among the Jehovah's Witnesses as well as the Mormons.) The Koran contains a slightly dif-

5. See *The Dialogue of St. Catherine of Siena*, "A Treatise on Discretion."

ferent teaching. It portrays Jesus as a merely human prophet, the greatest of prophets prior to Mohammed. The Koran claims that it is due to the corruption of the earliest Christian teaching by the later Catholic Church that Christians came progressively to believe that Jesus was God. A more sophisticated version of this idea was developed in nineteenth-century German historical-critical scholarship, in which some argued that the earliest "Christologies" of the New Testament were "low Christologies," that is to say, presentations of Jesus as an anointed messiah and spiritual sage. These were said to be supplanted eventually by the "high Christologies" of Paul and John, who taught explicitly that Christ is God. New books are published regularly from the sophisticated to the vulgar attempting to reiterate this line of thinking. The general purpose of such modern theories is to demonstrate that the early Church projected the teaching of the divinity of Christ back onto the historical Jesus, who did not himself truly claim to be God. The traditional Christian teaching is thus seen as a mere social construction of a religious community, one without a basis in Jesus' own historical words and deeds. To respond to these diverse forms of criticism of the Catholic faith, we should return to the New Testament itself and draw out a number of basic principles.

First, *the earliest "strata" of historical texts in the New Testament affirm clearly the Christian belief in the divinity of Christ.* Here we may take as a case in point the second chapter of Paul's letter to the Philippians. Paul wrote this letter while in prison, sometime between 50 and 55 A.D., a mere twenty years after the death and resurrection of Jesus. This letter contains what seems to be a hymn or ancient creed of the early Christian community that Paul is citing to his readers, a text already known to many.[6] Consequently, this passage gives us a window into what the earliest Christians believed in common only a generation after Christ.

6. Phil 2:6–11.

We find in it already the basis for the core Christological teaching of the Catholic Church.

Though he was in the form of God, [Jesus] did not count equality with God a thing to be grasped, [2:7] but emptied himself, taking the form of a servant, being born in the likeness of men. [2:8] And being found in human form he humbled himself and became obedient unto death, even death on a cross. [2:9] Therefore God has highly exalted him and bestowed on him the name which is above every name, [2:10] that at the name of Jesus every knee should bow, in heaven and on earth and under the earth, [2:11] and every tongue confess that Jesus Christ is Lord, to the glory of God the Father.

Notice that verse 6 affirms the pre-existence of Christ, who came into the world as one who is equal with God, himself the God of Israel. Verse 7 teaches that he emptied himself not by ceasing to be God but by humbly taking upon himself the "form of a servant," the "likeness of men." This verse implies that Christ was someone before he became truly human (i.e., he was God). However, it also points toward the suffering servant of Isaiah, and identifies Christ with that figure of Old Testament prophecy, a figure who "bore the sin of many."[7] Verse 8 teaches that the human obedience of Christ even unto death serves to redeem the human race, making atonement for human sin. Verses 9–11 affirm the resurrection of Christ, which is something that happened to him as man, in his crucified humanity. (Christ as God cannot be subject to resurrection from the dead!) Most astonishingly, though, these same verses speak of Christ resurrected being given publicly the "name above every other name," a name at which every knee will bend in worship. The "name" being referred to here is of course the name of God given in Exodus: "I am He who is," the name of the Lord of Israel (YHWH).[8] Isaiah foretells that in the end times, all the gentile nations will recognize the Lord of

7. Is 53:11–12.
8. Ex 3:14–15.

Israel and worship him, when "every knee shall bow, every tongue shall swear" that he is the Lord (YHWH).[9] Here, then, the early Christian community is clearly claiming that Christ crucified and raised from the dead is now recognized as God who became man, and as the Lord God of Israel who intervenes in history to save all the gentile nations. While we could give other examples of the early belief in the divinity of Christ in the New Testament, this one is particularly instructive because it is so primitive chronologically and at the same time so rich in teaching, foreshadowing so many of the major doctrines of the Catholic Church in centuries to come.

Second, *the earliest Christians were Jewish monotheists who worshiped Christ as God.* It follows from the point just made above that the earliest Christians *worshiped* Jesus. This idea is present in many books of the New Testament. It is a central theme in the book of Revelation, for example. In chapter 4 John the visionary sees a group of elders in heaven who worship the Lamb seated on the throne, clearly a reference to Christ crucified and resurrected. At the same time, the seer who records the vision is told by an angel that he should not worship the angel, who is a mere creature.[10] In the context of the late ancient Judaism of Jesus' time, it was clear to Jews that they should observe a principled form of monotheism and worship God alone. Exodus and Deuteronomy both prohibit worship of creatures and punish this transgression with death by stoning, a teaching that was taken seriously in the time of the composition of the New Testament. That the earliest Christians who were themselves Jews should practice the adoration of Christ could only mean one thing: that they took him to be God. And indeed we see unqualified affirmations of such worship in a variety of passages.[11] These references to worship of

9. Is 45:23.

10. Rv 22:8–9.

11. Not only in passages like Phil 2 and Rv 4 and 22, but also in Heb 1:6; Mt 14:33, 28:9, 28:17; Mk 5:6; Jn 9:38; Acts 7:59.

Christ are so pervasive in early Christian literature as to be considered a constitutive fact of earliest Christianity.

Third, *all four canonical Gospels teach (however implicitly) that Christ is God made man*. This is no doubt a controversial statement. Paul's letters are the earliest Christian writings and contain a clear expression of "high Christology," teaching that Christ is Lord and one with the Father. Since the nineteenth century, however, there has been a widespread claim that the earliest Gospel, Mark (perhaps written in the 50s), contains a different teaching, and that the subsequent Gospels (Matthew and Luke in the 70s, followed by John in the 90s) contain diverse visions of Christ, with John alone being unambiguous in his affirmation of the divinity of Christ.

In the twentieth century, however, this narrative began to evaporate under closer scrutiny of the texts. It became clear to all, for example, that Mark's Gospel is as "theological" as any of the other canonical Gospels. It is not a "mere" historical record written independently of theological influence. Furthermore, in an implicit but clear way Mark affirms the divinity of Christ. Jesus, for example, is shown to forgive sins, something normally reserved to God alone.[12] He heals others miraculously by his own decision, based upon the divine power residual in him.[13] Twice Jesus seems clearly to apply the divine name to himself: "I am."[14] Jesus claims to have authority even over the law of Moses, given by God.[15] He also teaches that he is not only the son of David (the messiah) but also his Lord.[16] When he dies, his expiration gives rise to the confession of faith of the gentile centurion, "Truly this man was the Son of God."[17]

12. Mk 2:6–10.
13. Mk 1:42.
14. Mk 6:50, 14:62.
15. Mk 2:27.
16. Mk 12:35–37.
17. Mk 15:39.

Undoubtedly the portrait of Christ in Mark is more practical and actualistic than speculative. Christ is portrayed performing miracle after miracle and his teaching is shown to confirm his authority as the messiah and "Son of Man" who is to bring in the eschatological age. But the teaching is clear nonetheless. In Jesus, the unique Son of God, it is the God of Israel himself who is truly active and present.

Matthew, Luke, and John are far more overt. In Matthew, the wise men from the East come to find Jesus as a child in Bethlehem and worship him.[18] In the Sermon on the Mount, Christ reinterprets the Torah of Moses, as one who stands above the law, just as God himself did on Mount Sinai.[19] He claims to have a unique relation with God as his Father, and to be his unique Son, who is the judge of the human race, and one served by angels.[20] In the resurrection narrative of Matthew 28, Christ encounters the apostles and tells them to "Go to all the nations baptizing in the name of the Father, the Son and the Holy Spirit."[21] Here the traditional name of God from Exodus 3:14 is now interpreted in Trinitarian terms: the three persons of the Father, Son, and Holy Spirit are the one God of Israel.

Luke portrays the revelation of the Trinity as occurring first to the Virgin Mary at the Annunciation.[22] She is told that the Holy Spirit will overshadow her in her virginity, and that by the power of God, she will conceive the Son of God in her womb. Here, then, God the Father, his Son, and the Holy Spirit are all referred to obliquely as God. In the following chapter, the Virgin Mary who is now pregnant goes to visit her cousin Elizabeth. The latter exclaims, significantly, "who am I that the mother of my *Lord* should come to me?"[23] The implication is that the God of Israel is

18. Mt 2:2, 2:11.
19. Mt 5–7.
20. Mt 11:25–27, 25:31–46, 26:53.
21. Mt 28:19–20.
22. Lk 1:26–37.
23. Lk 1:43.

personally present in the womb of Mary. Likewise, in Luke's book of Acts, when Stephen the first Christian martyr is dying, he prays to Christ (now raised from the dead) to receive his soul, addressing Christ not only as man but also as God.[24] Consequently, from first to last, Luke-Acts teaches that Jesus is God made man.

This teaching is presented in more overtly conceptual terms in John. The prologue of the fourth Gospel teaches that Christ is the pre-existent Wisdom or Reason through whom God made all things. "In the beginning was the Word [Logos], and the Word was God.... and without him not anything was made that was made ... and the Word became flesh and dwelt among us."[25] Jesus makes clear by his teaching and his miraculous actions that he is one with the Father. "The Father is in me and I am in the Father."[26] Christ claims that he has authority to teach "in my Father's name" and appeals again to the divine name, affirming that "before Abraham was, I am."[27] In the resurrection narratives, Christ is recognized by his apostles not only as one who was dead and is now alive again, but *as God himself* personally present among them.[28]

Of course one may object that these are only the New Testament *portraits* of the historical Jesus and need not reflect accurately what the historical Jesus truly said or did. It is true that while the four Gospels claim to be historical testimonies, they are not "photographic" portraits. Rather, they are theological documents written for the earliest Christian communities, intended to reveal the deeper truth about the historical Jesus. However, here we should make three important qualifications. First, we have no other textual access to Christ of a more historically primitive nature other than the documents of the New Testament. Conse-

24. Acts 7:59.
25. Jn 1:1–3, 1:14.
26. Jn 10:38, 14:10–11, 10:30.
27. Jn 5:43, 8:58.
28. Jn 20:28.

quently, there is no evidence for an alternative historical Jesus to the one Christianity proclaims. In fact, speculative attempts to discern the "real" historical Jesus are often comically transparent projections of twenty-first-century preoccupations. Second, the four Gospels each claim to bear witness to a divine revelation that cannot be understood adequately without the grace of God. This was true even for those who were eyewitnesses to the life of Jesus. Their belief in the mystery of Christ did not derive merely from natural experiences or historical arguments. It required the illumination of grace, since his mystery is something that transcends the competence of unaided natural reason. The Gospels themselves make it clear that Christ's historical life was only perfectly understood by the apostles after the event of the resurrection shed divine light on all that had come before. Third, the affirmation of this last point does not mean that belief in Christ is not grounded in history, or that modern historical study of Jesus is irrelevant. There are a great number of features of Jesus' behavior as reported by the four canonical Gospels that seem difficult to dismiss historically, and that clearly suggest that the historical Jesus made extremely high claims about his own identity. Faith in Christ is a grace, but it is not a grace opposed to historical realism.

For example, almost all historical scholars accept that Jesus of Nazareth must have preached about a coming "kingdom of God," a term that is eschatological, signifying the approaching end times. In speaking this way, Jesus seemingly took himself to be a final emissary of God at the end of the ages.[29] At the same time, Jesus is depicted in all four Gospels and in the letters of Paul as someone who spoke of himself as "the Son" of God and who called God his *abba* or "Father," thus suggesting that the historical Jesus took himself to be in some way the unique Son of God.[30]

---

29. See the extended arguments to this effect by N. T. Wright in *Jesus and the Victory of God* (Minneapolis, Minn.: Fortress Press, 1996).

30. See Martin Hengel, *The Son of God: The Origin of Christology and the History of Jewish-Hellenistic Religion* (Philadelphia: Fortress Press, 1977).

Furthermore, many scholars accept that Jesus seemingly thought his own ministry of healing and forgiving sins was in some way displacing the Temple as the locus of sacrifice and reconciliation with God.[31] This is particularly manifest in his repeated action of forgiving sins apart from the norms of the Mosaic law (in which forgiveness is typically accomplished through Temple sacrifices), and in his institution of the Eucharist, in which Jesus claimed to institute a memorial of his own death as a sacrifice "for the many, for the forgiveness of sins."[32] Finally, it seems likely that Jesus saw in his own death the coming of the eschaton or end times, and taught that he would himself stand as a judge over the nations.[33] One can deny any of these teachings as pertaining to the historical Jesus, but then if one does, it is required that we eradicate almost all the typical first-century Jewish sayings from the Gospels that may reasonably be attributed to Jesus of Nazareth in his historical context. Such skepticism is unreasonable. If we begin to admit any of them, however, then we also allow that we are dealing with a person who claimed to have a very unique historical status and to stand in an utterly unique relationship to the God of Israel, as his final emissary, and in a real sense as his very presence in history. The fact that Jesus did speak and act in such a way as to communicate such a high set of claims is explanation enough for the divisions caused by his presence and mission. They help us to understand historically why Christ was crucified: because he claimed in implicit and explicit ways to be one with God.

Fourth, *there are no other "Gospels" that can rightly claim to originate from the earliest Christian community.* The modern suspicion that alternative ancient Gospels exist that would put the canoni-

---

31. See, for example, Wright, *Jesus and the Victory of God*, chaps. 11 and 12.

32. Mt 26:28. See Martin Hengel in *The Atonement: The Origins of the Doctrine in the New Testament* (Philadelphia: Fortress Press, 1981).

33. See Ben Witherington III, *The Christology of Jesus* (Minneapolis, Minn.: Fortress Press, 1990).

cal accounts of the Church in question is based largely on historical ignorance. This issue is not new but arose in the second century as novel accounts were first being created. The bishops of the second-century Church affirmed the norm of the New Testament canon precisely so as to safeguard the "apostolic doctrine," that is, the teaching received from the apostles who knew Christ personally. Already in 110 A.D. Ignatius of Antioch cites from Mark, Matthew, Luke, and John as authorities in his letters to the churches of Asia. In the 180s Irenaeus of Lyons lists the four Gospels as indicative of apostolic teaching, over against late-second-century fabrications of the Gnostics, such as the Gospel of Truth of Valentinus. Irenaeus tells us that as a child he learned from St. Polycarp, who was himself the disciple of the apostle John, author of the fourth Gospel.[34] He speaks then, as someone at two generations' distance from the apostles themselves.

For, after our Lord rose from the dead, [the apostles] were invested with power from on high when the Holy Spirit came down [upon them], were filled from all [His gifts], and had perfect knowledge: they departed to the ends of the earth, preaching the glad tidings of the good things [sent] from God to us, and proclaiming the peace of heaven to men, who indeed do all equally and individually possess the Gospel of God. Matthew also issued a written Gospel among the Hebrews in their own dialect, while Peter and Paul were preaching at Rome, and laying the foundations of the Church. After their departure, Mark, the disciple and interpreter of Peter, did also hand down to us in writing what had been preached by Peter. Luke also, the companion of Paul, recorded in a book the Gospel preached by him. Afterwards, John, the disciple of the Lord, who also had leaned upon His breast, did himself publish a Gospel during his residence at Ephesus in Asia.[35]

It is true that some other writings may be of Christian origin (the Gospel of Peter) or may retain true sayings of Jesus (the Gospel of Thomas). In these documents, however, the overall perspective is fundamentally Hellenistic in origin and cannot derive from a

34. Irenaeus, *Against Heresies* III, 3, 4.
35. Irenaeus, *Against Heresies* III, 1, 1.

first-century Jewish, Palestinian context. They are later works from subsequent centuries. Consequently, they contain little that could realistically be attributed to the historical Jesus under any reasonable pretext.

The Hypostatic Union

What does it mean to say that God became human? Is this a reasonable belief? Can God become human without ceasing to be God? The Incarnation cannot be "explained" like a geometric demonstration or the constitutive parts of a chemical bond. It is a mystery. However, it does have an intrinsic intelligibility, and belief in it is in no way contrary to natural reason. Here we should consider briefly three basic traditional teachings regarding the mystery of the Incarnation.

First, *Jesus Christ is one divine person subsisting in two natures, truly God and truly human*. The Church confesses that Jesus Christ is personally the eternal Son, who has become man. In saying this, she means that he is not a creature who became God or a saint who somehow resembles God. Rather, he is the eternal Word, the second person of the Holy Trinity, who became human. The dynamic is primarily one of God descending to us, and not of us ascending to God. When Christ teaches in parables, then, it is the Son of God who teaches. When Christ suffers crucifixion on the Cross, it is the Son who is personally crucified. What happens to Jesus happens to God. What Jesus does personally, God does personally. The second person of the Trinity lived a human life among us, suffered death by crucifixion, and was resurrected in his human flesh.

Since the Council of Ephesus in 431 A.D., the Church speaks of this mystery by employing the term "hypostatic union," meaning "the union in the person." The Incarnation is not a mixture or fusion of human nature and divine nature. Christ is truly God and truly human (two distinct natures), but he is one being, one concrete subject. The divine and human natures of Christ are united in one person. Jesus of Nazareth is a divine person, the eternal Son of God. In this way, Christianity places personhood at the center of everything: ultimate reality (the Trinity) is personal and God became human to reveal himself to us personally.

The mystery, then, is that God should come to express to us who he is from all eternity (in his very identity as God) in and through a human historical life, as an individual human being like us, with a physical body and spiritual soul. Christ is the person of the Word, but he expresses who he is by his human thoughts and desires, actions and words, but also by his human vulnerability and suffering. The Son of God, without ceasing to be one with the Father, was conceived as a human embryo in the womb of the Virgin Mary, developed *in utero*, was born and matured, lived in many ways a very ordinary human life and died a human death as one of us. The *person* who did all this was God the Son. He is eternally one with the Father and the Holy Spirit, by virtue of his divine nature that he shares with them. He is able to be born, live and undergo change, death and physical resurrection by virtue of his human nature that he shares with us. In short, God the Son came to share our human life so that we could share in his divine life.

Second, *in Christ, the divine and human natures remain entirely distinct.* Christ is truly God and truly man, and so possesses the divine nature (with the Father and the Holy Spirit) and a human nature (with the rest of the human race). However, it is one thing to be God and another to be human. The Father and the Holy Spirit are truly God. We are truly human. The Son is truly both God and human. The divine nature and the human nature are not identical but remain distinct.

It is important to note that Christ's divine nature or divine life was not either altered or perfected by the Incarnation. God does not have to cease to be God in order to become human, nor does God have to undergo some kind of change of his eternal identity to do so. It is also a mistake to think that God undergoes improvement in his infinite perfection as a result of becoming human, as if God should need to be human in order to become morally superior. The mystery has to be understood in a contrary sense. Because God is infinite and omnipotent, God can become truly human without diminishing or lessening his divine perfection in any way. The Incarnation does not improve on what God is, but is the greatest expression *for us* of the creator's eternal power and perfection. Because God is eternally perfect in his goodness and power, he can become human to save us, without ceasing to be God.

Furthermore, God became truly and entirely human, meaning that he took on a complete human nature, consisting of a body and spiritual soul. Christ is not a mutilated human being, lacking a real human body or human spiritual soul. He is a complete human being like us, as one who is identical with us in all things but sin. In fact, because of his grace, moral perfection, and sinlessness, Christ is in truth the most human of all of us. In short, God has become the most human of us all so as to reveal to us who God is in a most human way. He also wants to reveal to us what man can be in fellowship with God. Holiness is a real possibility for human beings because Christ is the most holy of all men, and in another sense because Christ alone is God. By his holiness Christ shows us how human nature can participate in God.

Third, *all the natural properties of Christ—whether human or divine—are attributed to the one person of the Word, Jesus Christ as their concrete subject.* This is what is known as the "communication of idioms" or the attribution of properties. Jesus is fully God and fully man, and so whatever he does or undergoes whether by virtue of his divinity or by virtue of his humanity is attributed to the one person of the Word incarnate. So, for instance, if Christ heals a man born blind, as depicted in John 9, he does so by the power of God residing in him, and does so in union with the Father and the Holy Spirit. But he also does such actions as man, by saying words or by stretching out his hands. So, as a result, it is true to say: "This man is omnipotent. He heals the blind and raises the dead," or to say: "God incarnate heals by stretching out his hands."

Likewise, we must attribute all of Christ's human vulnerability and suffering to the second person of the Trinity. It is God the Word who was born of the Virgin Mary in a cave in Bethlehem. This is why it is literally true to say that she is the Mother of God. God the eternal Word also begged alms, walked to Jerusalem, slept in a boat, and underwent torture and physical execution. We must also say that God underwent suffering and death on the Cross. This is not to say that the divine nature of God suffered or was altered by crucifixion. The divinity of Christ, his very deity, cannot be altered by our sins. But Christ as man could suffer and die by virtue of his human nature, and the person who underwent this is God. Consequently, we can say that God suffered personally, but that he did so uniquely by virtue of his human nature, and not by virtue of his deity or his divine nature. Pope Leo the Great, whose writing deeply influenced the fifth-century Council of Chalcedon, states things in this way:

To be hungry and thirsty, to be weary, and to sleep, is clearly human. But to satisfy 5,000 men with five loaves, and to bestow on the woman of Samaria living water, draughts of which can secure the drinker from thirsting any more, to walk upon the surface of the sea with feet that do not sink, and to quell the risings of the waves by rebuking the winds, is, without any doubt, divine .... [It] is not part of the same nature to be moved to tears of pity for a dead friend, and—when the stone that closed the four-days' grave was removed—to raise that same friend to life with a voice of command. Or, to hang on the cross, and turning day to night to make all the elements tremble; or, to be pierced with nails, and yet open the gates of paradise to the robber's faith. So it is not part of the same nature to say, "I and the Father are one," (John 10:30) and to say, "the Father is greater than I" (John 14:28). For although in the Lord Jesus Christ God and man is one person, yet the source of the degradation is one, and the source of the glory is another. For His manhood, which is less than the Father, comes from our side. His Godhead, which is equal to the Father, comes from the Father.[36]

The communication of idioms does not entail the confusion of natures. The human nature of the Son is not omnipotent. The divine nature of the Son does not suffer and die. The Son is omnipotent uniquely by virtue of his divine nature and capable of suffering and death uniquely by virtue of his human nature. But he the Son is one person who both raises the dead by his divine power, and who undergoes death (the separation of body and soul) in his human nature. The two affirmations are not incompatible. On the contrary, they are deeply interrelated. Because Christ is God, he can act to redeem the world by his divine power even in the midst of acute human suffering and death. God descends into our misery as one who is truly human, so as to bring into this domain "from within" the power of God. In making himself humanly subject to death, God also makes his own death on the Cross an event from which to recreate the world, by the mysterious presence of his holiness, power, and love, which can never be overcome or thwarted, even in the crucifixion.

The Humanity of Christ

The Apostles' Creed states that Jesus of Nazareth "suffered under Pontius Pilate." This means that Jesus is not a figure of mythology, but someone who lived and died within human history. If Christ is God made man and is physically resurrected from the dead, then these things are said about a real person who lived in

---

36. Leo the Great, Letter 28 (*The Tome of Leo*), in *Nicene and Post-Nicene Fathers, Second Series*, vol. 12, trans. C. Feltoe, ed. P. Schaff and H. Wace (Buffalo, N.Y.: Christian Literature Publishing, 1895); translation slightly modified.

first-century Israel two thousand years ago. Modern scholars of all stripes typically agree on a number of particular facts. Jesus of Nazareth was a first-century Jew whose public ministry took place around the years 30–33 A.D. He was baptized by John the Baptizer (who is attested to in non-Christian sources) and assembled followers around himself. Early witnesses claimed that he worked healing miracles as well as nature miracles. His teaching was eschatological in tone (concerned with the end times), and he spoke frequently about the "kingdom of God." He claimed to have the authority to forgive sins, and spoke about God as his father, in a seemingly unique sense. At some point in his ministry he most likely confronted religious authorities in Jerusalem with a dramatic action in the Temple. He was put to death by Roman crucifixion. His earliest followers claimed shortly after his death that his tomb was empty and that he appeared to them physically alive by resurrection from the dead. From documents written as early as twenty years after the death of Jesus, the early Christian community can be observed to identify him with the God of Israel, and to worship him as someone whom they believe to be one with God.

Christians should have a vested interest, then, in acknowledging that Jesus of Nazareth was a first-century Jew, and very much a figure of his own historical epoch. It is a false alternative to think that we must believe *either* in the divinity of Christ *or* consider Jesus as a human being fully immersed in his historical epoch. The point of the Incarnation is that God did live among us as man in a particular historical individuality. Jesus presumably thought and spoke in Aramaic. In his preaching and parables he made use of the agricultural symbols and biblical imagery that were commonplace in his culture. His beliefs reflected many of the common convictions of the Jews of his time: that there is one God who created all things, that Israel is a chosen people, that the Mosaic law is of divine origin. But even though Jesus was entirely immersed in a particular human culture and religious tradition, he also interpreted and made authoritative judgments about that culture and tradition from within. He did this in light of his elevated knowledge of his own identity as the Son of God, and in keeping with his supernatural mission as the messiah and savior of mankind. Consequently we must acknowledge that the historical Christ also challenged his culture and called it to convert to the Gospel, which is universal and is for all peoples.

Furthermore, although the New Testament teaches that Jesus as man possessed extraordinary graces, it also emphasizes that he was subject to ordinary human trials. These were both physical and emotional. Jesus underwent fatigue, and was capable of undergoing physical suffering and death.[37] He was subject at times to profound grief (John depicts him weeping for a friend at the tomb of Lazarus).[38] He also experienced anger (seemingly without sin) in the face of human hard-heartedness and religious infidelity.[39] The New Testament underscores all this vividly so that we understand that God has become subject to our own human condition in all of its reality.

St. Paul speaks about Jesus as the new Adam.[40] Paul is "looking back" on the historical life of Jesus in the light of his resurrection. This is the perspective of Christianity: not an artificial projection of alien ideas onto the historical Jesus, but a realistic perception of the true depths of the mystery of Jesus that is only made possible by faith, and that is given to us in light of the knowledge of the resurrection of Christ from the dead. Seen in this light, Paul establishes a profound parallel. The first Adam fell into sin and forfeited the life of grace. The second Adam brings about a new creation.[41] This means that Jesus Christ is the human being in whom

37. Jn 4:6, Lk 22:42.
38. Jn 11:34–36.
39. Mt 21:12–13, Mk 11:15–18, Jn 2:13–22.
40. Rom 5:12–18.
41. Gal 6:15, 2 Cor 5:17.

God is re-establishing in a fundamental way a new universal order of creation, and refashioning the human race.

It follows from this perspective that Jesus as man is filled with the life of grace not only after the resurrection, but in his historical life among us, and indeed, even from the first moment of his conception, as suggested by Paul.[42] John's Gospel contains a similar affirmation: "From his fullness have we all received, grace upon grace. For the law was given through Moses; grace and truth came through Jesus Christ."[43] Christ as man shares his grace with us, and it is for this reason principally that he is called the "Head of the church."[44] Jesus is the Head who lives in his members by grace, and makes us alive to God the Father as those who participate in his grace. If we consider the Gospel portraits of the historical Jesus from this perspective, we can see that even in his relatively ordinary historical life among us, Jesus of Nazareth possessed extraordinary grace.

In his human intellect, for example, we can note a number of distinctive features. First, Christ is a uniquely profound teacher. The widespread historical influence of his words is not accidental. His moral and spiritual teaching is simultaneously accessible and deeply perceptive. Second, Christ claims to understand the historical unfolding of the mystery of our redemption. This is most evident when he interprets the symbols and prophecies of the Old Testament in a definitive way, often applying them to his own person and to the events of his own life. Third, he has the capacity to read the secrets of human hearts, and foretells prophetically key events that are yet to unfold, such as the crucifixion and resurrection. Finally, Jesus has an unambiguous human awareness of his own identity as the Son of God. Jesus does not wonder who he is. He knows he is the Lord, and knows who the

42. Gal 4:4–5.
43. Jn 1:16–17.
44. Col 1:18, Eph 5:23.

Father and the Holy Spirit are. As depicted in the four Gospels, then, the historical Jesus in some real sense knows himself to possess divine authority. Consequently, he asks his disciples to follow him unconditionally.[45] His authority is not received from another human being, nor is it below that of any other human being.[46]

In his human will, Christ possesses a plenitude of the grace of charity. According to the Gospels, Christ is a human exemplar of moral perfection. We see this most especially in the way the Gospels depict the moral visage of Christ: he has in his personality a beautiful balance of meekness and fortitude, humility and truthfulness, wisdom and simplicity, asceticism and joy, justice and merciful forgiveness. There is in Christ a perfect love for and obedience toward God, and a perfect love for his neighbor. In all his words, actions and sufferings, a radical perfection shines through. The soul of Christ possesses unique moral beauty, a truth that even secular thinkers who grapple with the Gospels find difficult to deny.

The New Testament teaches repeatedly that Jesus of Nazareth is without sin, and wholly innocent.[47] This claim is not something that could merely be inferred experientially from those who encountered Jesus of Nazareth historically. Rather, it depends upon a deeper understanding of who Jesus is, one revealed to the apostles by the Holy Spirit and perceptible to us in the light of faith. Jesus' sinlessness is one of the effects of the plenitude of grace that the Lord possesses as man. In fact, seen at the deepest level, Jesus' moral perfection manifests to us the human face of God. His human gestures of compassion and mercy are a visible sign of the divine love that he has for the human race as God. In his charity as man Christ thereby shows us how to live as human beings. To live an authentic human life is to seek to love in the truth, as Christ loved us, and gave his life for us. "Love one another ... as

---

45. Mt 10:37–38, 12:30, 25:31–40.
46. Jn 5:27, 8:28, 12:49, 14:10.
47. 1 Pt 2:22, 2 Cor 5:21, Heb 4:15, 1 Jn 3:5.

I have loved you."[48] The imitation of Christ stands at the center of Christian life. It is not possible by our own power, since we are weak and wounded by sin, but it is made progressively possible due to the power of Christ's grace working in us, through the life of faith, hope, and charity, and by recourse to the sacraments of the Church.

Christ's Life and Teaching

The whole of Christ's life is a mystery that is meant to reveal to us the very identity of God, as well as what it means to be truly human. Here we can consider briefly some of the touchstones of that mystery as depicted in the New Testament.

Virginal Conception and Hidden Life

The virginal conception of the child Jesus in the womb of his mother is something that could only have been revealed to the disciples of Jesus by his mother, the Virgin Mary, or other close family members, presumably after the resurrection of Christ. This mystery is recounted in both the Gospels of Matthew and Luke, but seems to be alluded to in passages in the Gospel of John and Paul's letter to the Galatians.[49] Since the teaching is attested to in more than one early, independent source in the New Testament, and was also reaffirmed in a geographically widespread fashion universally through the second-century Church, we should presume that it is of apostolic origin and something that pertains to the Catholic faith.[50]

---

48. Jn 13:34.

49. Mt 1:18–2:22, Lk 1–2, Jn 6:42, Gal 4:4.

50. *Catechism of the Catholic Church*, par. 496: "From the first formulations of her faith, the Church has confessed that Jesus was conceived solely by the power of the Holy Spirit in the womb of the Virgin Mary, affirming also the corporeal aspect of this event: Jesus was conceived 'by the Holy Spirit without human seed' (Lateran Council of 649). The Fathers see in the virginal conception the sign that it truly was the Son of God who came in a humanity like our own. Thus St. Ignatius of Antioch

It is sometimes objected that the teaching that Jesus was conceived miraculously by the power of the Holy Spirit (without a
human father) is a bit of mythology or a superstitious projection
meant merely to underscore symbolically (in an archaic way) the
significance of Jesus' life. However, there are no real analogies to
the virginal conception and birth of Jesus in Greco-Roman literature in the ancient world, where gods were depicted mythologically as interacting sexually with human women. The idea in
the New Testament is distinctively Jewish: not that God took on
human features of reproduction, but that the one God, creator
of all that exists, began something new in the human race by his
direct activity, acting omnipotently upon nature as the transcendent creator. Jesus' embryonic body and gestational development
are typically human and natural, but they have their beginning
by the power of the Holy Spirit overshadowing the Virgin Mary,
and giving her to conceive miraculously without a human father. This real absence of a human father marks *symbolically* that
Christ is the eternal Son of God become man, and that a new creation has been initiated by God in human history. The notion
of the virginal conception is consonant with the notion of God
found in the Old Testament. The idea was not accepted readily by
Greco-Roman pagans (who frequently took their own religious
myths to be highly symbolic allegories). On the contrary, the
Christian teaching regarding Jesus' conception was frequently
mocked by non-Christians, suggesting that the early Church did
not promote the teaching for apologetic reasons, but because they
believed that it was true.[51]

at the beginning of the second century says: 'You are firmly convinced about our
Lord, who is truly of the race of David according to the flesh, Son of God according
to the will and power of God, truly born of a virgin ... he was truly nailed to a tree
for us in his flesh under Pontius Pilate ... he truly suffered, as he is also truly risen'
(*Ad Smyrn.* 1–2)."

51. See on this Joseph Ratzinger, *Jesus of Nazareth: The Infancy Narratives*, trans.
P. J. Whitmore (New York: Image, 2012), 51–57.

If Christ became human in such an extraordinary way, why was his subsequent life so hidden in the midst of ancient Israelite society, in the nondescript town of Nazareth, and draped in the domestic labors of manual work and agricultural labor? The virginal conception is something understood "after the fact" of the resurrection, because it was only after Jesus was glorified that his true identity and salvific significance were fully revealed and understood. The new beginning represented by the virginal conception of Jesus makes sense looking back at Jesus' life, death and resurrection, in light of the plenary revelation that he is "Emmanuel," or God with us. Initially, however, the true identity of Christ was made known only to his mother Mary and his foster father Joseph. God came into our world discreetly. C. S. Lewis compares this to the allied invaders landing on the beach of Normandy in the dead of night.[52] God's new presence among us in Christ is disarmingly subtle and hidden, made progressively manifest, especially in the apostolic life of Jesus. There is another meaning to the hidden life of Jesus, however, which is that God came among us not as someone famous or recognized but as someone ordinary and even raised in poverty: born in a cave, living in modest circumstances, a person of manual labor, silence, and prayer. The humility and "ordinariness" of the life of Christ is a sign that the ordinary lives of Christians can be completely given over to the project of discipleship and holiness.

Baptism and Temptations

The public apostolic life of Jesus began with his baptism by John in the Jordan River. The site John chose to administer his baptism was significant but also controversial. His ritual was meant to recall the initial settlement of Israel by Joshua and the disciples of Moses who crossed the river to enter Israel. The washing signified repentance but also the "re-founding" of Israel, in expectation of

52. C. S. Lewis, *Mere Christianity* (New York: HarperCollins, 2001), chap. 2.

the messianic end times. "I baptize you with water for repentance, but he who is coming after me is mightier than I, whose sandals I am not worthy to carry; he will baptize you with the Holy Spirit and with fire."[53] John's baptism was controversial because it constituted a forum for the forgiveness of sins not mandated directly by the sacrificial code of the Mosaic law. This is why the religious authorities of the time came down to the Jordan to question John.[54] His practice suggested that the law of Moses was to be relativized in the coming messianic age.

The baptism of Jesus is presented in the New Testament as both a historical event and a profound mystery. By receiving baptism from John, Jesus humbled himself in a sign of solidarity with sinful human beings. Although sinless, he signified by this prophetic gesture that his public mission in the world would make reparation to God for human sinfulness. This is why the "heavens open" at the baptism through a vision of the Holy Spirit descending on Christ, accompanied by the voice of the Father, "This is my beloved Son."[55] This vision signifies that the Holy Trinity is being revealed newly to the world in and through the mission of Jesus as messiah.

Soon after his baptism, Jesus went into the wilderness east of Jerusalem for forty days, subjecting himself to a time of prayer and fasting, in which he underwent temptation by the devil.[56] Presumably the way we know about this historical incident is due to Jesus' direct communication of it to the apostles. The story is recounted in two slightly different ways in Matthew and Luke, where it is interpreted theologically. In Matthew, the forty days of the fast are understood to be symbolic of Israel's forty years in the wilderness. Jesus is the new Israel, the messiah and sinless one in whom the law of the Torah is perfectly obeyed. In Luke, Jesus

53. Mt 3:11.
54. Jn 1:19–22.
55. Mt 3:16–17, Lk 3:21–22, Jn 1:32.
56. Mt 4:1–11, Lk 4:1–13.

is the new Adam, the human being who is tempted by the devil—now not in a garden as the first Adam, but in a wasteland that is the result of human sin. Where the first man was subject to temptation, Jesus is victorious over the tempter and refashions humanity in the image of God.

The struggle between Christ and the devil uncovers "meta-temptations" that threaten humanity: the devil seeks to assail Christ with lust, vanity, and pride, "basic places" that the devil seeks generally to exploit human moral weakness. "For all that is in the world, the lust of the flesh and the lust of the eyes and the pride of life, is not of the Father but is of the world."[57] In Jesus these temptations take on highly refined forms, not crude ones, since the devil seeks to tempt those he perceives to be more morally pure by seductions they are more apt to heed. The temptation to change stones into bread represents the lust for power over the material order, placing human efficacy and comfort above the love of God. By failing to orient their material lives toward God, human beings may satisfy their many desires but fail to live out their embodied life in the image of God. The temptation for Christ to throw himself off the Temple (which Origen thinks took place in a vision and not physically) is representative of spiritual vanity.[58] The temptation is to turn the legitimate goods of religion or society away from their true end (the service of God), toward the glorification of one's self. The temptation to abandon true obedience to God and to serve the devil in exchange for "all the kingdoms of the world" is one of pride. Pride is the desire to place one's self first in whatever domain, a disordered thirst for autonomy without reference to the truth about one's self, others, and God. By conquering the devil with obedience to God, in humility and temperance, Jesus re-establishes a profound order in the human race. His grace of victory over the tempter is commu-

---

57. 1 Jn 2:16.
58. Origen, *Homily on Luke* XXX (PG 13:1877; cf. PL 26:309).

nicated to the Church through baptism, penance, and the other sacraments.

The Kingdom of God and the Twelve

Even the most casual reader of the four canonical Gospels will note quickly that Jesus speaks frequently of the "kingdom of God" and that he is depicted as regularly performing miracles, either physical healings (like the restoration of sight to the man born blind) or nature miracles (like the calming of the storm on the Sea of Galilee). The two go together because the miracles are intended as "signs of the kingdom" meant to confirm the teaching of Christ. The notion of the kingdom of God in Jesus' teaching and preaching is both messianic and eschatological. That is to say, first, it is meant to signify the restoration of the kingdom of Israel, which is being made present in the ministry of Jesus. Jesus is himself the last king of Israel. And at the same time, this is the Israel of the end times, in which the final state of creation is seen breaking through in the activity and judgment of Christ.

Much of Jesus' miracle working and teaching is best understood against the backdrop of the prophecies of Isaiah in the Old Testament, many of which were written during Israel's exile in Babylon in the sixth century B.C. There God promises a restoration of the covenant with Israel after the exile and a vindication of Israel's mission to be a light to the nations, announcing through the prophet that the final end times will come upon the world through the mission of Israel. The nations will all come to acknowledge the truth about God as the God of Israel, and the final age of the world will be initiated.[59] Isaiah has specific symbols for the fulfillment of this prophecy, such as the blind receiving their sight and the lame walking, as well as the promise of a period of renewed holiness in the life of the people of Israel.[60] These are

59. Is 42, 49, 52, 55–56.
60. Is 35:5–6, 35:8.

just some of the images to which Jesus appeals in his miracles and preaching, and they are also referred to by John the Baptist. In short, Jesus claims to be ushering in the final age of the world by his own actions and in the course of his own ministry.

His choice of twelve apostles, then, is significant, as a symbol of the reconstitution of Israel.[61] The number is representative of the twelve tribes of the earliest Israelite community as depicted in Exodus 24. Of course it is significant that the twelve apostles are not twelve biologically descended tribesman but are a kind of analogical symbol: both like and unlike the "twelve" of the older covenant. The important difference becomes clearer in the Last Supper, where Christ institutes a new rite (the Eucharist) that is intended to open the covenant with Israel to all the gentile nations. Biological descent will no longer be the form of inclusion in the one covenant of God with Israel. Now that will take place through the life of the apostolic Church and the sacraments. Jesus' decision to have the twelve who represent Israel as his disciples naturally places him in a symbolic place above the chosen people, as one who is choosing them, that is to say, as one who identifies himself with the God of Israel.

Parables of the Son: Revealing the Father

Central features of Christ's mission and intentions are revealed through his parables. Jesus told a vast array of parables throughout his ministry, many of which are remembered in the Gospels. These stories are symbolic and therefore have multiple significations. They can communicate simple truths about divine revelation but simultaneously have deeper meanings that Christians have continued to ponder for centuries. At the center of the parables is the mystery of Jesus himself: the "kingdom" that Christ typically refers to in the parables ultimately implies the king or messiah who is at the center.

61. Lk 6:12–16, 1 Cor 15:5.

Two examples will suffice for our purposes. First, consider the parable of the wicked tenants in the Gospel of Luke.[62] There the owner of a certain land (Israel) sends his messengers through history (the prophets) to the tenants (the chosen people), asking them to pay homage to the owner (through the observances of the Torah as interpreted by the prophets). When they fail to obey, and in fact reject or kill the messengers, the owner finally sends his Son, whom the tenants kill so that they can possess the land as its inheritors. What is revealed in this simple story is that Jesus sees himself as the culminating point of the history of revelation, the Son of the Father, in whom the final judgment of Israel and humanity is coming to a head. He will be rejected and killed, so he tells the disciples, but God will be vindicated through his death.

Another example is found in the parable of the prodigal son.[63] In this famous story, the son of a wealthy landowner goes to a far country with his inheritance and squanders it in loose living, before falling into starvation and desperation. He then returns to his father to ask forgiveness but when his father sees him, he runs out to meet him, cloaks him in mercy, and has a feast in his honor to celebrate the fact that he "was dead, and is alive again ... was lost, and is found."[64] The older brother of the prodigal son refuses to come to the feast out of spite at the irresponsibility of the younger brother, but the father comes out to get him, insisting on the principle of mercy. In this parable, the prodigal son is of course fallen humanity, particularly the gentiles, while the older brother represents the faithful people of Israel, who might resent the profligate mercy of God that will be shown to humanity in Christ, calling all to enter into the covenant with God. However, on a deeper level, the prodigal son also represents Christ. Jesus

62. Lk 20:9–19.
63. Lk 15:11–32.
64. Lk 15:24.

is without sin, but Jesus does go out into the far country of the fallen world created by human sin, and from within that world he turns us back toward the Father. His approach to the Father occurs through his death for our sake on the Cross and through his resurrection. In other words, it is ultimately Jesus who is the beloved Son who was dead, but who has come back to life. His resurrection will reconcile us to the Father.

There are many examples of this pattern of teaching in the life of Jesus. He slowly reveals the power of the kingdom in and through his miracles and teachings, implying by them that "[He] and the Father are one," and that through his own ministry he is bringing about the end times.[65] This is also why Christ insists on radical poverty for his disciples, and on their leaving everything to follow him: the final judgment of the world is coming and the demands of Christ's love are absolute. An "either/or" decision must be made in the face of the preaching of Jesus. It is on his authority that the hinge of history turns.

Conflicts over the Law: Opening the Covenant

From the beginning of his ministry, Jesus performed controversial actions that suggested a unique interpretation of the Mosaic law and a judgment of Temple sacrifice as it existed at his time. We should recall that the Jews of the time of Jesus rightly understood the Temple sacrifices to be of divine origin, and understood the system of purification and forgiveness of sins encoded in the Mosaic law to be of ultimate authority. However, we see from the beginning of the Gospels that Jesus renders the law relative in key respects. First, he participates in a baptism for the repentance of sins administered by John, one that is not prescribed in the Mosaic law.[66] Next, he claims to have the authority to forgive sins of

---

65. Jn 10:30.
66. Mk 1:4–11.

himself over and above the Torah precepts.[67] He performs miracles on the Sabbath and permits his disciples to collect food on the Sabbath, both of which are interpreted as working on the Sabbath by some of the religious authorities of his time.[68] Jesus proclaims all foods clean, or at least gives an oblique indication of the doctrine of the subsequent apostolic Church: that Christians are not bound by the food purity laws of the Torah.[69] Most especially though, Jesus predicts the destruction of the Temple and claims that the "new temple" is his own body, which will be destroyed by his crucifixion and subsequently raised up.[70]

At heart, all of this behavior points toward a deeper goal: the opening of the covenant to non-Jews and the inclusion of gentiles in the mystery hitherto reserved to Israel. Jesus clearly saw his own death and resurrection as the linchpin of sacred history, the culmination of the mission of Israel to the world and the principle through which forgiveness would be offered to the gentile nations.[71] This is also the interpretation of the early Church, which claimed that gentiles could enter into the saving covenant of God by grace, through faith in Christ and obedience to his word, and no longer merely through circumcision and inclusion in the chosen people of Israel. Given what we have said above, it is clear why Jesus instituted the sacraments of the Eucharist and of holy orders on the night before he died, as well as the sacraments of baptism and of penance (according to Matthew and John respectively) after his resurrection.[72] These are the means by which the Church can give the nations a way of participating in the covenant of grace.

67. Mk 2:10.
68. Mk 2:23, 3:1–6.
69. Mk 7:19, Acts 15:1–29.
70. On destruction, see Mk 13:2, Lk 21:5–36; on the "new temple," see Jn 2:19–21, Mk 14:58.
71. Mk 8:31, 10:45, 14:22–24.
72. Mt 28:19, Jn 20:21–23.

Instituting the Eucharist and the Priesthood

The night before he died Jesus instituted the sacrament of the Eucharist. "And he took bread, and when he had given thanks he broke it and gave it to them, saying, 'This is my body which is given for you. Do this in remembrance of me.' And likewise the cup after supper, saying, 'This cup which is poured out for you is the new covenant in my blood.'"[73] Paul speaks for the earliest Christians when he confesses the faith of the Church: the Eucharist renders present in a mysterious way the true body and blood of Jesus. "The cup of blessing which we bless, is it not a communion in the blood of Christ? The bread which we break, is it not a communion in the body of Christ? .... For anyone who eats and drinks without discerning the body eats and drinks judgment upon himself."[74]

The Eucharist was instituted by Jesus as a symbol of his death: the two distinct consecrations of bread, first, and then wine, second, signify the separation of his body and blood in the suffering of the crucifixion. The communion in his body and blood initiated the apostles into the mystery of his death and resurrection. By stating that his death constituted the "blood of the covenant" and was a redemptive offering "for the many," Jesus made overt reference to the foundational sacrifice of the old covenant in Exodus 24:8 (where the phrase "the blood of the covenant" is first used), and to the notion of the sacrifice of the mysterious "suffering servant" who dies for the redemption of "the many," according to Isaiah 53:10–12.[75] In other words, Jesus treated his death as the uniquely fundamental sacrifice at the heart of the covenant of Israel, a sacrifice memorialized in the Eucharist. Sacrifice in the Old

73. Lk 22:19–20.
74. 1 Cor 10:16, 11:29 (translation slightly modified).
75. "For the many," Mt 26:28; "blood of the covenant," Ex 24:8; "suffering servant," Is 53:10–12.

Testament implies an offering to God of something valuable to us, and an inner disposition of spiritual worship and voluntary love. Christ makes such sacrifice most concrete by offering his own physical suffering and death to God out of love for human beings.

By commanding his apostles to "do this in memory of me," Jesus spoke a word that was intrinsically efficacious: that is to say, it accomplished what it signified. The Council of Trent notes that in making this command, Christ ordained the apostles, and thus constituted the apostolic hierarchy and the sacrament of holy orders (the episcopacy and the lower orders that come from it: priesthood and the diaconate).[76]

Naturally, this action was scandalous to some, since Jesus' "new sacrifice" inevitably displaced the centrality of the Temple cult and the Levitical prescriptions of the Torah. Presumably Judas, who betrayed Jesus to the high priests, intuited something of the radicality of Jesus' actions in the Last Supper, and reacted against what he rightly perceived as Jesus' high claims of authority and historical uniqueness. The high priests followed suit. Meanwhile, the apostles who remained loyal to Jesus were unable to withstand the threats of torture and death from the religious authorities who arrested Jesus. All of them fled except one.[77]

Atonement

When Thomas Aquinas considers why Jesus Christ is to be considered the high priest who alone has redeemed all of humanity from its sins, he gives three basic reasons.[78] Fundamentally, the reason that Christ is the unique mediator of salvation, and the savior, is that Christ alone is God. Because he is God made human, Jesus' human actions and sufferings have an infinite dignity

76. The Council of Trent, Session 22, On the Sacrifice of the Mass, chap. 22.
77. Jn 19:26.
78. Aquinas, *ST* III, q. 48, a. 2.

of a mysterious kind. There is no human sin that is so great that God cannot make reparation for it in his human actions and sufferings.

Second, Christ as man has a plenitude of charity in his human heart or will, by which he is able to love the Father as man, on behalf of all other human beings. Jesus is the new Adam in this respect, as the one who was obedient to God in love, there where the rest of humanity has collectively failed to love God authentically and to be obedient to God in the truth. The truth of Christ's love for God serves to "re-instantiate" the relationship of human beings to God in a remarkable way.

Third, Jesus suffered in particularly acute ways in his passion and death. This is due in part to the sheer physical and psychological tortures Jesus endured in his death by Roman crucifixion: prolonged and intense torture, piercing of the most sensitive parts of the body, death by hanging on a tree, rejection by many of his fellow people, abandonment by his friends, mocking and humiliation, and the suffering of his mother. However, there are also profound internal sufferings of the human mind and heart of Christ that come about due to his plenitude of grace. Jesus can experience contrition for the sins of the whole human race in a more acute way than any other, due to his higher prophetic knowledge and due to the intensity of his love for the whole human race. We might say that in his passion and crucifixion, Christ is given to peer into the mystery of our sinfulness and abandonment of God and to make reparation for the human race by love, offered to God from within that "place" of dereliction. "My God, my God, why have you abandoned me?"[79] At the same time, Christ's vision of God from the Cross is luminous: he is able to offer himself to God in the most profound inner peace and moral stability, as the Lord who knows that he is one with the Father. "Father, forgive them; for they know not what they do .... Into your hands

79. Mk 15:34 (translation slightly modified).

169

I commit my spirit."[80] "What shall I say? 'Father, save me from this hour'? No, for this purpose I have come to this hour. Father, glorify thy name."[81]

We should note that none of this entails that Christ suffers the wrath of God the Father, or that he is punished as one deemed guilty on our behalf. This is a theory of penal substitution that was popularized especially by John Calvin, and that some Catholics have held, but which differs from traditional Catholic teaching about the atonement. It is true to say that Jesus takes upon himself our punishments, in the sense that he endures consequences of original sin that are collective punishments for human sin (suffering and death). He also confronts the horror of our moral iniquity with unique insight, due to his understanding of the damage done by human evil, and he mourns for our human guilt with intense suffering of contrition of heart, due to the perfection of his charity. Fundamentally, though, Christ's mystery is in no way one of his own guilt, but of his infinite innocence in the face of our sinfulness. The passion is not a mystery of divine wrath and vengeance but of divine justice, mercy, and reparation. There is no problem with the use of the language of "substitutionary atonement," but there is a question of what this language connotes. Jesus' substitutionary atonement for our sins is above all something positive, not something negative. He substitutes his love, his justice, and his obedience there where the human race has lacked love, justice, and obedience. He "remakes" our condition from within, "justifying us," presenting us anew to the Father as authentic "children of God" by grace, grace merited for us by the only-begotten Son, in and through his passion.

The Apostles' Creed states that after his saving passion and death, Christ "descended into hell." What is meant by this? Traditionally three things are denoted by this article of the Creed.

80. Lk 23:34, 23:46.
81. Jn 12:27–28.

First, that Christ experienced a true human death like that of other human beings. To save us from death, God himself underwent a human death, which consists in the separation of the physical body and the spiritual soul. While the body of Christ is buried in the tomb by Joseph of Arimathea and the holy women, the soul of Christ "descends into Hades."[82] God overcomes our death not by avoiding true human suffering but by subjecting himself to the greatest human trial. His solidarity with us in death is the source of our authentic hope in God for participation in eternal life.

Second, the "descent into hell" that is spoken of here entails a state of being, not a place. The special imagery of a "descent" is metaphorical, not mythological. On Holy Saturday, following his passion, the soul of Christ is subjected to the state of all those in the human race who have suffered death before him. He does not experience eternal damnation. This would be impossible for the eternal Son of God whose human soul is united to the Godhead and possesses a plenitude of grace! Rather, the soul of Christ is the instrumental principle through which God illumines the souls of all the just who died prior to the time of the coming of Christ. We noted in the previous chapter that the grace of God is offered in some mysterious way to all human beings, down through history. Those who came before the time of Christ were offered a participation in his mystery of redemption through grace working in their human lives, often in concord with the inward inclinations of the moral law, to do good and to avoid moral evil. All those who died in a state of grace prior to the time of Christ died in an "anticipatory state" that was incomplete, awaiting the plenitude of the redemption. The "descent into hell" then refers to the illumination of all the just, all those who had rightly cooperated with the grace of God prior to the time of the coming of Christ. In his death and resurrection from the dead, then, Christ leads into the

82. Mk 15:43, Jn 19:38.

light of heaven (the beatific vision) all the souls of the faithful departed who had died in a state of grace.

Finally, the mystery of Jesus' descent into hell affects each of us in an eminently personal manner. By joining himself to our death, Christ allows each of us to experience the mystery of death united to God in him. Throughout our lives, even in our darkest moments of solitude, human sinfulness, and seeming God-forsakenness, we are not abandoned by God, nor are we obliged to live apart from God. The grace shown to us in Christ's death and descent into hell provides us with evidence of God's mercy, which reaches to the further horizons of creation. If we confide ourselves to that mercy with living faith, we can have confidence that, in the words of St. Paul, "neither death, nor life, nor angels, nor principalities, nor things present, nor things to come, nor powers, nor height, nor depth, nor anything else in all creation, will be able to separate us from the love of God in Christ Jesus our Lord."[83]

The Resurrection

Those who are truly Christian believe in the physical resurrection of Jesus from the dead. The resurrection of Jesus is not just a symbol. Rather, in the words of the *Catechism of the Catholic Church*, it is an event that is at once both "historical and transcendent."[84] God intervenes definitively in human history in the resurrection of Jesus, and in doing so reveals definitively the transcendent mystery of who God is and of what he intends for humanity.

The ancient world had no illusions about the reality of death. The Jews of the time of Jesus experienced the Roman political oppression and execution as regular features of ordinary life. Jews knew the difference between the idea that a martyr who has died

---

83. Rom 8:38.
84. *Catechism of the Catholic Church*, pars. 639–47.

lives on with God in his immortal soul (awaiting resurrection), and the claim that a person who has truly been put to death is now truly alive physically, in a transformed state, by the power of God. For the Jews of the time of Jesus, resurrection was associated with the end times, the eschaton, and with God's final judgment of the entire human race. It was looked forward to as a mystery of God's vindication of Israel, his glorification of the physical world, and the definitive salvation of the human race. This is why Christ's disciples find strange his foretelling that he will be crucified and rise from among the dead.[85] They cannot understand the idea that only one person would rise, and not the entire human race at the end of the world. In short, the resurrection of Jesus upsets the expectations of the religious Jews of Jesus' age: it inaugurates the end times, but it does so in a curious fashion, by initiating the time of the "ekklesia": the ecclesial gathering of all the nations in the universal or "Catholic" Church.

The resurrection of Jesus is a mystery of faith that is not subject to historical proof, but belief in the mystery does help to explain reasonably the historical genesis of the early Christian movement. In the time of Jesus, various messianic claimants had come and gone (mostly political revolutionaries), and after their deaths their movements died out. The early Christians told a very different story: they claimed that their own leaders had fled in fear of death when Jesus was arrested. They claimed to have lost faith in him almost immediately. Their argument that the tomb he was buried in was found empty three days later went uncontested by their adversaries, who seemingly accepted the truth of this statement.[86] Their assertion that Jesus appeared to many of them after his death was not something that made them popular either with Jewish religious leaders or with gentiles, be they political leaders or the intelligentsia. On the contrary, the early Christians were

85. Mk 9:10 (translation slightly modified).
86. Mt 28:15.

mocked, beaten, and killed systematically for their beliefs, which gained them no worldly honors or accolades. And yet they willingly gave their lives for what they took to be an irrefutable truth: that God had raised Jesus from the dead. Furthermore, their ministry was encompassed by public miracles that confirmed the message they preached: that God had acted definitively in history in the mystery of the resurrection.[87]

Historical belief in the resurrection, then, is not irrational but is historical. It does mean putting one's faith in the testimony of the apostles, but that act of belief is not unreasonable. What, however, is the resurrection of Jesus? What does it mean to say that Jesus is glorified in his humanity, in both his spiritual soul and his body?

The resurrection is not merely a return of Jesus to an ordinary human life. It is a mystery of the radical transformation and glorification of our human state. In the diverse apparitions of the risen Christ that we can find throughout the New Testament (the Gospels, Acts, Paul, Revelation), there are two basic modes or contrasting states in which the life of the risen Lord is presented. In one set of apparitions, such as with Mary Magdalene in the garden of the tomb in John 20, Jesus appears as an ordinary human being. The emphasis of such apparitions is on the reality of Jesus' physical body. He is truly alive. So he asks for food to eat or makes the doubting apostle Thomas place his hands in his side.[88] In another set of apparitions, particularly in Christ's appearances to Saul of Tarsus and to John, the seer at Patmos receiving the apocalyptic vision of Revelation, Christ appears in his unhindered glory, and is overwhelming.[89] Here the emphasis is on the transformed character of Christ's glorified flesh and on the new royal authority he possesses as the universal judge of humanity

87. Acts 3:1–11, 9:36–41, 19:11–12.
88. Lk 24:41, Jn 20:24–29.
89. Acts 9, 2 Cor 12:2, Rv 1:9–17.

and of the Church. The diverse apparitions, then, attest to both ordinariness and glory. Jesus is the new Adam who was dead and who is now alive. He is also the principle and source of a new creation, he in whom all things are being remade.

Medieval theologians spoke about four properties of the resurrected body of Christ, each revealed either explicitly or implicitly in the New Testament. *Impassibility* is a characteristic denoted negatively: in his risen body Jesus is now incapable of being subject to suffering or death. The transformed state of his risen flesh is one in which he can die no more. The Lord is present to his Church throughout the ages, then, in his perennial risen life. *Subtlety* is a property concerned with the spiritualization of the material body. The physical body of Jesus is still material, but the matter of his body is so transformed by the glory of the resurrection as to be perfectly subject to the influence of the spiritual soul and the movements of the spiritual life. From this, there follows *agility*: we see in the Gospels that Christ can make himself present where he wills: to the apostles on the road to Emmaus, in the cloister of the Upper Room, on the shores of the Sea of Galilee. There is a mysterious power of the risen Lord to manifest himself to us as one who is no longer of this physical world and who lives in a glorified physical state. Finally, there is *clarity* or translucence. Jesus in his glorified state can illuminate those to whom he manifests himself, not only by his words but also by the very presence of his glorified body. This is true especially in his overwhelming appearances to Saul on the road to Damascus and to John on the island of Patmos. Through his human body, the Lord enlightens the hearts of his disciples to his radiant and triumphant presence.

The resurrection of Jesus from the dead affects all of humanity in at least two very basic ways. First, the resurrection of Jesus signals to the human race the definitive victory of God over all powers of evil, sin, and death. It is true that we still live in a world in which it often seems that death and injustice have the last say. However, the resurrection of Jesus reveals the final end of the world in an anticipatory fashion, and so it promises to us all the victory of God's power, employed in the service of his mercy and love. In the end, as Julian of Norwich famously says, "all manner of things shall be well," because in the end, the resurrected Lord is victorious over even the worst of evils.[90] We might even go as far as to say that in the crucifixion of Jesus, humanity has done the worst thing possible: we have killed God. And from that greatest of evils, God has brought forth the greatest of possible goods: the forgiveness of sins, the restoration of grace, and the universal possibility of eternal life with God in the resurrection. Human history is still subject to immense and intense human and natural evils. Yet all of these real evils, however tragic and scandalously unjust they are, take place against the backdrop of the scandal of the Cross: of God's subjecting himself to human suffering and death, and of God's own ineffaceable and eternal victory of life, charity, and mercy.

Belief in the resurrection, then, is central to the Christian life and colors everything else. All suffering, all trials, and all of our finite historical existence are conditioned by knowledge of the glorification of Christ. If one believes that death is final, then one ultimately works by a different moral calculus. Neo-Gnosticism is characterized by a despair of the salvation of the body. The body then has its significance only in this world. "If the dead are not raised, 'Let us eat and drink, for tomorrow we die.'"[91] If one believes that physical death is not the final word, then this changes all of one's practical decisions. "Do you not know that your body is a temple of the Holy Spirit within you, which you have from God? You are not your own."[92] The acceptance of the mystery of Easter changes one's life radically, and gives a horizon to human existence that is uniquely hopeful and joyous.

90. Julian of Norwich, *Revelations of Divine Love*, trans. E. Spearing (New York: Penguin, 1999), Short Text, 15.
91. 1 Cor 15:32.
92. 1 Cor 6:19.

Second, the resurrection of Jesus reveals to us the final purpose for which the physical world was created in the first place. In and through a vast cosmic history God created a world in which living things could exist, and through a long, complex process God governed a world in which increasingly complex forms of life evolved. However, in the project of man, God elevated the material world into the realm of spirit and offered the human being living contact with God, spiritual friendship in a shared life of grace. This initial creation of the physical cosmos would allow human beings to marry and procreate reasonably and freely, educating their offspring as persons in communion with God. However, this initial mystery was itself meant to "evolve" spiritually and morally toward glorification: union with God by grace, and inward transformation of the physical life of man by the mysterious power of God. The mystery of the original sin of humanity brought this history of original grace to a crashing halt, and subjected man to the natural processes of decay and death. However, through the dynamic of the Cross, the Holy Spirit acts upon fallen humanity to remake us after the pattern of Christ. We can now become cooperators with the grace of God even in death, in view of the mystery of the resurrection. "We know that the whole creation has been groaning in travail together until now; and not only the creation, but we ourselves, who have the first fruits of the Spirit, groan inwardly as we wait for adoption as sons, the redemption of our bodies."[93] Jesus the new Adam, then, is the "Omega point" of the universe: the place that we see our lowly bodies transformed and divinized, where man is rendered fully alive by the power of God. In the resurrection of Christ we come to see the apex of the cosmic edifice, the orientation point that gives perspective to all else that is present in creation.[94]

93. Rom 8:22–23.

94. See on this idea, Joseph Ratzinger, *Introduction to Christianity*, trans. J. Foster (San Francisco: Ignatius, 2004), 234–43.

There are real presences of the resurrected Christ in our world. In his glorified life of the resurrection, Jesus is no longer a part of this physical cosmos, if by that we would mean that he would be somewhere "within" the physical world or contiguous with other physical realities. The glorified bodies of Christ and of the saints (such as that of the Virgin Mary) are of another order. However, the glorified body is not entirely "extrinsic" or outside the physical cosmos either. Jesus' body remains in a mysterious relationship to the ongoing life of the Church, and he can render himself present to human beings in a variety of ways. First, there is a simple, almost indefinable, but utterly real presence of the risen Lord to all those who have the grace of supernatural faith. Even in its darkness and obscurity, the faith makes us aware that Christ is personally present to each of us, not only in his reality as God, but also in his sacred humanity, as a human being like us, in body and soul. This sense of his presence can be more faint or more acute at various times, and it can grow in us the more we are given to contemplative prayer and conversation with Christ. But it is enduring and undeniably real.

Second, Christ is present in and through his sacramental activity. The sacraments are instrumental causes of grace, as we will explore in the next chapter. Christ is present in us by his grace which he shares with us, and this in an especially clear way through his sacraments. Christ acts not only as God but also as man, to communicate grace to the faithful, in and through all seven of the sacraments. In six of these (baptism, confirmation, reconciliation, marriage, holy orders, anointing of the sick), the presence is *operative* in nature: it is Christ who *acts or operates* by grace, in and through the minister of the sacrament. However, in the unique case of the Eucharist, the presence is not only operative, but also *substantial*: the glorified body of Christ is mysteriously and truly present substantially, under the appearances of bread and wine. By reserving the host in the tabernacle, every parish or chapel maintains the presence of Christ in the midst of our world. In this way, the Lord in his glory accompanies the Church down through the ages, sustaining her in her journey with his concrete presence. It is one that is perceptible only through the grace of faith, but it is eminently real all the same.

Christ is also present to the Church through the lives of his holy ministers, bishops, priests, and deacons in whom he may act, especially through the proclamation of the word of God and by holy preaching. He is present in his saints, who can be found in each age of the Church, manifesting the transformative holiness of Christ in the midst of our world. He is present also through special apparitions where he makes himself known to particular persons, often great saints like Francis of Assisi, Catherine of Siena, or Pio of Pietrelcina, but also great sinners like Jacques Fesch, who was transformed by such an experience. Catholics are not obliged to believe in any particular post-apostolic apparition of Christ or the Virgin Mary. All such "events" are subject to the reasonable judgments of Christian prudence, as well as the sound discernment of the ecclesiastical hierarchy.

Jesus Christ is alive. He has the power to manifest himself in extraordinary ways to his closest friends, as well as those who consider themselves his enemies. He is present in his mystical body, the Church. We can see his face in the actions of ordinary Christians who act with charity. If we want to encounter the risen Lord ourselves, it is not difficult. Every human being can do so in the simplest and most direct way possible: by beginning to pray to Jesus.

5

THE CHURCH

The Holy Spirit and the
Apostolic College

At many points in his apostolic ministry, Jesus spoke about the Holy Spirit as a person distinct from both the Father and himself.[1] The night before he died he promised that he would send the Holy Spirit upon the apostles after his death and resurrection.[2] He spoke of the Holy Spirit as "the Spirit of Truth" who would lead the apostolic Church into the fullness of the truth, and called him the "Paraclete" or "Counselor" who would convict the world of its sins and act inwardly to justify the human race by grace.[3]

This subsequent sending of the Holy Spirit upon the apostles is depicted in two distinct ways in the New Testament. In the Gospel of John, Jesus sends the Paraclete on Easter night, after he is raised from the dead, breathing the Spirit upon the apostles so that "if you forgive the sins of any, they are forgiven; if you retain the sins of any, they are retained."[4] In this way he instituted the apostolic mediation of reconciliation with God, which would

---

1. Mt 12:31–33, 28:19; Jn 3:6–8, 15:26.
2. Jn 14:16–17.
3. Jn 16:13–15, 16:7–11.
4. Jn 20:23.

later come to be termed the sacrament of penance. A second event is depicted in Acts 2. Here, fifty days after the resurrection of Christ (the "Pentecost"), the Spirit is sent upon the apostles gathered in prayer with the early Christian community and the Virgin Mary, the Mother of God. The apostles are given illumination and fortitude, as well as charismatic gifts to preach the gospel to all the nations, without fear of persecution or death. The bold and clear preaching of Peter cuts his auditors to the heart, "so those who received his word were baptized, and there were added that day about three thousand souls."[5]

The mission of the Holy Spirit is to accompany the work of the visible, apostolic Church, acting in the preaching and sacramental life of her members, sanctifying them by works of love, and leading them into the fullness of truth. The mission of the incarnate Word was especially visible, outward, and public in his human life among us. The mission of the Spirit is more typically invisible, inward, and intimate. He comes forth from the resurrected Christ and is the invisible soul of the visible Church. He indwells in the hearts of human beings, prompting them by grace to recognize the truth of the Gospel, the reality of Christ, and their need for conversion. He inhabits mystically within the hearts of the saints, giving them the graces and virtues necessary to accomplish works of grace for the sake of Christ. Therefore, the pattern of "return" follows in inverse the pattern of "origin." Just as the Holy Spirit is sent forth from the Father through the Word made man, into the world, so he acts interiorly to lead human beings to recognize Jesus as the Son of God, and to live in the Son.[6] In this way he makes them adoptive sons and daughters of God turned toward the Father. "And because you are sons, God has sent the Spirit of his Son into our hearts, crying, 'Abba! Father!'"[7]

The Holy Spirit is given to the Catholic Church both in the

5. Acts 2:14–47, quotation at 2:41.
6. On being sent into the world, see Jn 15:26.
7. Gal 4:6.

"apostolic age"—the time when the apostles founded the Church—and in the "post-apostolic age," which stems from the time of the death of the last apostle and will continue until the end of the world. The apostles, however, received two types of privileges from the Spirit: those that pertained to them only during the apostolic age (meant for the founding of the Church) and those that they transmitted to their successors, the *episcopoi* or bishops, whom they appointed and ordained by the laying on of hands.[8]

What pertained to the apostles alone was: first, to receive the plenitude of revelation; second, to recognize as being from Christ the sacraments that are of divine institution (coming from God himself); third, to found the one, holy, universal (that is to say "Catholic") Church. This means that after the time of the apostles there cannot be any additional new revelation that adds to the initial apostolic deposit of faith. The Church can understand more *explicitly and conceptually* what was contained implicitly and intuitively in the apostolic doctrine. But this "development" of Church doctrine can only take place because it stems from what is truly contained in the primal revelation of the apostolic Church. Consequently, appeals to "new revelation" whether in the form of private visions or new religious movements (Montanism, Islam, Mormonism) are always in some sense fundamentally erroneous. Nor can there be any new Church founded by a new Christian reform movement. Catholicism is not denominationalist. There is only one Church founded by Christ, and though her members can be subject to internal weaknesses, schism, and even significant betrayals of the truth of the Gospel, she will continue to endure down through the ages until the end of the world.[9]

In the post-apostolic age, then, the Holy Spirit guides the "apostolic hierarchy," the validly ordained bishops who remain in communion with the pope, so as to guide the Church. Here the

8. 1 Tm 3:1–7, Ti 1:7–9, 2 Tm 1:6.
9. Mt 16:18.

Spirit gives assistance to the bishops to teach the truth of Christ faithfully, to discern falsehood from error, to preserve the unity of the faithful, and to govern the ecclesial body with stewardship so as to preserve her in existence until the end of time. Already in 110 A.D., the letters of Ignatius of Antioch bear witness to the threefold hierarchy instituted by the apostles of bishops, presbyters, and deacons. It is they especially who are charged to safeguard the communion of the Church, which is founded in the eucharistic body and blood of Jesus.

Since therefore I have, in the persons before mentioned, beheld the whole multitude of you in faith and love, I exhort you to study to do all things with a divine harmony, while your bishop presides in the place of God, and your presbyters in the place of the assembly of the apostles, along with your deacons, who are most dear to me, and are entrusted with the ministry of Jesus Christ, who was with the Father before the beginning of time, and in the end was revealed. Do all then, imitating the same divine conduct, pay respect to one another, and let no one look upon his neighbor after the flesh, but continually love each other in Jesus Christ. Let nothing exist among you that may divide you; but be united with your bishop, and those that preside over you, as a type and evidence of your immortality.[10]

Take heed, then, to have but one Eucharist. For there is one flesh of our Lord Jesus Christ, and one cup to [show forth] the unity of His blood; one altar; as there is one bishop, along with the presbyters and deacons, my fellow-servants: that so, whatsoever you do, you may do it according to [the will of] God.[11]

A few qualifications are in order. People are not bishops (or priests or deacons, for that matter) simply because they wish to be or because they assisted at a ceremony in which there was a laying on of hands. Valid ordination of a bishop, priest, or deacon requires that the ordaining minister (the ordaining bishop) have the sacred power to ordain, a grace that is given only to those who were themselves ordained by a validly ordained bishop. The no-

10. Ignatius of Antioch, *Letter to the Magnesians*, c. 6, in *Ante-Nicene Fathers*.
11. Ignatius of Antioch, *Letter to the Philadelphians*, c. 4.

tion is not circular but historical: all bishops must be ordained by validly ordained bishops, going back to the apostolic Church itself. Indeed, we find in texts of the second and third century that the earliest Catholic Church was itself immensely concerned to preserve this practice faithfully, so as to maintain the "apostolic succession" of bishops from the time of the apostles.[12]

Second, valid ordination is not identical with holiness. Aquinas says that bishops are to be chosen for their prudence and stewardship, primarily, and their holiness secondarily.[13] The former quality is especially needed to govern the Church well, while someone may very well become holy but remain ill-suited to the governance of the Church. A bishop should have thorough knowledge of the Christian faith and a good deal of practical wisdom, as well as charity for others, and holiness of life.

Finally, we should note that the claim we have made does not entail that each bishop is personally doctrinally infallible. It is the collective unity of the bishops over time, with and under the jurisdiction of the bishop of Rome, that can discern the truth of the Catholic faith across the ages. The creeds and councils of the Catholic Church are clarifications of what pertains to the apostolic deposit of faith, of what the Church believes infallibly. But this discernment takes place through a complex process of reflection, argument, and decision by the collective consensus of the bishops. It is true that the bishop of Rome has the special prerogative to affirm infallible teachings of the Church from himself, in the name of all the bishops of the world. However, when he does so (and this privilege has been used rarely in fact), he must do so in organic continuity with what his predecessors and the worldwide episcopacy have taught before him. In other words, the seeming

12. For only two poignant examples, see Irenaeus, *Against Heresies* III, 3, 1–4; III, 4, 1; IV, 26, 2; IV, 33, 8; Hippolytus of Rome, *The Apostolic Tradition*. See also *The Treatise on the Apostolic Tradition of St. Hippolytus of Rome, Bishop and Martyr*, ed. G. Dix (London: Alban Press, 1992).

13. Aquinas, *ST* II-II, q. 185, a. 3.

"novelties" of the pope, when he truly teaches something infallibly, are never doctrinal "innovations," but always truly organic developments of the teaching that has come before.

A good example of this is the twentieth-century proclamation of the dogma of the bodily Assumption of the Blessed Virgin Mary. This teaching is an expression of what the tradition has always affirmed for the Virgin Mary, and for all human beings in our capacity to participate in divine life. Our bodies are not an impediment we need to shed for shared intimacy with God. From the earliest times the Church taught that all human beings will be resurrected from the dead in the end times and that the Virgin Mary was the new Eve, fully redeemed by the grace of Christ her Son (a teaching we will return to below). From the seventh century the widespread liturgical celebration of the bodily Assumption of the Virgin Mary marked the broad emergence of an ecclesial consensus that began centuries before. Christ has worked perfectly in the Virgin Mary what he intends to work more broadly in all of humanity at the end of time. The teaching was developed organically out of elements of the primitive faith of the Church, and affirmed subsequently by the bishops, only to be confirmed solemnly by Pope Pius XII in the twentieth century.[14]

The Petrine ministry is a genuine mystery of faith, something instituted by Christ himself directly. Chosen by Christ himself as the "Rock" upon whom the faith of the Church rests, Peter has the vocation to strengthen his brethren in the faith. He is portrayed throughout the New Testament as the central authority of the early Church, the primary apostolic teacher, upon whom the others depend for the final decisions in matters of governance.[15] The earliest Church of the second century very clearly acknowledged the primacy of the successor of Peter, the bishop of Rome,

---

14. See on this subject, Matthew Levering, *Mary's Bodily Assumption* (Notre Dame, Ind.: University of Notre Dame Press, 2014).

15. Mt 16:18–19; Jn 21:15–19; Lk 22:32; Acts 1:15–22, 5:3–10, 8:14–17, 10:11–15.

who was also considered to be the successor of the apostle Paul since Paul was martyred in Rome.[16] In addition to his irreplaceable role in safeguarding the infallible teaching of the Catholic Church with regard to faith and morals, the successor of Peter is also the guarantor of Church unity. The Catholic Church endures down through the ages united across time, place, and peoples. She remains undivided by the splintering of doctrinal divisions (as one finds in Protestantism), or the warring loyalties of nationalism (as one finds in the sister orthodox Churches, despite their great proximity in most things to Roman Catholicism). The *principal* origin of this is the Holy Spirit himself, who assures the unity of the Catholic Church down through the ages (in spite of the frailties or failings of many of her members), as a visible sign of her miraculous origin and of the power of the grace of Christ. The *instrumental* origin of this unity is the Petrine ministry. Or rather, the Holy Spirit binds the Church together through a communion of charity and love, united in the truth of Christ. But he does so in part through the instrumental service of the pope, the "servant of the servants of God," whose primacy in the Church is meant to assure her mystical unity throughout time. God has no need of the papacy and need not have instituted it. But he did institute it, and given that he is committed to it until the end of time, we ourselves are dependent upon the acknowledgement of this biblical and mystical reality if we wish to become complete and authentic disciples of the living Christ, on his terms and not upon those of our own making. Understood rightly, the teaching of the popes is a source of continual wisdom for the Church and of authentic freedom for the Gospel, so as to know the revelation of Christ most perfectly and serve God alone unconditionally.

16. See, for example, Clement of Rome, *First Letter to the Corinthians*; Ignatius of Antioch, *Letter to the Romans*; Irenaeus, *Against Heresies* III, 3, 1–4.

The Seven Sacraments

The sacraments of the new covenant are sacred signs or symbols which are of divine origin and that act as "instrumental causes," or channels, of grace. That is to say, sacraments are not only outward signs of inward graces. They also transmit or convey the grace that they symbolize, at least when the recipient accepts them worthily and is in a properly disposed state. The Catholic Church teaches that there are seven sacraments, each instituted by Christ either during his earthly life or after his resurrection during the apostolic age. We can find references to all of them in the New Testament.[17]

Here we should make some qualifications. Citations of scripture are not proof texts meant to compel a skeptical mind. That Christ directly instituted seven sacraments cannot be proven empirically because no one can go back two thousand years to verify that Christ rose from the dead, that he founded the Church, or that he instituted the sacraments. These are all truths of the Catholic faith that can be believed by grace alone, or disbelieved by the rejection of that grace. Intellectually speaking, however, such references act as signs that denote real historical continuity between the earliest life of the Catholic Church and her subsequent development in later ages. The seven sacraments are all of derivation from the apostolic age, but they also each have a subsequent historical development in form. We can look back, then, from later sacramental practices and see the initial seeds of these

---

17. On baptism, see Mt 28:19–20, which serves as an echo of Mt 3:13 and Jn 3:3–8. On confirmation, see Jn 20:22 and Acts 2:1–4, 8:15–17, 1C:38, 19:5–6. On the Eucharist, see Lk 22:7–20, Mt 26:17–29, Mk 14:12–25, 1 Cor 11:23–26, and Jn 6. On reconciliation, see Mt 16:19, Jn 20:23, 2 Cor 5:18, Jas 5:16. On the anointing of the sick, see Mk 6:12–13 and Jas 5:14–15. The sacrament of holy orders is contained implicitly in the eucharistic institution narratives: "*Do this* in memory of me." We also find subsequent references to it in Acts 1:8, 2:4 (where the apostles receive the fullness of enlightenment); Jn 20:22–23; 1 Tm 4:14; 2 Tm 1:6–7. The sacrament of matrimony is referred to in Mk 10:8, 1 Cor 7:39, and Eph 5:31–32.

practices in the New Testament and the early Church. The sacrament of confession provides a good example. Christ clearly gives the apostles the power to "bind and loose" the sins of penitents, and the early Church understood the bishop to be the safeguard of communion, determining who was fit to receive communion and who was not. In the first centuries of the Church, then, the sacrament of penance was frequently administered only by bishops and accompanied by public penance. The penitent performed public acts of penance to show his or her disposition to receive communion in a worthy fashion. In the early medieval Church, however, it gradually became customary for the bishop to delegate the power of absolution to priests and to permit the penance to take place in purely private settings, a practice that endures to this day. Once one perceives the "history" of the sacrament, there is a clear account one can give of its developmental form, from the time of the early Church until today.

Some sacraments are contained virtually and implicitly in others. As noted above, the Gospels make overt references to Christ's institution of baptism, the Eucharist, holy orders, and the sacrament of penance. Meanwhile, the sacrament of marriage is contained implicitly within the sacrament of baptism, for when two baptized Christians marry, they wed "in Christ" and so form a living image of Christ and the Church.[18] The sacraments of confirmation and anointing of the sick, meanwhile, are referred to in Acts, seemingly in passing. When were they originally instituted? They are sacramental capacities transmitted implicitly by the power of holy orders and are reserved to bishops and priests. Consequently, we can say that they were instituted by Christ when he established the apostolic college and the sacrament of holy orders. They are not later inventions of the medieval Church, since their usage was common from the earliest centuries of the Church.[19]

18. Eph 5:31–32.
19. See, as examples, St. Ambrose, *On the Mysteries* VII, 41–42; Origen, *Homilies on Leviticus*, 2:5.

To say that sacraments "effectuate what they symbolize" means that each sacrament has a particular effect of grace. This complexity may seem arbitrary. Why should there be different ways to participate in the unique grace of Christ? However, the sacraments are of divine institution, not human innovation, and their diversity has a profound wisdom enshrined within it. As Aquinas notes, there is a unity to the whole "sacramental organism," with some sacraments that are more fundamental, and others that are more ultimate. Some are aimed at our sanctification, others at our healing. Some sanctify more immediately the individual, others are at the service of the common good. His overview merits an extended citation:

The sacraments of the Church were instituted for a twofold purpose: namely, in order to perfect man in things pertaining to the worship of God according to the religion of Christian life, and to be a remedy against the defects caused by sin.

And in either way it is becoming that there should be seven sacraments. For spiritual life has a certain conformity with the life of the body: just as other corporeal things have a certain likeness to things spiritual. Now a man attains perfection in the corporeal life in two ways: first, in regard to his own person; secondly, in regard to the whole community of the society in which he lives, for man is by nature a social animal. With regard to himself man is perfected in the life of the body in two ways: first, directly [per se], i.e. by acquiring some vital perfection; secondly, indirectly [per accidens], i.e. by the removal of hindrances to life, such as ailments, or the like. Now the life of the body is perfected "directly," in three ways. First, by generation whereby a man begins to be and to live: and corresponding to this in the spiritual life there is Baptism, which is a spiritual regeneration, according to Titus 3:5: "By the laver of regeneration," etc. Secondly, by growth whereby a man is brought to perfect size and strength: and corresponding to this in the spiritual life there is Confirmation, in which the Holy Ghost is given to strengthen us. Wherefore the disciples who were already baptized were bidden thus: "Stay you in the city till you be endued with power from on high" (Luke 24:49). Thirdly, by nourishment, whereby life and strength are preserved to man; and corresponding to this in the spiritual life there is the Eucharist. Wherefore it is said (John 6:54): "Except you eat of the flesh of the Son of Man, and drink His blood, you shall not have life in you."

And this would be enough for man if he had an impassible life, both corporally and spiritually; but since man is liable at times to both corporal and spiritual infirmity, i.e. sin, hence man needs a cure from his infirmity; which cure is twofold. One is the healing that restores health: and corresponding to this in the spiritual life there is Penance, according to Psalm 40:5: "Heal my soul, for I have sinned against Thee." The other is the restoration of former vigor by means of suitable diet and exercise: and corresponding to this in the spiritual life there is [anointing of the sick], which removes the remainder of sin, and prepares man for final glory. Wherefore it is written (James 5:15): "And if he be in sins they shall be forgiven him."

In regard to the whole community, man is perfected in two ways. First, by receiving power to rule the community and to exercise public acts: and corresponding to this in the spiritual life there is the sacrament of holy orders, according to the saying of Hebrews 7:27, that priests offer sacrifices not for themselves only, but also for the people. Secondly in regard to natural propagation. This is accomplished by Matrimony both in the corporal and in the spiritual life: since it is not only a sacrament [which sanctifies the human couple] but also a function of nature [which unites the political community].[20]

Baptism, then, is the doorway into the sacraments. Being baptized is like becoming the citizen of a new country. Christ acts upon a person to communicate the "character," or permanent mark, by which a human being is claimed for Christ and incorporated into the mystical body of the visible Church. This gives a person the power to receive other sacraments, since only those who are baptized are ontologically capable of receiving confirmation, penance, the Eucharist, anointing of the sick, marriage, or holy orders. In addition, baptism sanctifies the human being by communicating the infused graces of faith, hope, and charity, which allow for the indwelling presence of the Holy Spirit.

20. Aquinas, *ST* III, q. 65, a. 1.

The soul is redeemed from original sin and no longer morally estranged from God. In small children the grace of baptism is given in a merely "habitual" way, that is to say as a capacity or seedling of potency. The activity of faith, hope, and love must be awakened in the child through external education, which is why parents and godparents must promise to raise the baptized child as an authentic Catholic Christian.

Confirmation deepens the grace of baptism by granting a capacity to witness publicly to the Gospel. It is the sacrament aimed at granting the recipient fortitude for public testimony. Aquinas thinks that this sacrament had its initial actuation in the apostles on the day of Pentecost, when they no longer feared to preach the Gospel in public.[21] By sending the Holy Spirit upon them as his apostolic and episcopal witnesses, Christ in his glory gave them the power to confer the sacrament upon others. In the early Church this sacrament was often denoted by the Greek word *sphragis* ("seal"), a term also employed for a Roman soldier marked with the seal of Rome. Confirmation marks the new adult convert out as a spiritual combatant for Christ, devoted to the works of charity in the grace of the Holy Spirit.[22] In the Eastern Church, confirmation has traditionally been delegated to priests and performed at baptism, while in the Western Church it has typically been reserved to the bishop and conferred once Christians reach the age of reason (often in adolescence). Both practices are deeply meaningful. The Eastern custom symbolizes the sheer gratuity of the grace of belonging to Christ and the fact that confirmation brings baptism to perfection. The Western custom denotes the fact that Christian witness to Christ links us to the bishop, and that it is a privilege and responsibility of mature Christian life.

21. Aquinas, *ST* III, q. 72, a. 1, ad 1, and a. 5.
22. See on this Jean Daniélou, *The Bible and the Liturgy* (London: Darton, Longman and Todd, 1956), 201–2.

The Eucharist is the summit of the Christian life: it is the sacrament of the real presence of the body, blood, soul, and divinity of Christ, in which the glorified Christ is rendered substantially present. The Church communes truly, then, in the body and blood of Jesus, and in doing so is given a particular participation in the charity of Jesus. The Eucharist is the sacrament of charity, in which the Church is united with God by grace, and the communion of the entire Church is renewed in fraternal love.

Two sacraments are connected to particular needs of healing. Penance is a sacrament that restores the soul of the penitent to a state of grace after a moral failing. It is traditionally referred to as a "plank given after a shipwreck."[23] This sacrament has an irreplaceable and unique supernatural capacity to restore the soul to a state of peace with God, particularly after serious sin, and allows for the grace-filled consolation of the conscience. Over time, regular practice of the sacrament of penance refines the moral conscience of the practitioner and makes him much more likely to avoid serious sin altogether. The anointing of the sick, meanwhile, is for ailments of the body, particularly when in grave danger of death. This sacrament is intended principally to strengthen the recipient to undergo physical suffering and even death in union with Christ, and to bear sufferings patiently with grace, in reparation for one's sins and for the sins of others.

Finally, two sacraments are concerned with the sanctification of individuals within the larger society of persons. The sacrament of marriage unites two people within an indissoluble bond of grace, until death, so that their spousal friendship, and the generation and education of children, can become a locus of grace in the world. This sacrament creates within each human family a "domestic church" in which Christ can dwell by grace. Finally, the sacrament of holy orders is the sacrament that provides for the administration of the sacraments named above, as well as for

---

23. Aquinas, *ST* III, q. 84, a. 6.

the instruction and governance of the Church. It is because of the priesthood that there can be an enduring presence of Christ in the Church: in the Eucharist, in penance, and in the graces of confirmation and anointing of the sick. All of these sacraments depend immediately upon that of holy orders, and so the latter forms a kind of vertebral column in the Church—not the heart of the Church, but its backbone, without which the rest cannot stand.

The sacraments are a beautiful mystery because they address human beings simultaneously as animals (who have need of our senses to encounter others) and as spiritual beings (who can live inwardly by faith in the spoken word of God). Although some say that the sacramental organism is a purely human construct, the truth is that the sacraments were instituted by Christ as a mercy, so that the Church might always remain God-centered, in spite of all our human limitations and moral frailties. It is not the clergy who maintain the sacraments in being, at least not principally, but God and Christ, alive at the heart of the Church. The sacraments are sources of grace *ex opere operato*, that is to say, by the very working of the sacraments. This means that lay recipients of the sacraments who are well disposed can receive grace from their celebration whenever the minister simply has the intention to do what the Church intends in celebrating a sacrament correctly. Thus the sacraments never depend upon the moral worthiness or supernatural faith of the minister. This may seem like a cynical view of the ministers of the Church, but in fact it simply underscores a basic distinction. It is one thing for a priest to be an instrument of grace, and another for him to be personally holy. All those in holy orders should tend toward personal holiness, and the grace of the sacrament of holy orders can always assist them in this. But the Church's continued existence does not depend per se on their holiness. It depends upon God who continues to act in the sacraments, drawing human beings to himself and sanctifying them down through the ages, over and above any and every limitation of men.

The Sacrifice of the Mass

A sacrament effectuates the grace that it signifies. In other words, a sacrament does what it promises in symbolic fashion. When a person is washed by baptismal water, the grace of baptism is effectively given to cleanse the soul from the effects of original sin. When a person is anointed with the oil of confirmation, he is sealed with the Holy Spirit so as to be fortified to bear witness to Christ publicly.

Aquinas notes that there are three distinct significations present in the sacrament of the Eucharist, and so correspondingly, the sacrament has three effects.[24] First, the sacrament signifies symbolically the sacrifice of Christ: the double consecration of the body of Christ, followed by that of his blood, signifies the separation of body and blood that took place at Golgotha when he gave his life for us. This is hardly a controversial claim, theologically speaking. It is Jesus himself in the Gospels who makes clear that the institution of the Eucharist on Holy Thursday is a symbol of his death: "This is my body which is for you. Do this in remembrance of me.... This cup is the new covenant in my blood. Do this, as often as you drink it, in remembrance of me."[25]

Second, the Eucharist symbolizes food. In the Eucharist God changes bread and wine into the very substance of the body and blood of Christ. "It is not the power of man which makes what is put before us the Body and Blood of Christ, but the power of Christ Himself who was crucified for us. The priest standing there in the place of Christ says these words but their power and grace are from God. 'This is My Body,' he says, and these words transform what lies before him."[26] What we consume is the body

24. Aquinas, *ST* III, q. 79, a. 1.
25. 1 Cor 11:24–25.
26. John Chrysostom, *Homilies on the Treachery of Judas* I, 6, in *The Faith of the Early Fathers*, vol. 2, ed. and trans. W. A. Jurgens (Collegeville, Minn.: The Liturgical Press, 1979), 104–5.

and blood of Christ in his glory, present in a sacramental mode. However, the accidents or properties of bread and wine remain. Consequently, in communion, the human being consumes Christ's body and blood under the signs of bread and wine. The symbolism is important: in the Bible, in Exodus in particular, bread is the symbol of sustenance. The Eucharist sustains our soul in the spiritual life of grace during our pilgrimage in this world. Wine is the biblical symbol of joy: the Eucharist is also something ultimate, our joy, the heights of our spiritual life, our place of deepest communion in the love of God.

Thirdly, the Eucharist symbolizes the unity of the Church. St. Paul writes: "Because there is one bread, *we who are many are one body, for we all partake of the one bread.*"[27] Common reception of the body and blood from one altar binds believers together into a communion of persons. The Eucharist creates this unity inwardly by bestowing supernatural charity, allowing us to participate collectively in the love that Christ has for the Father and for other human beings. And so the Church is sustained by the Eucharist as a mystical body, a spiritual and visible communion of truth and love. In this way Christians themselves, despite the fact that they are all sinners who depend entirely upon the grace of Christ, become a collective, visible sign of Christ's presence in the world.

What is of key importance is to see the order between these three effects of the grace of the Mass. First, the grace of the Eucharist is sacrificial: it flows forth from the sacrifice of the Cross of Christ, and it conforms us inwardly to that sacrifice. Second, the unity of Christ crucified with the Church is one of communion in charity: the love of Christ sustains and rejoices. Finally, the Eucharist then is the sacrament of charity that binds all of Christ's faithful into one body.

The Mass in which the Eucharist is confected is a true sacrifice, then, because in the celebration of the Mass, during the

27. 1 Cor 10:17.

double consecration of Christ's body and blood, the Church offers the merits of the unique sacrifice of Christ to the Father, and the grace of the Cross is poured out upon the Church. We should not think that the Eucharist is called a sacrifice because it constitutes any addition to the one saving sacrifice of Christ. On the contrary, the Mass just is the one saving sacrifice of the Cross rendered present to Christ's faithful. In the mystery of the Mass, the grace of the one self-offering of Christ crucified (who has died and is now glorified, and suffers no longer) is communicated to the Church. This grace is "Christ-conforming." It works inwardly to move the faithful by charity to offer their lives to God in Christ, and to conform their lives to the love of Christ under the agency of the Holy Spirit. This is why the Church intercedes for the world in the prayers of the Mass: there she is called upon by God to unite herself by charity with Christ crucified, in his grace alone and by his grace alone, so as to intercede on behalf of the world. The greatest saints, from Catherine of Siena to Teresa of Calcutta, have always had the deepest devotion to and reverence for the Mass, because it is there they received their spiritual sustenance and were enabled by the grace of the Cross to undertake heroic sacrifices on behalf of the Church and the world. The greatest of blessings in this life for Catholic Christians is that each day in the Mass, they can unite their ordinary or extraordinary experiences of joy and suffering to the Cross of Christ, bringing their lives into union with Christ's own sacrifice. In the Mass, then, the Church offers to the Father the merits of Christ's passion (as he himself instructed us to do in the Last Supper), and in doing so, she also offers herself, supported and motivated uniquely by the grace of Christ.

Justification and Sanctification

Prevenient Grace

We cannot attain true spiritual intimacy with God by our own natural powers. There is a twofold distance between ourselves and God. One is the distance of creature to creator. We are finite and God is transcendent. A second is the distance of sin. Our nature is not only finite but also wounded, fallen, and alienated from God. Consequently, the New Testament teaches that despite our natural capacity to know that there is a God, no one can come to know God personally and approach God with genuine love for God unless God first acts upon a person's mind and heart by grace. Grace is a participation in the very life of God, not such that we come to be God himself (we are always mere creatures), but such that we come to know and love God in a way analogous to the way God knows and loves himself.[28] Grace makes us friends with God.[29] Aquinas notes that all grace is in some sense one: it is a mystery of God working in us to draw us out beyond ourselves into his mystery.[30] But this one mystery of grace has many effects and so it is reasonable to name grace from its diverse effects, based on the process of conversion to God that it realizes in our lives.

"Prevenient grace" is a term used frequently by St. Augustine. It denotes a central New Testament teaching: we cannot take any initiative to turn toward God unless he first takes the initiative to turn us toward himself.[31] This mystery does not entail a denial of free will, but its affirmation: God's grace inspires us to use our freedom well, in search of God. This insistence on the divine initiative is true for everyone, from the child who is baptized into the grace of Christ, to the hardened sinner whose heart is soft-

28. On participation in the life of God, see 2 Pt 1:4.
29. Jn 15:15.
30. Aquinas, *ST* I-II, q. 111, aa. 1–2, esp. a. 2, ad 4.
31. Jn 6:44, 16:8–11; Phil. 2:13; Acts 16:14; 1 Cor 4:7; Eph. 2:8.

ened progressively, to the critical skeptic who begins little by little to take the question of the truth of Christianity seriously. Such changes are an effect of the preemptive activity of God, who mercifully comes toward us to draw us toward himself. Prevenient grace is like the dawn of a new sunlight that gently begins to illumine and warm our soul, or like a new rain that begins to loosen and nourish the rocky soil of our hearts.

Justification

The grace of inward righteousness or "justification" is that which makes us adoptive children of God in Christ. It is the grace that stabilizes us, so to speak, in turning us toward God in an integral and authentic way. If prevenient grace is like the dawning of light, justification is like the kindling of a living flame, a fire of faith and love that burns steadily in the human heart. The Catholic Church teaches that justification occurs in a human person by grace alone and not by any natural moral agency or works of self-righteousness.[32] This is not a subject of contention between Catholics and Protestants, at least so long as the true teaching of the Catholic Church is accurately understood! However, there is a point of difference on the question of what this righteousness of grace consists in. The Church confirms in her dogmatic teaching what the New Testament truly reveals. Justification occurs by the grace of faith, acting in our hearts through hope and charity.[33] "For in Christ Jesus neither circumcision nor uncircumcision is of any avail, but faith working through love."[34] God justifies us by infusing into our minds a habitual capacity to believe in Christ and the apostolic testimony. By this grace we are given intimate knowledge of who God is. But integral to this process is also a conversion of heart: that we should love God above all things by

32. *Catechism of the Catholic Church*, pars. 1987–2005.
33. Ibid., par. 1991: ""With justification, faith, hope, and charity are poured into our hearts, and obedience to the divine will is granted us."
34. Gal 5:6.

grace, renounce all attachment to serious sin, and hope in God effectively as our true good and ultimate end.

This Catholic view of justification suggests then that the conversion to belief in Christ by the grace of faith is fundamental to justification, but is not the whole picture. We cannot be "simul justus et peccator" in the words of Luther: simultaneously just and sinners. Yes, human frailties and tendencies toward sin remain in the faithful until death and must be struggled against. But if a Christian commits a serious sin (fornication, neglect of the weekly and daily worship of God, grave damage done to the reputation of another) then the person loses the grace of justification in charity. He may possess the grace of faith, but it is now in a weakened state, a state of wounded or lifeless faith. "He who does not love abides in death"; "So faith by itself, if it has no works, is dead."[35] This does not mean that we can merit salvation by our own powers. It means that works of charity (themselves a grace) are the living form of faith, and without them our faith becomes inert, and in that sense dead. In these circumstances, faith needs to be reawakened by the grace of charity, and reoriented back toward God.

This vision may seem unrealistic. After all, don't most baptized Christians commit serious sins at some point in their lives, or even regularly or habitually? Yes, they do. This is why the Church also rightly insists on the importance of regular sacramental confession and absolution: the grace of the sacrament of reconciliation acts, among other things, to restore the penitent to a state of grace, by infused charity poured anew into the heart. The life of charity is a precious gift given in baptism that should be protected, but if it is lost, the life of grace can be restored by the sacramental forgiveness of sins. Of course God can do this by his own initiative *outside* the sacrament of confession, but he has promised to do so always and everywhere in the sacrament,

---

35. 1 Jn 3:14, Jas 2:17.

and so recourse to the sacrament gives the repentant soul freedom from incertitude and a way of assurance so as to regularly encounter and be touched by the mercy and grace of God. This vision of justification affords great hope. Little by little Christians who regularly go to confession and communion can live lives free from grave sin, and can begin a process of deeper conversion: toward sanctification in Christ. This also allows us to see why the Church is not only a Church of saints but also a Church for sinners: for the weak, the broken, or the lost God offers unconditional forgiveness and the grace of charity, over and over again, "seventy times seven [times]."[36] The sacrament of penance is a key place we learn our own continual need for God's grace, but also where we experience the fidelity of God's mercy and love, and the power of the Cross of Christ to heal us of our infirmities and make us progressively stronger in the way of holiness.

It is important to see the soundness of this claim. It is true that the efficacy of the sacrament of confession is almost mechanical: if the penitent is properly disposed, he will receive grace. Here objectivity triumphs against the prevailing subjectivity of so much modern "spirituality." A ritual that ultimately derives from Christ and that truly communicates grace is a consolation in the face of the unreliability of our subjectivity. Modern culture typically focuses on authenticity and sets it up over against normative rituals. Often such an emphasis constitutes a form of terrible self-righteousness, and ultimately a kind of lie, that covers over our human weakness and need for the mercy of God. The Church's teaching on justification is wonderfully balanced because it insists that the human person can be changed and transformed, but that this transformation can come about only by the work of the Holy Spirit in us, not by human self-designation.

36. Mt 18:22.

Sanctification

Catholicism especially insists on the real possibility of progressive sanctification and growth in the spiritual life. The great Catholic saints are an especially powerful testimony to the reality of the grace of Christ at work in the world, bearing fruit in the lives of people who are extraordinary friends of Christ. When St. Francis of Assisi left everything to follow Christ in radical poverty, when Therese of Lisieux lived in joy through an intense trial of the dark night of the soul, even to the point of death, and when St. Vincent de Paul created a nationwide mission to catechize and feed the poor of his country, these people acted by the grace of Christ. They became saints. Sanctity is not something locked behind a glass case and accessible only to a few. It is true that the greatest mystics, miracle workers, and founders of religious orders are far from commonplace. But each baptized Christian, indeed each human person, is called by Christ to a life of holiness and sanctification, each in his or her own way, more discreet and hidden or more radiant and manifest. In the lives of most people this takes the form of a daily struggle, sometimes with a mixture of progress and regress. The search for sanctification in Christ, however, is what is most profound and interesting in human existence, and without this "project" at the center of our human lives they lose their deepest zest and glow, or as Christ himself says, their "salt" and "light."[37]

When Thomas Aquinas talks about the grace of sanctification he characterizes it especially in terms of what he calls "infused habits" of faith, hope, and love. "Habit" here refers to a stable disposition or capacity, in the sense of the Latin *habitus*. A person who has the natural habitus of riding a bike can do so without falling off. A great jazz musician has the stable capacity to play in an ensemble with others, changing keys fluidly and cleanly in the

37. Mt 5:13–14.

midst of complex improvisations. An *infused* habitus, however, is not natural, but something supernatural that is a gift of God. The infused habit of faith gives us the stable disposition and capacity to believe in Christ, to find his personal presence, and to assent to all of the Christian mystery as taught by the Church of Christ. The infused habit of hope orients us toward God as our true homeland and gives us the stable disposition to desire one day to see God face to face in the beatific vision, making use of all that we live and undergo in this life in view of union with God in the world to come. The infused virtue of charity allows us to participate in divine love, loving God as God loves himself and loving others by grace in the light of the love God has for them.

The infused virtues are not something static. They initiate us into a vital participation in the life of God. What is alive grows over time, and often becomes stronger only in the face of adversity. It is common for God to stimulate the development of faith, hope, and charity in us not only by acting within our souls, but also by obliging us to confront challenging external circumstances of trial or hostility. In the midst of these he invites us to grow in faith, hope, and love.

Over time, the effects of sanctifying grace in our lives can stabilize us in a Christian life of self-gift, of self-offering to God and the service of others, in increasingly intensifying charity. It is here, and only here, that Catholic theology speaks of "merits" that are the effects of grace. The notion of "merit" has biblical roots, since the New Testament tells us that we are justified and sanctified by grace alone but also that we will retain a "reward" or punishment on the basis of our actions.[38] The only way to make sense of this dual teaching is to hold that grace works in us so that we may walk in the path of righteousness and sanctification that God wills for each of us. The "merit" in question comes about through the intensification of the infused virtues operative with-

---

38. Mt 6:6, 6:18; Lk 6:35; Rom 2:7–8.

in us, especially the virtue of charity. "If anyone says, 'I love God,' and hates his brother, he is a liar."[39] "By this all men will know that you are my disciples, if you have love for one another."[40] Works of charity are the source of genuine Christian reward and are themselves the ultimate effect of the grace of Christ present in our earthly lives. God gives us grace to accomplish the very works that he wants in turn to crown with his reward.

"No Salvation Outside the Church"?

If salvation comes about by grace alone, then what are we to make of the ancient adage, *extra Ecclesiam nulla salus* (outside of the Church no one is saved)? Does this saying imply that God offers the possibility of salvation only to some, perhaps a minority of the human race, and that it is these alone who are members of the visible Church? Are only those saved? Just how vast or how small should we consider the "Catholic Church" to be?

The phrase itself, "no salvation outside the Church," has its origins in the third-century A.D., in the writings of Origen in the East and St. Cyprian in the West.[41] Here the phrase has a particular context: the Church was under intense persecution from the Roman government, and Christian writers were making it clear to *Christians themselves* that they must not forsake the Catholic faith. In leaving the Church, they are forfeiting salvation. Beginning from this principle, then, subsequent generations of thinkers in the Western Church began to expand on the teaching in light of St. Augustine's doctrine of predestination. Only those who enter into full communion with the Catholic Church and who die in a state of grace can be said to be saved. They are the elect and predestined. Even in this theology, however, there were important

39. 1 Jn 4:20.
40. Jn 13:35.
41. Origen, *Homilies on Joshua* III, 5; Cyprian, *Letters* 4, 4 and 73, 24; *The Unity of the Catholic Church*, c. 6.

qualifications. First, the Western Church at the Second Council of Orange in 529 A.D. and at the Synod of Valencia in 855 A.D. underscored that God never sentences anyone to eternal damnation who has not first culpably rejected the aid or the grace of God. Second, even the Augustinians who affirmed predestination of the members of the visible Church alone had a rather expanded vision of the "visible Church." They, like Augustine himself, considered that all human beings prior to the time of the coming of Christ were offered the grace of inchoate participation in the redemption of Christ. Consequently, those gentiles and Jews who came before Christ and cooperated with God's grace active in their lives (often in unseen ways) were in fact directed discreetly toward full inclusion in the one, visible Catholic Church, and thus could be saved.[42]

Nor was this a rare view in the Middle Ages. Thomas Aquinas signals in several texts that he thinks that God offers not only to the baptized but to each person in history the grace sufficient that they might attain to eventual salvation.[43] He is also sober about the real possibility of the refusal of grace, and emphasizes the culpability of the damned for their own eventual reprobation. God does not abandon human beings unless they first abandon him, and even when God permits a creature to sin, and then withdraws his grace (in just respect for a human creature's freedom to sin), he does still maintain that creature in being out of respect for its spiritual dignity.

Ultimately it was in confrontation with the restrictive atonement theory of Jansenism in the seventeenth century that the Catholic Church began to develop a more complete theory of

---

42. See Augustine, *On the Catechising of the Uninstructed* III, 6; XIX, 31; and the study of this theme in the medieval Augustinian tradition by Yves Congar, "Ecclesia ab Abel," in *Abhandlungen über Theologie und Kirche: Festschrift für Karl Adam*, ed. Marcel Reding (Düsseldorf: Patmos-Verlag, 1952), 79–108.

43. See, for example, *In I Tim.* II, lec. 1; *In Heb.* XII, lec. 3; *Summa Contra Gentiles* III, c. 159; *ST* III, q. 48, a. 2; q. 46, a. 6, ad 4.

these matters. The Jansenists claimed that Christ did not die for all human beings, but only for the predestined, uniquely living members of the visible Catholic Church. Against this position, Pope Innocent X affirmed that Christ died for all human beings, a teaching that clearly implies that grace is offered in some mysterious way to all, throughout history. As noted above, this does not mean that all human beings are or will be saved, but it does imply that if they are not saved it is due to a culpable rejection of the grace of God on their part.

In the nineteenth century Pope Pius IX gave the famous phrase a qualification: there is no salvation outside the visible church, presuming that a person has knowingly and culpably refused to enter into (or remain in) communion with the grace of Christ, in the Catholic Church. Pope Pius IX was thinking of cases of "invincible ignorance" in which a person acts without fault, not due to willful or culpable ignorance, but due to a morally blameless absence of understanding.[44] Now we see a more complex portrait begin to emerge: God offers grace to all human beings. All salvation is in the Catholic Church or in some way directed toward it. Those who culpably fail to acknowledge this in their lives cannot be saved, since they do effectively reject the grace of Christ, and life in the Catholic Church. Those who are invincibly ignorant may, through a mistaken sincerity of conscience, still approach God imperfectly but really under the effects of grace working in their lives. Even in the latter case, however, the process of salvation is only ever completed by the person being incorporated into the one mystical body of Christ, the visible and invisible communion that is the Catholic Church. It was this more nuanced version of the notion "no salvation outside the Church" that was presented by the Second Vatican Council in the document *Lumen Gentium*.[45] Reformulating the teaching positively, the Council

---

44. See, for example, Pope Pius IX, *Quanto Conficiamur Moerore*, Encyclical Letter, 1863, par. 7.

45. See *Lumen Gentium*, nos. 14–16.

taught that all salvation whatsoever that occurs takes place in the grace of Christ and either incorporates a person directly into the Catholic Church or places the person in some kind of directed relationality to the Church. This does not eradicate the real possibility of eternal damnation. On the contrary, "if someone should refuse to enter the Church as through a door ... [he] could not be saved."[46] Invincible ignorance may excuse many who cooperate with God's grace sincerely in their conscience and action, but all human beings have an obligation to seek the truth in all things, including especially the truth about God, whose existence can be known imperfectly even from natural reason. Religious indifference and intellectual sloth, then, are never good precedents for claiming innocence in the face of the calling of Christ.

The visible Catholic Church is the one true Church of Christ, that in which the mystery of his grace most perfectly subsists in this world. At the same time, there are elements of the true Church present in other churches and ecclesial communities, and God can and does work through them in significant ways. This is the case most especially with regard to the Orthodox sister churches, which have maintained the presence of the apostolic hierarchy (valid episcopacy and presbyterate), the Eucharist and all other sacraments, who honor the Virgin Mary as the Mother of God, and who have maintained practices of monastic life and the ancient liturgy of the Church. It is true in another way of those ecclesial communities that have issued from the Reformation which perform the sacrament of baptism and that maintain a profound devotion to and study of sacred scripture as the Word of God. To the extent that the grace of God is deeply active within these Christian communities, their members are drawn more closely toward the Catholic Church and her teachings, and their pattern of life begins to resemble more deeply or converge with the lives of Catholic Christians who live in a state of grace and

---

46. *Lumen Gentium*, no. 14.

perpetual friendship with God. It is true that some non-Catholic Christians live lives that are more morally exemplary than those of many Catholics, but it is also true that these same non-Catholic Christians would live even more complete and holy lives if they were to enter into full communion with the Catholic Church and receive the abundance of grace that this communion alone is able to provide.

The Catholic Church also teaches that grace can be at work in the world outside of the visible Christian community. Biblical evidence of this principle is found in Hebrews 11, where we are told that "without faith it is impossible to please [God]," but also that there have been "pagan saints" such as Abel, Noah, Job, and Rahab who were pleasing to God due to their faith.[47] The text also states that pre-Christian pagans could attain salvation when they acknowledged the existence of God and believed that he would reward those who sought to do his will. Based on this passage, medieval theologians rightly distinguished between "explicit faith" and "implicit faith": both terms designate the unique supernatural grace of saving faith, but in different modes.[48] For example, the Catholic faith that is received from the apostolic Church represents the "explicit faith" that saves, but this explicit faith itself undergoes a progressive development of doctrinal expression, and so things that Catholics come to believe explicitly over time are considered logically implicit in the earlier teaching of the Church. More to the point, however, is the example of the faith of the ancient Israelites, who believed in the Mosaic covenant. They believed explicitly in the revelation given to the Old Testament prophets, but implicitly they also believed in Christ insofar as they believed in the early revelation of the God of Israel, who promised in time to come to deliver the entire human race, through what in fact was the Incarnation and passion of the Lord.

47. Heb 11:6.
48. See, for example, Aquinas's analysis in *In Heb.* XI, lec. 2.

Similarly, then, in our own age, the time since the coming of Christ into the world, the grace of God may be at work in the natural moral and religious dispositions of human beings, leading them invisibly and in a hidden way toward the encounter with Christ and the Church. This orientation toward salvation comes from the grace of Christ, who is the unique savior, and must take root in some way in the personal actions of non-Christians, in their understanding and free decisions. However, it may be at work as a form of "implicit faith" in the true and living God, present in people with only an imperfect knowledge of the truth. This might be the case, for example, when non-Christian monotheists confide themselves to God truly in poverty of heart, or seek to live by authentic truths of the natural law. Such acts are natural in kind, so their outward appearance need not imply the presence of grace at all. However, the grace of God might work in and through such natural pursuits, in which human beings seek to find God, the absolute, and to order their lives morally in the light of what is most ultimate.

The Church also teaches that non-religious persons need not be excluded from salvation. As Pope John Paul II noted in his 1993 encyclical "Veritatis Splendor," the light of the Holy Spirit shines in the conscience of every human being, especially when confronting daily decisions of good and evil actions.[49] Such an observation should give us reasons for sobriety: human beings typically make any number of poor moral decisions, and the secularization of the human person often leads to a very problematic moral calculus. Consequently, atheism, agnosticism, and religious indifference are not usually dispositive aids to moral development or helpful dispositions in any way to the life of grace. However, the desire for truth and the inclination to do the good and avoid evil cannot be eradicated from the human mind and heart. It is entirely possible then for the grace of Christ to work secretly within

49. John Paul II, *Veritatis Splendor*, pars. 2–3.

the heart of the non-believer.[50] Such work is evident, at least in cases where non-religious people become progressively open to Christianity, explicitly aware of Christ, and convert to the Gospel. The Holy Spirit is at work in all humanity.

This "catholic" or universal vision of grace, then, is all-encompassing in one sense, but there is also a concentration in the center. The "ordinary means" of salvation by incorporation into Christ are found in the Catholic Church: the apostolic deposit of faith, the seven sacraments, and the communion of the visible mystical body of the Lord, maintained through the Petrine office. Many of these "ordinary means" exist outside the Catholic Church (that is to say, among other Christians) and these can produce effects of grace that incline persons toward full communion with the Catholic Church. "Extra-ordinary means" of salvation also exist: grace working through elements of natural truth found in non-Christian religions or present in the moral consciences of all human beings. The ordinary means of salvation are those that are more secure. It is objectively much safer and easier to be saved within the Catholic Church. Those furthest from belief in God, Christ and the Church are those most deprived, objectively speaking, and therefore in some real sense those most threatened by eternal damnation. Faith in the universal presence and activity of the Holy Spirit and the grace of Christ is not a reason to desist from evangelization, but is the greatest reason to engage in it, believing in the real possibility of conversion for all human beings. "Preach the Gospel to the whole creation."[51]

---

50. "Nor does Divine Providence deny the helps necessary for salvation to those who, without blame on their part, have not yet arrived at an explicit knowledge of God and with His grace strive to live a good life. Whatever good or truth is found amongst them is looked upon by the Church as a preparation for the Gospel." *Lumen Gentium*, no. 16.

51. Mk 16:15.

States of Life:
The Vocations of Priests,
Laity, and Religious

If we think of the Church as a musical composition, we could say that God writes his symphony across a diverse spectrum of persons and states of life. The Christian life is polyphonic, not monotone. The more that human beings are sanctified by the grace of Christ, the more unique they become. The saints are each examples of remarkable moral beauty and personal uniqueness, which anticipates the uniqueness of each human being in heaven. The radiant individuality of each person sanctified by the grace of God is also always relational: it is oriented deeply toward the love of God and the good of others. What is said here of individual persons is also true of the three major states of life: holy orders, the life of the Christian laity, and that of religious life. These states of life each present unique pathways toward holiness, distinct but harmonious, each deeply related to God and to one another.

The priesthood is above all a mystery of participation in the grace that Christ gives the Church to sustain her throughout her earthly pilgrimage. This occurs principally by means of the celebration of the sacraments, the pastoral governance of the Church, and the preaching and teaching of the Gospel. In these various activities, the priest seeks to act "in Christ" to various degrees. The priest is an agent of Christ more certainly in the administration of sacraments, where the mere celebration of the rites of the Church is sure to communicate grace to those who are of good will. Paradoxically, then, the human action of the priest in the celebration of the sacraments is very modest, almost mechanical, and yet the effect is more exalted. The priest can be an instrument of Christ also, however, in teaching and in governing or giving pastoral counsel. Here however the personal sanctity, theological

learning, natural gifts, and human preparation of the priest all
enter in as key factors. A priest who has lived a life of prayer and
spiritual discipline, who is humanly empathetic, who has studied
and gained knowledge from experience, is more likely to be a con-
duit of the grace of God to others. That being said, God in his
mercy often acts in extraordinary ways even through the modest
limitations of priests, for the good of the larger Church.

One way of thinking about this mystery is to say that the
priest is an "instrumental efficient cause" of grace. He is an "instrument" (like the violin in the hands of a musician or a brush
in the hands of a painter) because Christ himself is the primary
cause of grace, and the Lord gives grace through his priests as instrumental ministers. He is an "efficient cause" because his office
consists in transmitting graces to others. The role of the priest is
one of mediation of the truth and grace of Christ. We should note
how particular this vocation is. The way the priest serves God
and seeks personal holiness is as being at the service of the larger
ecclesial body, through sacramental ministry, the teaching office
of the priesthood, and pastoral care of others. Once we understand this, it is easy to see why the priesthood is a privileged life
of conformity to Christ, but is not a normative ideal that everyone is called to. The priest exists in a sense so that the laity and
the religious of the Church may have regular access to the sacraments and might receive regular evangelical instruction as well
as sage counsel. We might say then that priests are sanctified by
their service of the Church, but we should also add that the priest
who lives only for this work may become imbalanced if he does
not have a deeper life of personal prayer, rest, study, and healthy
friendships. When these other features of existence are in place,
they give the priest spiritual stability and peace as he exercises his
ministry on behalf of the Church.

The lay state of life may seem initially to be one primarily of
reception, if we contrast the lay person to the priest with regard

to preaching and the sacraments. However, this vision of things is too reductive and "clerical" in its fixations. The laity certainly do receive the sacraments and the teaching of the Church through the mediation of the episcopacy and the ministerial priesthood. However, it is they who primarily are active in bringing the Gospel into the world in a great variety of ways. We might characterize this vocation in terms that are sacramental by mentioning the grace of matrimony and the grace of confirmation. Married lay persons are those who principally receive the grace of matrimony, one that allows them to build up the "domestic church" which is the human family. In Christian marriage Christ sanctifies the human friendship of a man and woman, dwelling in them by grace, and strengthening them spiritually in both their marital joys and trials. He offers them the grace not only to educate their children in the faith, but also to bear witness to him in the wider world through their personal examples of faith, their fidelity to one another, and their outward welcome of others into their home.

Confirmation is above all the sacrament of the lay person who brings the Gospel out into the world of human culture, work, and political life. The lay person receives the grace to be at home with Christ even in the midst of the world, to bring Christ (discreetly or overtly) into the domains of business, law, education, manual labor, artistic creation, media, or the service industries. That is to say, the lay person has the challenging and irreplaceable task of forging his or her character for Christ in the heart of human society, and so also of seeking to forge human society anew according to the heart of Christ. Christians who seek in their daily lives to be just and merciful, truthful and discerning, generous and patient—and who seek above all to bear open witness to their faith—all bring the mystery of Christ into the world around them in various ways.

The religious life is distinguished by the vows of poverty, chastity, and obedience, by which religious men and women place their entire lives at the service of the contemplation of God and the evangelization of culture. This form of life has its basis in Jesus' own example as one who was poor, obedient, and chaste. We find early followers such as St. Paul imitating Christ in his celibacy, and noting that the Lord's example is not an aberration, but one that many in the Church are called upon to embrace.[52]

Because it forsakes any number of natural goods and turns radically toward God, the religious life is traditionally considered preparation for the life of the world to come. The radicalism of the vows is meant to free human beings for a more intensive form of devotion to Christ. Because they do not have children, religious are not obliged to take on ordinary forms of work and can instead live in communities dedicated to particular "charisms" or evangelical forms of life. These forms of life seek to serve God in this life and to prepare for perfect union with God in the life to come.

Contemplative monks and nuns, then, live a life of contemplation, liturgical prayer, study, and manual work, all aimed at a profound union with God, daily repentance for sins, and personal sanctification, as well as continual intercessory prayer on behalf of those in the world. Active religious may perform spiritual works of mercy, such as when they teach, catechize, and give solace to the suffering, or they may perform corporal works of mercy, in providing material aid to the poor and indigent, or medical care to the ill or the dying. The core of the religious life in all its forms, however, is union with God, and the practice of fraternal charity. By living in community, Catholic religious help one another to pray more regularly and fervently. They cooperate in profoundly meaningful lives of beautiful liturgical worship of God, evangelization, service of others, and common study. They are also challenged to develop the social virtues of mutual affability, forgiveness, obedience to superiors, and humility. In all

52. 1 Cor 7:7–8, 7:32–35, 11:1; see also Mt 19:12.

this, they seek to conform their lives more deeply to the grace of Christ and to his example, living realistically in the face of death and personal judgment by God, preparing with hope for the life of the world to come.

When lived authentically as pathways to salvation and sanctification, the lives of priests, laity, and religious are of great mutual aid to one another. The priest is an agent of grace at work in the life of the Church, whose ministry serves as a constant support to laity and religious. The laity bring the Gospel into the world, and by their witness to Christ in all aspects of society they manifest in a unique way the power of the grace of Jesus at work in our midst. The religious orders, meanwhile, are meant to recall to their fellow human beings the final purpose of human existence, the possibility of personal sanctification, and the mystery of charity lived out in its most intense form. Of course all human beings have terrible limitations in the face of the exigencies of the Gospel. Our evangelical ideals coexist with patent mediocrity. But this should not lead us to despair. Quite the opposite: the Christian states of life are lifelong projects of intense struggle, and gradual progress in sanctification. They bear testimony to the fact that daily human existence can have a real meaning precisely through the effort to conform one's life to the mystery of Christ. In this way, any Catholic vocation well lived (even in the midst of our moral and psychological fragilities) is a testimony to the deeper sense of human existence, and a valuable witness to one's fellow human beings.

The Virgin Mary

Devotion to the Virgin Mary is as old as the Church herself. The early Church uniformly recognized the Virgin Mary as the most perfect example of human holiness and redemption in the grace of Jesus Christ. As John Henry Newman pointed out, she is referred to in the second and early third century as the new Eve by St. Justin Martyr in Rome, St. Irenaeus in Gaul, and Tertullian in northern Africa. They are witnesses across a wide geographical spectrum to the uniform faith of the early post-apostolic Church.[53] By this term they mean to designate the Virgin Mary as the one who was distinctively sanctified by the grace of Christ. She is not God, but a poor creature. But where Eve fell, Mary was obedient to God in a particularly perfect way by the grace of God. Where Eve was a point of departure for the human race in the order of nature, the Virgin Mary was a new point of departure for the redemption of human beings, in the order of grace. In all of this, she is utterly dependent (as are we) upon the grace of the new Adam, Christ, who is the God-man.

Irenaeus is one of the clearest witnesses to this early belief of the Church in the sinlessness of the Virgin Mary:

Mary the Virgin is found obedient, saying, "Behold the handmaid of the Lord; be it unto me according to your word." (Luke 1:38) But Eve was disobedient; for she did not obey when as yet she was a virgin .... so also did Mary ... by yielding obedience become the cause of salvation, both to herself and the whole human race.... For the Lord, having been born the First-begotten of the dead (Rev. 1:5) and receiving into His bosom the ancient fathers, has regenerated them into the life of God, He having been made Himself the beginning of those that live, as Adam became the beginning of those who die. (1 Cor. 15:20–22) Wherefore also Luke, commencing the genealogy with the Lord, carried it back to Adam, indicating that it was He who regenerated them into the Gospel of life, and not they Him. And thus also it was that the knot of Eve's disobedience was loosed by the obedience of Mary. For what the virgin Eve had bound fast through unbelief, this did the virgin Mary set free through faith.[54]

---

53. See John Henry Newman, "Letter Addressed to the Rev. E. B. Pusey, D.D., on Occasion of His Eirenicon," in *Certain Difficulties Felt by Anglicans in Catholic Teaching*, vol. 2 (London: Longmans, Green and Co., 1900).

54. Irenaeus, *Against Heresies* III, 22, 4.

It is a pitiful error, then, to understand the traditional Catholic and Orthodox teaching regarding the Virgin Mary as one that makes of her a rival to Christ or an independent channel of grace or merit. In fact, in the official dogmatic teaching of the Catholic Church, the exact opposite is the case. The Virgin Mary is she who received the grace of the Word incarnate in a particularly perfect and intensive way so as to manifest most radiantly what redemption in Christ consists in. Therefore, the Virgin Mary is not only part of the mystery of the Church but is in a sense the most manifest realization of the Church. She shows us what humanity can become when redeemed most perfectly by the grace of Jesus. It is for this reason that the *Catechism of the Catholic Church* calls her an "eschatological icon of the Church": alive now in heaven with Christ, she is an anticipation of the final state of the Church.[55]

What are the theological reasons we should pay attention to the mother of Christ? Why is Mariology important to the Gospel? Most essential is the notion of Mary as the Mother of God. The ancient Greek term here is *theotokos*: literally, the God-bearer. This title is first and foremost about Christ. It denotes that Mary gave birth to a man who is God, the second person of the Holy Trinity, the eternal Son who truly lived a human life among us. However, the title also has implications regarding Mary's unique holiness. Based on New Testament teaching, the Church has always held that Mary was the *worthy* Mother of God, meaning that she was rightly disposed by grace to accept the Incarnation of the Son as her own mystery and to live deeply in accord with Christ as his most perfect disciple. This holiness of life was primordial in Mary, a gift of grace disposing her from the beginning of her existence to live out her vocation as the Mother of God. It allowed her to remain faithful to Christ to the end, interceding for sinners in the crucifixion, and being conformed to Christ even in his

55. See *Catechism of the Catholic Church*, par. 972, and *Lumen Gentium*, no. 68.

death and resurrection, by her bodily Assumption into heaven. In all of this, Mary depicts to the world what it means to be most perfectly redeemed by Christ. Her life is a microcosm of the life of the Church and an example to all Christians.

When thinking about the biblical foundations of Mariology, it is important to recall the Catholic principle that scripture is a book inspired within the context of the early apostolic community and rightly interpreted within the early tradition of that same apostolic Church. The scriptures bear witness, for example, to the Catholic teaching that the Eucharist is the real presence of the body and blood of Christ (Jn 6:53–55; 1 Cor 11:29), but this scriptural teaching is clearest when one finds very express witnesses to it in the teachings of Church Fathers such as Ignatius of Antioch, Irenaeus, Ambrose, and Augustine, who appeal in turn to scripture as the basis for their traditional teaching. We gain even better understanding, however, by a living participation in the liturgy of that same apostolic Church where there is the true confection of the Eucharist (by a validly ordained minister), and not merely a ceremony conducted by baptized lay persons that employs bread and wine symbolically. In the real presence of the body and blood of Jesus Christ, we can perceive in faith more readily the true teaching (found in Jn 6 and 1 Cor 11) regarding the Eucharist.

Likewise, the scriptures that refer to the Virgin Mary are intelligible for us when we read them within the larger community of the early apostolic Church that is devoted to the mystery of the Mother of God as a deep and non-negotiable aspect of the mystery of Christ. If we look back carefully at the Gospels from the vantage point of early Church tradition we can see evidence of high Mariology in the Gospels (in Luke and John particularly) as well as in the book of Revelation. Meanwhile, participation in the living devotion to the Virgin Mary in the Catholic Church (which is not worship, but veneration), by asking the Virgin Mary to intercede and pray for us, may make us aware of her personal presence as the Mother of God, who accompanies the Church in her earthly pilgrimage.

We might begin, then, by considering the annunciation scene found in Luke's Gospel, in which the Virgin Mary receives a revelation of the Incarnation from the archangel Gabriel.[56] The scene is purposefully portrayed in juxtaposition with the annunciation of John the Baptist's birth made to Zechariah in the inner sanctuary of the Temple in Jerusalem.[57] Where Zechariah questions in skepticism about the capacity of his elderly wife to bear a son, the Virgin Mary is depicted as questioning respectfully, as one who obeys the message of the Lord in her heart with faith.[58] Augustine says that she conceived the Word in her mind before she conceived him in her womb, and he sees this as a sign of her holiness: God has prepared her by grace to be the worthy Mother of God.[59] So likewise as St. Jerome noted in the fourth-century Vulgate, when the Virgin Mary is hailed by the angel as "full of grace" (in Greek, *kecharitomene*), it is a perfect passive participle that is employed, one having a very strong sense: literally, "Hail, one who has been fully or most perfectly graced."[60] The angel acknowledges that she is holier than he is. Accordingly, when she receives word of the Incarnation, Mary answers, "how can this be, since I do not know man?"[61] As St. Augustine noted, Luke has just told us that Mary is engaged to be married. But since the origin of children is something she would know, Luke's text seems to suggest that the Virgin Mary had previously decided "not to know man," that is to say, to live in perpetual virginity. She was to become the Virginal Mother of God.[62]

56. Lk 1:26–38.
57. Lk 1:8–22.
58. Lk 1:22, 1:38.
59. Augustine, *Of Holy Virginity*, chap. 3.
60. In Jerome's Latin: "gratia plena."
61. Lk 1:34 (translation by the author).
62. Augustine, *Of Holy Virginity*, chap. 4.

From the second century onward there was a uniform consensus in the Catholic Church, both East and West, that the Virgin Mary was virgin "before, during, and after" the conception of the Son of God in her womb. The idea is central to the second-century apocryphal legend, *The Protoevangelium of James*, which may or may not contain testimony to any historical truth about the early life of Mary, but which is testimony to the living piety and common belief in the virginal consecration of Mary in the earliest tradition of Christianity. From the earliest times, she was considered a model of virginity in the service of the mystery of Christ. This idea is constantly repeated, and thematized, for example, in the fourth century by authors like St. Ephrem in the East, and Sts. Ambrose, Jerome, and Augustine in the West.

It is true that in the Gospels there is occasional mention of Jesus' "brothers and sisters" from which some commentators conclude that the Virgin Mary had other children than Jesus. However, it should be kept in mind that ancient Aramaic had no distinct word for cousins or close family members other than the word for brothers and sisters, and this wider usage was common in Jesus' own time. Furthermore, the second-century Christian historian Hegesippus reports that these brothers and sisters were in fact the cousins of Jesus, children of Cleophas the brother of Joseph, and his wife, Jesus' aunt by marriage.[63] As St. Jerome noted in the fourth century, this depiction is actually consistent with the texts of Matthew and John, who describe an "other Mary" present at the Cross, who is not the mother of Jesus, but who is the mother of the brothers and sisters of Jesus.[64] John's Gospel in turn depicts this person as the "wife of Clopas."[65]

Early Christians were typically united in believing that the Virgin Mary was so radiantly blessed by the grace of Christ that

63. See Eusebius, *Ecclesiastical History* III, 11, 2.
64. Mt 13:55, 27:61, 28:1.
65. Jn 19:25.

she avoided all actual sin in her life. This was what it meant to be "full of grace" and the "new Eve." Mary is depicted as this "new Eve" figure three times in scripture. This occurs twice in John's Gospel: at the wedding of Cana where her petition to Jesus inaugurates his ministry, and where he calls her "woman" (that is to say, Eve) and at the Cross near the end of the Gospel.[66] In the latter passage he says to her "woman, behold your son," speaking of the apostle at the foot of the Cross, but also referring through him to the whole Church. Mary is the new Eve who is moved by God's grace to petition the adult Christ to begin his earthly ministry among us. She is the perfect disciple at the foot of the Cross, who stands (and does not wilt) as the perfect disciple in faith, even when her Son is crucified. By her loving consent to his mission as our redeemer, she becomes with him and in him an intercessor for the whole Church. "Woman, behold, your son."[67]

St. Augustine believed in the personal sinlessness of the Virgin Mary, but also posited that all human beings fell in Adam into the mystery of original sin. Consequently, he believed that the Virgin Mary was born in original sin but received the fullness of grace from early on within her human life so as to avoid any actual or personal sin.[68] He did not see this as a sign of her independence from Christ but rather as a confirmation that the grace of Christ was particularly at work in her by anticipation so as to prepare her to cooperate most fully with the mission of the redeemer. Subsequent theologians reflected on this question in the Middle Ages. Bernard, Bonaventure, and Aquinas held to the position of Augustine that the Virgin Mary was born in original sin but sinless in her personal action, by the grace of God. Anselm and Duns Scotus, meanwhile, appealed to an alternative patristic tradition, which is represented especially in Ephrem and Ambrose: the Virgin Mary was conceived without sin by the grace of God, given to

66. Jn 2:4 and 19.
67. Jn 19:26.
68. Augustine, *On Nature and Grace*, 42 (36).

her in view of Christ's merits.[69] This perfect redemption in Christ signaled not only the radiant victory of Christ over sin in the life of the Virgin Mary, but also her perfect disposition in grace to become by her free consent in faith and love, the Mother of God.

Scripture refers to the Virgin Mary as the "Mother of God" overtly. The title is employed by Elizabeth in the infancy narratives of Luke: "Why is this granted me, that the mother of my Lord should come to me?"[70] The visitation of the Virgin Mary to Elizabeth is a supernatural mystery, because the mere presence of the Virgin Mary (who bears the God-man in her womb) makes another person aware (by the grace of faith) that Jesus is Emmanuel, God with us. So likewise, John the Baptist is depicted as miraculously agitated in the womb of Elizabeth to react to the presence of Jesus, foreshadowing his later earthly mission as the forerunner of the Lord.[71]

As we have noted above, the crucifixion scene in John 19 depicts the Virgin Mary standing next to the Cross of Jesus, faithful and unwavering even in the most extreme of personal trials. In her perfect discipleship she becomes not only the Mother of God but now also the Mother of the Church. This idea is also shown symbolically but unambiguously in Revelation, where the Mother of God is depicted as a woman "clothed with the sun."[72] The image clearly refers to Mary because it pertains to the mother of Jesus.[73] Here she is the new Eve, the woman who is attacked by the ancient serpent, as was Eve.[74] She is also a figure here of the Church, persecuted by the Roman Empire, and she is protecting her "offspring," members of the Church, who are also the children of the Virgin Mary.[75]

---

69. Ephrem the Syrian, *Nisibene Hymns*, 27:8; Ambrose, *Sermon* 22, 30.
70. Lk 1:43.
71. Lk 1:41.
72. Rv 12:1.
73. Rv 12:5.
74. Rv 12:8.
75. Rv 12:17.

In the wake of this attack, the Virgin Mary is carried away to a place of protection from which she can intercede for the Church.[76] The "sun" with which the Virgin Mary is enrobed is the divinity of God himself. Just as the Lord was conceived in her womb and dwelt humanly with her, so she is assimilated by the resurrected Christ, her Son, into the life of God and by her bodily Assumption dwells spiritually with Jesus in the life of the resurrection. The idea that the Virgin Mary was perfectly redeemed by Christ in the resurrection from the dead is not an innovative one. Never in early Christianity did Christians claim that the Virgin Mary's remains lay buried in some part of the world nor were there ever shrines to honor her relics (as was the case by contrast for many saints such as Peter and Paul). On the contrary, the early Christians clearly believed from the beginning that she was uniquely holy, and therefore the one most perfectly redeemed by Christ, even in the resurrection from the dead. By the seventh century, there is widespread evidence in both East and West of an annual liturgical celebration of the mystery of the "dormition," that is to say, of Mary's assumption body and soul into the glory of heaven with Christ.

The Virgin Mary is not God, nor is any Christian saint who is "divinized" by Christ in the beatitude of heaven. But she is perfectly united with God in heaven, an image for us of the perfect life of the Church in the world to come. She can offer her prayers for us, like those of any other Christian whom we might ask (rightly and humbly) to pray for us. However, she intercedes for us with Christ not only as the Mother of God, who is filled with the grace of Christ and the presence of the Holy Spirit, but also as our mother, who loves the Church and who has a special solicitude for all our spiritual and temporal needs. She has nothing in herself except what she receives from God and from Christ and she adds nothing to the mystery of his grace. Rather, she is

---

76. Rv 12:14.

an expression of the richness of his grace present in his mystical body the Church, of which she is the primary created member. She shows us in a most perfect way what Christ wishes to do in us by the work of charity, to make us persons who accept his mystery completely and who act and intercede meritoriously (moved by grace alone) so as to bring others to Christ. Consequently, it is entirely biblical and entirely Christ-centered to say in unison with the whole Church, "Hail Mary, full of grace, the Lord is with you. Blessed are you among women, and blessed is the fruit of your womb, Jesus. Holy Mary, Mother of God, pray for us sinners, now and at the hour of our death."

6

SOCIAL DOCTRINE

The Perennial Controversy

Catholic Christianity has always been controversial, although for different reasons in different ages. The first apostles were put to death by the government authorities of the Roman Empire because they questioned the prerogatives of the theocratic state and challenged the mores of their time. In the age of high Christendom, the civil state often exiled or put to death Christian leaders (from St. John Chrysostom to St. Thomas More) who stood in its way by recalling the Church's social doctrine. Venerable cultures such as those of India and China have sometimes resisted a free Catholic presence in their midst because the Church's teaching inevitably challenges aspects of the religious traditions and customs of these civilizations. Muslims have opposed Christianity most especially due to Koranic objections to the mysteries of the Holy Trinity and the Incarnation, which are thought to violate the truth of monotheism. Enlightenment secularists of the eighteenth and nineteenth centuries objected in principle to any belief in supernatural revelation and opposed the civic influence of the Church. Modern fascist and communist states of the twentieth and twenty-first centuries have objected to belief in the existence of God and sought at times to eradicate any real presence of Catholic Christianity from human culture. Current adherents of secular liberalism are ill at ease with many facets of Catholic teaching regarding human sexuality, and fear that Catholic claims to moral normativity inhibit the exercise of authentic human freedom.

How should we account for the wide range of historical and cultural forces that are opposed to Christianity, some of which are in contradiction with one another? After all, is Catholicism not primarily a religion focused on the mystery of Christ, something that transcends natural reason and human politics, but that incites people to greater compassion, care for the poor, and responsible participation in the political life of society? It is true that the mystery of Christ transcends the natural world of human politics and society, but the Lord also makes absolute claims upon his disciples, a fact that in turn can affect every aspect of their lives, including their participation in human political life. The ancient Roman emperors who killed the Christians were prescient: when Christian revelation is taken seriously, it does change everything. Because human culture functions concretely under the effects of original and personal sin, there are many forms of collective blindness operative at the heart of every human society, no matter how noble or venerable. Furthermore, non-Christian methods of social organization, be they religious, monarchical, democratic, or authoritarian, tend to accept or even promote any number of forms of behavior that are contrary to the truth of the Gospel. Some of these behaviors function as de facto symbols of the authority and legitimacy of the regime or ideology in question. We might think here of Roman sacrifice on behalf of the emperor, or the modern liberal defense of the right to abortion, the former Soviet-bloc insistence that atheism be taught as the unique truth in public schools, or the law of the French revolutionaries (still in effect in most of France) that no university might have a department of theology and that no priest might teach in a university. These are stances of public authority that are symbolic of a larger cultural identity, and which exist in de facto tension with Roman Catholic teaching and practice. If the Catholic faith becomes widely accepted by many, the authority of a given state and its general moral legitimacy can be threatened. Consequently, the preaching of the Gospel and the visible presence of the Catholic Church can represent a potential stumbling block to many in the wider world of human culture and political life.

This does not mean that everything that Christians promote in the public square derives immediately from revelation, and even less does it suggest that Catholics wish to impose the acceptance of supernatural faith upon others by the force of law (a point we will return to below). On the contrary, the Church historically distinguishes between truths of divine revelation (which implicate all baptized Catholics by virtue of their faith) and truths of natural reason (which implicate all human beings by virtue of their natural reason). The latter truths include many pertaining to human ethics and the social order generally, but can include religious truths as well. For example, the Church affirms that it is a truth of natural reason that God the creator exists, and that he should be acknowledged by religious behavior.[1] Non-Catholics may come to know and acknowledge these truths by their natural powers, at least in principle.

Teachings on Catholic social justice, then, are derived primarily from the latter set of teachings: moral truths that are accessible to natural reason, in principle, but that might be very difficult to arrive at or accept in practice due to the effects of original sin. The moral ignorance of human culture, superstition, the force of custom, prejudice against difficult ethical teachings, the addictions of materialism and morally superficial eroticism, and the fear of submission to a transcendent moral law: all of these can

1. See on this matter *Dei Filius* and Second Vatican Council, *Dignitatis Humanae*, December 7, 1965.

coarsen the human heart and blind the human mind. However, all of this only demonstrates why it is all the more necessary for the Catholic Church to proclaim teachings of the natural law, teachings that the Holy Spirit may inspire persons to accept rationally, by the hidden presence of his grace.

Justice and the City of Man

The Nature of Justice

Authentic human justice is not a merely human construct or social convention. Nor is it derived from the arbitrary will to power of some privileged group. Real justice is grounded, rather, in the nature of the human person, the order of the universe, and ultimately the transcendent mystery of God. Here we can think of justice in two ways: as a virtue that characterizes human decision-making, and as something pertaining to the deeper order of the world. The former sense of justice is a species or kind of the latter sense. That is to say, just human decisions are just because they fit within a deeper order of the world and because they are indicative of that order in its human moral dimension.

Considered in the first sense, as a virtue of human persons and societies, justice pertains to rational, free creatures. We do not say that animals or trees are just or unjust. We say that human choices are just or unjust (be they the choices of individuals or the collective choices of societies). A choice is just when it respects the true nature of reality: principally, when it acknowledges the dignity and goodness of human persons and their needs, but also when it respects the integrity of natural realities as well as man's relationship with God. For instance, the betrayal of a spouse or the taking of innocent human life can be called unjust. But human cruelty to an animal is also unjust (in part because it disfigures the human agents), as is the destruction of the ecosystem. So too the failure to acknowledge God through acts of worship, gratitude, and thanksgiving constitutes a grave and often unnamed injustice that is systemic in human secular societies.

The deeper grounding of justice, then, is located in the order of reality itself, which a human person is capable of recognizing, and someone who fails to recognize this order is rightly deemed morally wanting. For example, due to his or her intrinsic dignity, each person should be treated with basic respect, affability, and friendliness (at least in ordinary circumstances). It is just to be affable to colleagues or even strangers, and in some way unjust to fail to do so. Likewise, it is in accord with the order of things that human beings have a greater dignity than animals and plants, and so it would be gravely unjust, for example, to kill a human being to feed to a herd of nonrational animals, while it is not unjust to herd and eventually kill animals (in humane ways) so as to feed human beings. Indeed, it would be unjust to allow a human child to starve to death uniquely in order to save nonhuman animals. At the same time, there is an order to the natural ecological environment such that it is unjust for members of the human community to pollute and destroy the ecosystem where further generations of human beings as well as animals and plants are meant to live. Nor is it just for human beings to eradicate whole species of animals due to their inconvenience. Even less is it just for members of the human race to eradicate some types of persons who are inconvenient to us: Jews, Tutsis, atheists, Christians, Muslims, the unborn, the elderly, and so on.

Finally, it is only right that human beings acknowledge the larger order of reality in its dependency: we are all given existence by God and are in a sense ordered toward God by our very nature as rational creatures, capable of acknowledging God intellectually by prayer and devotion. Thus, according to traditional Catholic social teaching, religious acknowledgment of God (worship, piety, the pursuit of true knowledge of God, avoidance of superstition) is part of the larger structure of justice in human civilization. In seeking to maintain an authentic religious sense of the transcendent creator, human society sustains a deeper order of justice with respect to the author of our being, who is also the providential governor of the world.

Aquinas, following Aristotle, distinguishes three forms of justice, each of which, he thinks, finds an objective basis not only in common experience but also in biblical revelation.[2] *Commutative* justice is primarily about relationships of pure equality or unilateral exchange. If one person pays a certain amount of money, he should receive a proportionate amount of goods in exchange. If one of the partners in a wedding ceremony honestly promises lifelong fidelity, the other should do so as well.

Distributive justice is concerned with the participation of many in a larger collective whole. Each individual should receive what is due to him proportionately (and this is often rightly unequal), and each should give to the common good in turn (again often unequally). Consider, for example, the changing relationship of a child to its parents. The young child should be provided for by his two parents in justice. As a young adult, however, he should justly seek employment and economic sufficiency. Later, as a mature adult, he should contribute to the needs of his elderly parents when circumstances require it. A person who is mentally handicapped must receive greater assistance from the state. A person who is either extraordinarily wealthy or extraordinarily talented may have obligations to contribute to the common good in ways that others do not.

Social or legal justice, meanwhile, pertains to the participation of individuals in the larger whole and is concerned with goods that one cannot possess individually but only collectively. For example, one can only enjoy the great happiness of living in a stable and loving family by participating in that family collectively. One

2. Aquinas, *ST* II-II, q. 58, aa. 5–7; q. 61. See Aristotle, *Nicomachean Ethics* V, 1–6.

cannot realistically take a "part" of the family and run away with it. But this means that there is an order of justice regarding mutual participation and inclusion in a larger community of love and the pursuit of collective goods. A family member has a right to participate in her family life, as well as a set of obligations to contribute to the happiness and stability of the family. This is the case with members of religious orders who make solemn vows: they have the right to participate in the life of their religious community (in prayer, study, work, and evangelization) as well as obligations that accrue to them. Ultimately this final form of justice is what is closest to love and frequently it gives human beings a tangible sense of meaning: the ordering of their lives toward inclusion in common goods alongside others and with others. It is a form of justice that stems from friendship and that has its term or purpose in sustaining and providing for the deepest forms of friendship among human beings.

The Common Good

This deeper philosophical notion of human justice brings us to a core theme in Catholic natural law theory: the notion of the common good.[3] This too is an analogous or flexible term. "Common goods" are the kinds of social goods that derive from multiple individuals who are arranged in a given order. They frequently exist only due to human interdependence. So, for example, a human family is a kind of common good, one made possible due to the stable, social bonds of wedded fathers and mothers, with their children. The common good of a local society provides a larger support system of commerce, education, agriculture, health care, and technology overseen by the local political government. A larger common good might be a large political entity, like a state or a nation, but could also denote a social organization like the Church or a university.

3. See the *Catechism of the Catholic Church*, pars. 1905–17.

Referring again to the broader definition of justice as pertaining to the order of reality itself, we can also speak about the world of nature and the cosmos as a common good. The larger physical world is marked by an intelligible order and by a complex web of interdependencies. This natural world provides a habitat for human persons. The living things that populate the world, and the deeper matrix of inanimate objects that sustains life: all of this is a kind of common good that we depend upon vitally, and participate in. Human happiness, then, depends upon the common good that is the cosmos.

Ultimately we can speak of God as the supreme "common good" of the whole universe.[4] The whole world derives its existence and goodness from God alone, and in a sense exists for God. Simply by being and tending toward their various perfections, inanimate natural realities, plants, and animals all bear witness to the existence of God and give evidence of his goodness. They exist as created participations of God's own goodness, and in doing so indicate ontologically (by their very being) that God is the transcendent purpose for their existence. (God created all things ultimately for himself.) Human beings also have God as their supreme good in an especially immediate way, since they can come to know God intellectually and love God above all things. God is the transcendent common good of the whole human community. The designation "common" here is significant. Because of the transcendence of God, he is a good that all human beings can hold in common in a way that necessarily includes all other human beings and unites them, each in his or her own dignity, without exclusion or opposition. God is the author of each human being and so any kind of "religious justice" that would deny basic human dignity to some subgroup of human beings would be inevitably unjust and erroneous. Likewise, the common good that is God "includes" or requires integral respect for the whole creation.

4. Aquinas, *ST* I-II, q. 109, a. 3.

One cannot rightly denigrate the natural order of the cosmos or the human social order of persons in the name of God or reasonable religion. On the contrary, right reason should move us not only to acknowledge God as the supreme good, but to respect the integrity and necessity of all "lesser" common goods: the family, the local society, the state, various human social organizations, the Church, and the whole of the physical cosmos.

Understood in this light, "justice" is not something simple and we do not master a sense of it merely by way of our initial instincts. Understanding the deeper order of ethics and the basis of morality in the world is a difficult and noble task that requires intellectual discipline and concentrated study. The perennial tradition of moral theology in the Catholic Church seeks to maintain such study at the heart of human society so as to sustain and advance a deeper sense of justice and the common good across diverse civilizations and from age to age.

Protecting Innocent Human Life

The most basic form of human justice pertains to inclusion in the common good and the most basic form of inclusion pertains to human life and existence. You cannot participate in the common good if you are dead. No one can participate in human society if she or he is forbidden even to live. Consequently, a basic responsibility of every human community is to protect innocent human life and to prevent the injustice of grave harm done to others by murder or physical violence.

This fundamental teaching of the natural law applies to special cases in various ways. The moral norm regarding abortion is clear. Each human individual life begins at conception. The embryonic person has a genetic identity distinct from the parents. It is from the first moment of conception that a person develops organically into maturity as a fetal human being and a newborn human child. There is no "personhood threshold" that begins at some point after conception and before birth. The human being is one entity from the first to the last. Consequently, abortion at any stage of the life of the newly conceived person constitutes the unjust taking of a human life, and is gravely wrong. It constitutes a species of murder.[5]

We may underscore the larger social complexity of abortion by noting that it is sometimes committed under external pressure or in circumstances of desperation. More often it is an act of convenience, so as to avoid the very real responsibilities entailed in having a child. Abortion is usually motivated by a clear acknowledgement that there is a new human being in the womb that is distinct from the mother: that is precisely why the procedure is undertaken. This distinct, new human being is going to be burdensome and so one wishes to do away with its presence.

Here, then, we should note three moral principles. Firstly, it is never morally warranted to do something intrinsically gravely evil in order to obtain a good.[6] We cannot take human life or accept that it be taken in order to safeguard our lifestyle or to obtain other reasonable goods. In these circumstances trust in God's providence entails cooperating with the acceptance of new human life. Secondly, persons who have had abortions or cooperated in obtaining them have sinned gravely and are wounded by that sin. They are in need of encouragement to embrace the truth and mercy of God. We human beings are all sinners and stand in

5. Furthermore, if we are aware that there is a spiritual soul that is the form of the human body, then it is philosophically reasonable to assert that the soul is created as the form of the body from the time that a new human body is conceived. Where there is a living human body, there is a soul that is the principle of life in that body. This claim regarding the presence of the spiritual soul is an additional reason to defend the dignity of human life from conception until natural death, but not the unique condition. Clearly when we are dealing with a newly conceived human being, everyone can tell that we are dealing with someone who is distinct from the parents, and whose life is put to an end by abortion. See in this respect Pope John Paul II, *Evangelium Vitae*, Encyclical Letter, March 25, 1995, pars. 58–60.

6. See John Paul II, *Veritatis Splendor*, pars. 79–83, who presents this principle as a commentary on Rom 3:8.

need of the compassion and mercy of God. Thirdly, every human person has an obligation to work actively to the ending of a society in which abortion is practiced and accepted as a normative procedure. Those with more political responsibility are especially obliged to seek the cessation of the practice of abortion, its funding, and its legality. All educators and healthcare professionals bear analogous responsibilities.[7]

The teaching that all innocent human life is to be protected is sometimes contrasted with traditional Catholic teaching regarding capital punishment and just war, which do identify circumstances in which it is morally defensible to take human life. One can wonder if it is consistent to affirm the exceptionless protection of human life in one domain while permitting the taking of human life in other contexts. In fact, the profound coherence of the teaching is clear if one considers everything in light of a unifying principle: human life is sacred and there is a just obligation of the state to defend innocent human life. This is why abortion is always wrong. It is also why just warfare (when it is truly just, which may be rare) is conducted for the same reason, to defend innocent human beings. A just war saves a victimized population from extermination or terrible violence and unjust exploitation. The traditional grounds for designating a war as "just" require that several factors be taken into consideration. They not only require that the cause is just, but also that the action taken is likely to be effective, and can be done without inflicting undue harm on innocent civilians:

1. the damage inflicted by the aggressor on the nation or community of nations must be lasting, grave, and certain; 2. all other means of putting an end to it must have been shown to be impractical or ineffective; 3. there must be serious prospects of success; 4. the use of arms must not produce evils and disorders graver than the evil to be eliminated. The

7. See, on this topic, the Congregation for the Doctrine of the Faith, "Doctrinal Note on Some Questions Regarding the Participation of Catholics in Political Life," 2002; available at www.vatican.va.

power of modern means of destruction weighs very heavily in evaluating this [final] condition.[8]

Capital punishment is an analogous case. Here society seeks to protect the innocent by punishing grave crimes against human life. The perpetrator of serious crimes who directly undermines the common good (especially by the unjust taking of human life) effectively cedes his right to remain an active participant in the community. The state can act with mercy to incarcerate the person, with hopes of spiritual rehabilitation. But the state also has the alternative of confronting the person with the gravity of his transgression through the just act of capital punishment. For a very serious crime there is a proportionate, retributive justice effectuated when a person is deprived by the state of his physical life. Here some qualifications are in order. For capital punishment to be truly just, there must be very clear evidence of very grave action on the part of the person. The punishment may never be arbitrary. Only legitimate state authority has the power to rightly conduct such action because only that authority is ultimately responsible for the political common good. Vigilantism is thus excluded. The act of the death penalty is always aimed fundamentally at the person's repentance before God and acceptance of divine mercy in view of eternal life. It is never permissible to wish the death of a human being in view of his eternal damnation.

Some Catholic popes, bishops, and theologians have argued that the death penalty can be made increasingly rare or even practically eradicated in modern societies with developed structures of incarceration. There is legitimate debate on this subject. In part this is because the question of the means of rightful punishment (long-term incarceration versus capital punishment) is subject to prudential determination on a case-by-case basis. Nev-

---

8. *Catechism of the Catholic Church*, par. 2309.

ertheless, one has the right as a Catholic Christian to maintain the traditional viewpoint that the state can protect innocent human life by occasional recourse to the death penalty in the case of major crimes. What is at stake in such decisions are deep values of justice, love, and mercy, both for the innocent victims and the protection of society, but also for the guilty and for those who have seriously offended the larger society. Ironic as it may seem, the traditional viewpoint does contain a profound message of hope: God's grace can be at work in our lives both through works of retribution and of forgiveness, both in lives of prolonged repentance as well as in the acceptation of death as a passage to God's mercy.

The Church's teachings on human life are united by a common thread. They all seek unequivocally to protect innocent human life in society, and forbid categorically the purposeful taking of innocent human life, even to achieve a good outcome. It is morally abhorrent to target innocent civilians in wartime in order to defeat an unjust aggressor (such as in the indiscriminate bombing of an enemy city), just as it is gravely unjust to execute a morally innocent person in order to protect the common good (for example through false government accusation). Likewise, it is never ethical to take the life of an innocent unborn child in order to ameliorate the life of the mother. Those who work in the government, in the military, or in health care, have a natural obligation in justice to seek to achieve good ends only ever through morally licit means, ones that never entail the unjust taking of human life.

The Universal Destination of Goods

Of course the preservation of human life is only a very fundamental or basic human good, one that permits human life in society. That life, meanwhile, consists in a world of shared human goods: physical resources, friendship and family life, human education, work and the economy, complex social organizations, laws and human government, abiding social customs, shared philosophical convictions and religious traditions. To exist as a human being is to exist within a larger social network of rational human animals who depend upon one another, each for his or her own existence, and who develop and thrive only through various forms of dependence upon one another.

Here the Catholic Church speaks about the "universal destination of goods."[9] This is not the idea that all property must be owned by the state or by collective institutions. Traditional natural law teaching affirms that there is a right to private property and personal ownership that stands at the heart of any just society. This idea, then, is one of a universally inclusive "distributive justice" of private property and personal advancement. Each person has the right to participate and be included in the larger common good. In practice this means that each person has the right to basic needs of human existence: shelter, clothing, adequate nutrition, and clean drinking water, but also an adequate education, meaningful work, just wages, and participation in the larger economic life of society.

If we expand this line of thinking, there is also a right to found a family (by heterosexual marriage) so as to seek to have children and educate them religiously. (No state has the right to tell married persons how many children they may have.) Likewise, there are rights to political participation in the larger society and to protection provided by the political state. People should be able to express themselves politically and ethically without fear of retribution. This is true also of larger social organizations such as the Church, the universities, societies of artists, etc., that have a right to participate in the public square.

All of these just rights also imply responsibilities on the parts of the individuals, families, and social organizations in question. Persons living in society ordinarily have the responsibility to

9. See the *Catechism of the Catholic Church*, pars. 2401–49.

make good use of their possessions, to pursue adequate education when it is provided, to work diligently and honestly, to provide for their children with care and intelligence, and to contribute reasonably to the welfare and protection of the larger state and community (e.g., through taxation, voting, contributions to social services, and military service).

These are of course all general principles. Most reasonable people will accept them without contestation. However, the concrete practical applications give rise to significant debates. Is democracy really the best form of government? Is a capitalist market economy that advocates for personal responsibility and individual creativity preferable to centralized government systems of wealth redistribution? What balance should exist between personal responsibility and the assistance of the state? In order to stimulate growth of an inclusive economy that helps all, how high or low should taxation be on the wealthy? What should a just minimum wage consist in? Should normative education goals include that of university education for all? If so, how are the dignity and importance of manual labor professions to be maintained in the larger culture?

Intelligent people can disagree sharply on these questions because they are typically subject to complex forms of prudential estimation, in diverse circumstances of time and place, and must take account of available resources. Debates frequently arise about varied means to achieve the just ends of life in society. In the modern era, the magisterium of the Catholic Church has tended to advocate for the choice of democratic forms of government in direct preference to atheistic totalitarian regimes that frequently dehumanize citizens and subject them to grave political injustices. At the same time the Church has warned against the banalization of human culture within secular democracies due to the rise of materialism, moral relativism, vast economic inequalities, religious indifference, and coarse disrespect for human life. Market economies have proven to be those that provide the best wealth creation for the most people and have given rise to great advances in medicine, security, and educational opportunity. Personal initiative and entrepreneurial creativity have a core role to play in wealth creation and should be respected as key elements to a healthy society. At the same time, those who have the most influence in society have a grave obligation to make the economic and educational opportunities of human culture sufficiently expansive and inclusive, not unduly restrictive or reserved uniquely to an elite minority. The Church is a consistent advocate for the poor and of those who are displaced or vulnerable because she has the obligation to recall their ineradicable human dignity and Christ's own predilection for and mysterious identification with the poor. "Truly, I say to you, as you did it to one of the least of these ... you did it to me."[10]

The Sanctification of Sex

Why Sexuality Matters:
Against Manichaeism

One area of Catholic teaching that tends to be very controversial in our current epoch is that which concerns human sexuality. The Church is often portrayed as prudish and resistant to the social upheavals that have occurred as a result of the sexual revolution (the prevalence of divorce, contraception, promiscuity, social acceptance of homosexuality, cohabitation, widespread use of pornography, etc.). It is true that the Catholic Church continues to underscore the problematic character of all of these developments.

However, the basic claim of the Catholic Church is true: human sexuality cannot be reduced to a mere source of pleasure, but is something of deeper importance. The way that people live

10. Mt 25:40.

in their sexual lives deeply impacts their relationship with God, their capacity to love other persons, the stability of family life (including the good of children), and each person's internal harmony and well-being. The spiritual stakes of sex are in some sense always high, never low. Why is this? Because human sexuality, while enrooted in our animal nature (our senses, instincts, and emotions) is never merely an animal action but also always inevitably personal. It engages human freedom and human reason. It touches immediately upon the capacity to love or to be self-centered, to be true or to be untrue, to transmit human life or to seek to avoid doing so, to relate to God or to refuse to relate to God. This is why sex has a "moral center" that cannot be eradicated. It always touches upon the spiritual dimension of the human person.

It is because of this fact that human sexuality is so frequently accompanied by deep moral sentiments: those of love and devotion or guilt and shame, fidelity and happiness or spiritual emptiness and disappointment. Human sexuality never really functions just as an aesthetic act of pleasure or an anesthetic buffer against the sorrows of the world. Such reductive views are false and lead down the pathway to moral superficiality and spiritual dissatisfaction. Furthermore, it is Manichaean or "dualistic" to think that the whole sphere of human sexuality is a zone separated from God or that has nothing to do with God, as if our physical body had nothing to do with the life of the Holy Spirit. God the creator is present in all things, and calls all to the spiritual vocation to love in charity. Consequently, the Gospel shines a ray of truth on our human sexuality and calls human beings to conversion—to the vocation to love God and others in truth, in the whole of their bodily life. Human sexual acts are capable of being deeply sanctified by grace and therefore profoundly oriented toward God. It is this pathway that can make human sexuality authentically joyful and a source of deeper human peace and happiness.

Chastity and Temperance

As Thomas Aquinas notes, the pleasure derived from human sexuality is what is highest in the order of sensate pleasures.[11] These cannot fulfill the deepest aspirations of the human heart, but if sought out as an end in themselves, they can serve as profoundly addictive distractions. Consequently, in our fallen condition, the sexual instinct can easily become tyrannical or addictive, and drag human freedom into patterns that are self-destructive. C. S. Lewis commented that when confronted with the random promptings of the sexual appetite, every human being must make a basic choice between rational self-governance and moral anarchy.[12] What he meant is that we must learn to govern our sensual appetites, informing them with authentic reason and personal love, or else face a life of moral self-unraveling. We need not look far to see the widespread negative impact of lust on human relationships.

But human sexuality can be governed maturely in view of the love of God and the good of others. This is the function of the virtues of temperance and chastity, sound habits of life that allow a person to love other people chastely and selflessly, in a non-exploitative way. Temperance is the virtue that regulates all the pleasures of touch, from eating and drinking to emotional flirtation and sexual pleasure. The temperate person retains the "primacy" of the spiritual life in all things, whether drinking and eating or in emotional relationships with others. Chastity is the virtue of temperance specifically with regard to sexual desires. A person is chaste when he refrains from any sexual thoughts and actions that are unreasonable or selfish, so as to maintain a balanced interior life, chaste external actions, and a respectful, caring disposition toward others. Chastity creates a kind of spiritual

11. Aquinas, *ST* I-II, q. 31, a. 6.
12. Lewis, *Mere Christianity*, 100.

refinement: modesty in appearance, emotional gentleness, altruistic love. It makes men more spiritually and emotionally sensitive (without betraying their manliness), and frees women from insecurity, competition, and manipulation (without betraying their femininity). Within marriage, chastity helps to safeguard fidelity and stability, emotional trust and lasting friendship.

While the culture of the sexual revolution often claims that chastity is impossible or that it stems from sexual repression, the truth is that chastity is of vital importance for a person's authentic moral development and psychological maturity. With prayer, careful effort and the help of God's grace, it is possible to live chastely in a joyful and balanced way. The decisions we make regarding sexuality impact our character and the development of our whole person. Without a stable form of chastity in our lives we cannot become truly mature, loving, and giving human beings.

Chaste Sexuality in Marriage

The way we live out our human sexuality inevitably affects the three central relations in our lives: how we relate to God, to other human persons, and to ourselves as beings capable of love and responsibility. Human sexuality relates us to God first and foremost because it is at base a reproductive power by which we are capable of transmitting human life. The inclination toward sexuality is forceful in human beings because it is meant to assure the continued presence of the human race. It presses human beings toward having children. At the same time, when a new human life is conceived in the womb, it is God that creates the spiritual soul of the new human being directly and immediately (without input from the human parents). This means that in human reproduction, there is something sacred: a cooperation with God in which the parents generate a new human being and God creates the spiritual soul, so that there results a complete human person made in the image of God. When human beings act sexually, therefore, they necessarily act in ways that make use of this power to procreate, which implicitly relates back to God the creator. This does not mean that every human sexual act of a married couple must be aimed at having a child. It does mean, however, that human sexuality always has a sacred dimension that lies in the background, and this does affect the moral meaning of every sexual act. (We will return to this topic below.)

Sexuality also of course affects one's relationship to other persons. It can be exploitative or self-giving, utilitarian or caring, violent or communicative, banal or spiritually significant. Mature sexual relations occur when the partners take seriously the true end of sexual activity. This is not mere pleasure, nor even an intense human friendship (of a shorter or longer time frame). Rather, the real purpose of sex is spousal and procreative. It permits a man and a woman to commit to one another for life, so as to have children together and raise them as mother and father.

When Aquinas talks about this he describes the friendship between the married man and woman as the "essence" of the marriage.[13] The mutual vows of fidelity and lifelong monogamy are the core or heart of the marriage. This form of life is sealed by conjugal union, in which human sexual actions express friendship, intimacy, and marital stability. Aquinas refers to the procreation and education of children, meanwhile, as the "final cause" or ultimate purpose of marriage. The friendship of the spouses aims at having children and at educating them together. This is the core purpose of the friendship that the spouses have together. This view is very balanced because it allows one to see a number of important traits of marriage.

First, marital friendship is unique in comparison with all other friendships because it alone is characterized by conjugal acts of love that seek to transmit human life. Consequently, where there

13. Aquinas, *ST* III, q. 29, a. 2.

243

is no intention to perform the kinds of actions that are naturally open to the transmission of human life (*coetus*), there can be no real marriage. Furthermore, where the spouses do not intend to commit permanently to one another to raise their children, they are not truly married (even if they in fact conceive children together). The intention to have children and raise them together belongs to the essence of spousal friendship.

Second, based on Aquinas's definition we can see why there can be profoundly meaningful marriage between spouses who try to have children but are involuntarily sterile or between older spouses that can no longer have children in the home. In these cases what transpires in the conjugal life of the couple is essentially marital, even though it may not produce children. Because such couples intend to have children or at least perform actions naturally oriented toward the transmission of life, they can be genuinely united as married partners, even if their marriages are not able to be perfected in the same way as the marriages of couples are who are able to have children. The incapacity to have children is often a serious cross in the lives of married couples, yet they can nevertheless grow closer to God and be sanctified by the grace of Christ in and through their married lives.

Third, Aquinas's definition allows us to see why marital love alone is the form of sexuality that can be directly oriented to God, and therefore sanctified by grace. Sexuality based on lifelong commitment and open to the transmission of life is self-giving rather than self-referential. It is human physical love that is given to the other person as an expression of permanent commitment, but also in acceptance of the other person's capacity to be a mother or father, and in the gift of one's self to maternity or paternity. So it is also love that is open to the good of children and of the larger society. It is even most fundamentally a form of physical love open to cooperation with God (through procreation) and not sealed off from the transcendent. The sign of this is that when people do have children, they become responsible for the future care for their children, and so more dependent upon the divine providence of God, with which they must cooperate in their day-to-day lives. Having children and caring for them leads to progressive spiritual maturity. In the larger plan of things, then, sexuality is meant to have a religious function. Lived out rightly, it contributes to the profound spiritual development of the parents as well as their children.

Contraception

Given the complexity of the human being as a spiritual animal, it takes a fair amount of moral discipline to sanctify human sexual relationships. There are also a lot of ways these relationships can go wrong. Contraception is frequently seen as an uncontroversial way to manage human reproductive choice. However, it is much more spiritually damaging than it may first appear to be. What do we mean here by "contraception"? Technically defined, contraception is any action—either before, during, or after sexual intercourse—that specifically intends to subvert conception. Of course the typical aim of such an activity is to enjoy human sexual relations without fear of pregnancy. Fundamentally, it is problematic because it severs the connection between conjugal union and procreation, intentionally sterilizing human sexuality. This affects sexual acts in a number of ways.

Most fundamentally, contraception changes the meaning of the sexual act by making it essentially about mutual sexual pleasure. Even if the contraceptive sex act takes place between two people who love each other very much, it is basically a consensual act of shared mutual pleasure. The pleasure of human sexuality is not a bad thing, but when it becomes the unique aim in a sexual act, even within a marriage, the act inevitably becomes self-referential. Due to the couple's use of contraception their actions are no longer open to life in a way that would entail the receptivity to each other's procreative capacities, and the vulnerability and commitment that go with this. The genuine gift of self is undermined and replaced by a logic of control and even mutual use. This is why contraception in a subtle (or often not so subtle) way tends to degrade human relationships over time. A contraceptive mentality emerges that seeks to be with the other person because the other is a source of pleasure and consolation. This can render human relationships permanently immature (as in the case of long-term cohabitation without commitment). It can also contribute to the development of habitual selfishness. Human sexuality is often addictive, especially when it is not integrated into a lifestyle of self-giving. Contraception allows this addictive element to develop in a one-sided way, so that human relationships are frequently marked at their core by self-referential lust.

Contraception is particularly problematic because it severs the direct connection with God as the creator of new life. In effect, it secularizes sex, sterilizing it so as to remove the "threat" of new human life. When contraception use becomes widespread and habitual it leads to a contraceptive mentality: sex should be readily available without children and without commitment. This mentality explains why the rise in contraception use leads to a rise in abortion rates. Contraception use creates the expectation of the right to have sex without consequences, and abortion becomes a stopgap measure for assuring sex without children when contraception fails. It also leads to the ready permissibility of premarital sex (often deeply immature in nature), cohabitation, adultery, and the facilitation of a culture of pornography. Its constant use makes people progressively blind to the inherent natural relation between sex and procreation, so that forms of sexuality that are not procreative (sodomy and homosexuality) seem theoretically equivalent in people's minds to heterosexual monogamous marriage.

The Catholic Church teaches that contraception is seriously morally problematic and leads to bad outcomes both within marriage as well as outside of it. This does not mean, however, that a married couple must intentionally aim at conceiving a child in every human sexual act. That is a caricature of the Catholic tradition that is deeply inaccurate, but which contains a grain of truth. The grain of truth is that unitive love between the spouses should not be severed from openness to life. The falsehood is to claim that this means that the couple must intend to conceive in every instance. The Catholic Church only claims (rightly) that human sexual acts should be the kinds of acts that can produce children (heterosexual intercourse), and that they should take place in the context of a committed marital relationship. If the couple does not purposefully sterilize their actions, their lovemaking is inherently natural and good, and can contribute to the development of the friendship that exists between the married couple.

The Church does teach that a married couple may refrain from human sexual relations at certain times that they know they are more likely to conceive, if they do so for a serious enough reason.[14] Due to modern scientific knowledge, so-called natural family planning can be as highly effective in this regard as any artificial method. A couple may abstain from sexual relations for approximately eight days a month and so avoid conceiving children. People often object that this is just another form of artificial contraception or something nearly equivalent. Concretely, however, that is not true. There is a basic difference between *refraining* from performing a natural action, and engaging in a disordered action. A couple who abstain from time to time from sexual relations do not engage in a purposefully sterilized sexual act. Instead they grow in temperance and in mutual love for one another and for God through periodic times of abstinence. They do not make use of pleasure divorced from their life-giving powers as spouses and as human beings made in the image of God. Couples who

14. Such reasons could be economic, psychological, and/or health-related. See Pope Paul VI's discussion in *Humanae Vitae*, Encyclical Letter. July 25, 1968, par. 10.

regularly have recourse to natural family planning, so as to space the birth of children reasonably, testify frequently to the fact that the practice deepens their spiritual life and requires deeper love and communication between them. Contraception does not make these ethical demands of its users and frequently has negative short-term and long-term consequences in married life.

One may object that this whole vision stands at odds with the experience of many married couples who love each other very deeply, and who have children, but who also use contraception periodically in their relationship. It is true that married people who use contraception do frequently love each other and remain successfully faithful to one another in enduring, life-giving relationships. Here, however, three things should be kept in mind. First, the Church's teaching on this matter has to do with ways that married couples can orient the *whole* of their lives toward God, including even their sexual intimacy, in union with the grace of Christ. Contraception disrupts this process in discrete instances, even in those who otherwise seek to do what is good and right. Couples who accept the teaching of the Church in this domain frequently testify to its spiritually and emotionally beneficial fruits. Second, various forms of physical and chemical contraception that are commonly used by married couples function not only to thwart the conception of new human life, but act in addition as abortifacients. They impede the implantation of a newly conceived human zygote in the wall of the mother's uterus, or cause the lining of the uterine wall to shed after the implantation of the zygote, thereby destroying a newly conceived human life. This kind of contraception, which is not rare, is disdainful of the dignity of human life. In addition to harming children, hormonal contraceptives have been shown scientifically to have very detrimental effects upon the bodies of women.[15] Finally, even

---

15. See references to the negative health effects of protracted use of hormonal contraceptives by the Centers for Disease Control and Prevention (www.cdc.gov).

if a married couple use contraception within the context of an otherwise fruitful and faithful relationship, they contribute to a cultural redefinition of sexuality in doing so. Their children and friends can readily perceive from their example that sexuality can be divorced from openness to life. Therefore, sexuality in principle can be severed from marital commitment and transformed into a uniquely aesthetic act performed between consenting adults. In the end, contraceptive sexuality in marriage has a very different *context* than contraceptive non-committal sexuality, but it is not a specifically different kind of act, and so it contributes by its example to the redefining of human sexual relationships within the wider culture.[16]

From what has been said above, it should make sense why certain forms of sexual acts are morally problematic. Having children outside of marriage is vastly ethically superior to abortion, but it does introduce children into an unstable environment, one where they often grow up aware of being abandoned by one of their parents. Cohabitation is a form of ethical dilettantism based on a mutual lack of commitment. Frequently it stems from the fact that a man is unwilling to have children with a woman and is keeping her suspended in a relationship that is subtly manipulative. Relationships of this kind do not foster persons of self-giving, and tend to result in moral paralysis and spiritual and physical sterility. Sexual acts that are not reproductive (various forms of sodomy and oral sex) are not subject to sanctification by God because they do not transmit human life. No matter how much personal affection animates them, such acts as such are basically aimed at consensual self-gratification. While true human lovemaking should be motivated by *eros* or strong mutual desire, the pursuit of the erotic for its own sake is problematic, especially

16. See, on this topic, the British philosopher G. E. M. Anscombe, "Contraception and Chastity" in *Faith in a Hard Ground: Essays on Religion, Philosophy and Ethics*, ed. M. Geach and L. Gormally (Exeter: St. Andrews Studies, 2008), 170–91.

when it becomes divorced from openness to life, and subtly undermines one's relationship with God and with other people. People who treat each other as pornographic objects inevitably become isolated in the prison of their own imaginations, like Peter Pan, the boy who refused to grow up, living in an imaginary world. Sexual maturity can only take place when human instincts are governed by a deeper and more irrepressible drive: the spiritual drive to love others and to give one's whole life to God.

Homosexuality

Homosexuality is a complex phenomenon that requires nuanced consideration, one that is often lacking in public discussion of the topic. Broad distinctions should be made. Some people find themselves strongly attracted uniquely to members of the same sex, even from a young age. Others develop an attraction to either sex or predominantly to the same sex. This can take place for some people especially during the course of adolescence and early adulthood, while for others it endures as a lifelong phenomenon. Some people who have strong same-sex attractions confidently locate the origin of these attractions in a childhood or adolescent experience (sometimes based on problematic relationships they had with one parent). Others note that their attractions are hormonal and affirm resolutely that they are unrelated to any developmental problems.

The Catholic Church makes no claims on the subject of the origin of homosexuality, or its various possible causes. Instead she stresses two basic teachings.[17] First, homosexual acts by their very nature can never be considered morally equivalent to heterosexual acts of married persons. They are by nature sterile acts (not based on the complementarity of the sexes), and as such are not oriented

---

17. See in this respect the Congregation for the Doctrine of the Faith, "Letter to the Bishops of the Catholic Church on the Pastoral Care of Homosexual Persons," October 1, 1986; available at www.vatican.va.

towards procreation. This means that even when they take place in the context of a friendship between two consenting adults who love each other, they are not well-ordered sexual acts. Just because they cannot serve as the catalyst for a reproductive family life, such acts inevitably have a kind of self-referentiality to them. They procure mutual pleasure but are not acts oriented toward the cultivation of self-giving through a friendship based upon paternity and maternity. Because they misuse the sexual power of reproduction, these acts also tend to alienate people from God and from a deeper spiritual relationship with Christ. There is an analogy here to fornication. Just as heterosexual acts that take place outside of marriage typically are not oriented toward committed love and the procreation of children, so too homosexual actions are structurally incapable of being turned toward the generation and procreation of children, in a reproductive union, and in cooperation with God.

Second, however, the Church also insists resolutely on the inherent dignity of human beings who have pronounced same-sex attractions. She recognizes that many persons with strong same-sex attractions find themselves affected by these attractions involuntarily, independently of anything they might intend. Some find it nearly impossible, or very difficult, to embrace heterosexual marriage. Others feel psychological alienation from the opposite sex for any variety of reasons that are understandable in light of their histories. People with strong same-sex attractions can suffer from grief since they are unable to have heterosexual relations that would give them their own children to raise. In addition, they may sometimes suffer from social stigmas, serial relationships, or a sense of futility (especially in their older age). The promiscuity that is present in some sectors of the same-sex community can also give rise to spiritual experiences of disillusionment, despair, and alienation from God. The Catholic Church's teachings on sexuality can appear strange or offensive to many people with same-sex attractions, and some respond to them with a hostility that is motivated by genuine sincerity. Nevertheless, the Church's teaching is motivated by a sincere love that is not condescending but truthful and demanding.

The Catholic Church rightly notes that persons with strong same-sex attractions are not only loved by God as much as anyone else, but are also called to friendship with God and to personal holiness. For them this passage can entail great struggle that Christians should address with compassion and understanding. They must seek to have uniquely chaste human friendships, and can suffer from periods of loneliness, as well as their experience of human fragility. They sometimes experience crosses that people with pronounced heterosexual inclinations do not have to face (though the contrary is true as well). By recourse to the grace of God in prayer and the sacrament of reconciliation, people with strong same-sex attractions can learn to live in profound spiritual friendship with God, and in deep Christian charity for other persons. One should not underestimate the greatness of the grace and mercy that God shows people who struggle in this domain, nor the heights of sanctity and consolation that he can lead people to, in and through their effort to respond wholeheartedly to the love of Christ. The biblical teaching on homosexuality is a "hard saying" but it is also one that can lead people to a higher plane of life, one of inner peace and fulfillment through friendship with God.

Human Sexuality and Divine Mercy

Due to the effects of original sin, all human beings find it difficult to govern their sexual lives well and to habitually make good decisions in this domain. Our human nature is weak and our mind is sometimes clouded by the vagaries of sexual desire. Therefore, the vast majority of people pass through at least certain times in life in which they live out their sexuality in immature or selfish ways. Temptations to sexual thoughts and actions that are morally destructive are a virtually inevitable feature of human existence. Furthermore, in this domain most human beings harbor a strange mixture of unresolved forms of desire and guilt, an unstable, evolving terrain that they carry with them throughout their lives.

Consequently, when considering the subject of human sexuality, it is always important to recall the mercy of Christ for all human beings, and the irreplaceable role of sacramental confession. Only grace can truly heal the human person interiorly, and such grace is available to us through this sacrament in particular. Sacramental confession permits us to experience in a truly supernatural way that we are loved and forgiven by God. This forgiveness is regenerative or life-giving. The sacrament infuses into our hearts the grace of authentic contrition, and stimulates growth in the infused virtues of temperance and chastity. In this way, confession strengthens our authentic love for God, as well as our authentic love of self, directing any destructive feelings of guilt or shame back toward confidence in the mercy of Christ and the victory of his passion.

Religious Freedom

The traditional teaching of the Catholic Church on religious freedom is comprised of two central principles. First, each human being has an obligation to seek out the truth about God and religion and to adhere to the true religion when he discovers it. Consequently, just as truth should have a privileged place in society over falsehood, so the true religion objectively has a right of privilege in human society. This is why the Church has taught down through the ages that a civic population has the right to enshrine Catholicism as the official religion of the state, and to employ instruments of the state (such as schools or universities) in order to promote the truth of the Catholic religion.

The second principle is that our real acceptance of religious truth, in order to be genuine, must be assimilated freely through our conscience and personal deliberation. For example, it is not wrong to baptize a child prior to the age of reason because baptism communicates a great grace to the baptized child. But this grace is not brought to perfection without a progressively rational assent to the faith. Consequently, authentic Catholic education must seek to bring people to a deep and mature understanding of the faith and a thoughtful, free embrace of all that they are taught. Moreover, adult conversion to Catholicism must never be forced, and should not be the product of manipulation of the conscience or of external compulsion.

Here someone may object, of course: what about the Inquisition or the crusades? What about the Church's past human rights record? Is it really true that she traditionally respected the role of the freedom of conscience? Or is this a modern innovation? The answer to this question is nuanced. On the one hand, yes, the principle of the respect of the personal religious conscience stems back to the earliest stages of the new covenant. Jesus Christ himself died at the hands of the religious and political authorities of his time for bearing witness to a truth that the "rulers of this age" rejected.[18] Primitive Catholicism was primarily a religion of adult conversion, in which Christians regularly were put to death by the Roman state due to their convictions of conscience. Even after the rise of Constantinian Christianity, in Byzantium and in the high Middle Ages, there were protections given to the religious consciences of non-Christians. Christians were forbidden by the Church from forcing Jews to convert (a principle that Aquinas underscores forcefully).[19] Christian governments did engage in wars with Muslims in the Middle East due to conflicts about the Christian populations in the Holy Land (wars of questionable jus-

18. 1 Cor 2:8.
19. Aquinas, *ST* II-II, q. 10, aa. 11 and 12.

tice or prudence). But even in the crusades it was formally forbidden to force Muslims to convert to the Catholic faith. Even at the high-water mark of Christendom, Christianity was never a "religion of the sword" in this respect.

However, there have been two qualifications to this viewpoint historically. One concerns polytheism, and the other concerns Christian heresy. Regarding polytheism: there have been different theological opinions among Catholic theologians on this issue. Sixteenth-century Jesuits, for example (Robert Bellarmine and Francisco Suarez) argued that polytheism and many of the rites that accompany it are instances of religious irrationality. There is no obligation of the state to tolerate them. In practice, however, missionary efforts of the Church in Africa, Asia, and South America have frequently adopted a gradualist approach, emphasizing many of the positive aspects of indigenous religion. Furthermore, the Second Vatican Council document *Dignitatis Humanae* insists on the importance of a general respect and legal protection for the religious conscience of all human persons, including those who are not monotheists.[20] This is important especially in a modern political context, where minority religious groups are frequently persecuted severely or even put to death for their religious practices, either by anti-religious secular regimes or by adherents of other religious traditions.

Historically it is with regard to Christian heresy that the Church has been the most reluctant to consider the principle of appeal to conscience as a unilateral first principle. The problem of Christian heresy *internal* to the Church is that it can destroy the moral fabric of the Church itself. If a Catholic priest teaches or practices something seriously contrary to the Catholic faith, it can be a source of scandal, division, or schism. Consequently, from earliest times the Church has maintained the possibility of penances or canonical penalties for those who gravely contravene

20. *Dignitatis Humanae*, no. 2.

the Church's teachings or practices. This practice is ever alive in the Church, since it is possible still to be excommunicated or placed under a special form of penance, or simply to suffer penal sanctions such as expulsion from the religious life or loss of the material support of the Church. Belonging to the Church does not give people a blank check so that they can live in irresponsibility to the vows they make or in hypocritical disregard for the Church's teaching that they have promised to uphold. This disciplinary side of the Church is undoubtedly illiberal, but it is a sign of the seriousness with which the Church takes the truth of Christ, as well as the concern she has for the salvation of souls, especially for those who may forfeit their salvation if they are not warned of the gravity of their transgression.

While this general principle about internal obedience is sound, there have been historical *applications* of the principle that have been unsound or unreasonable. The Inquisition is a key example and a complex one. The Inquisition was started not only to prosecute heretical movements but also in part in order to *defend* persons accused of heresy from vigilante movements that might take their lives (or livelihood) without warrant. The modern system of trial by jury based on the presumption of innocence until proven guilty was actually initiated in part by the medieval Inquisition. Furthermore, studies of inquisitional practices have shown that many of the penances that were assigned to persons in heretical movements were extremely modest (such as the saying of a few prayers).

At the same time, medieval inquisitors did frequently work hand-in-hand with the state, adopting means that were violent, such as torture or execution. Some local governments in turn made use of the Inquisition as a form of social control, particularly in the Spanish Inquisition, which persecuted the Jews in particularly infamous ways. Here we should make some important observations. First, the Catholic Church never taught that torture is morally acceptable, but she never condemned torture explicitly until after the medieval period. Torture was a widespread penal practice inherited from the Roman Empire that Christian culture came to disavow only progressively. However, as the modern magisterium of the Church rightly underscores, physical torture is inherently inhuman and objectively evil, so that the civil recourse to torture in the Middle Ages by certain "Christian" regimes must be condemned as unchristian and inhumane.[21] (Nor should torture be employed in our supposedly more "enlightened age" of secular liberalism and atheist communism, where it is statistically far more frequent!)

Second, the fact that the Church does have a right to have recourse to some means of discipline does not mean that she should always make use of this right, or that all such licit means are equally evangelical in nature. Christian culture should maintain a deep sense of divine and human justice (and so make real requirements on her ministers). For example, priests who commit serious crimes ought to be punished in proportionately serious ways. But more generally speaking, the Church must also maintain an even greater sense of divine and human mercy. Christ commands the love of enemies. It is essential to the Christian life to maintain a humane respect and even zealous charity for those who disavow the Christian faith, who betray the Church, or who hate and persecute the Church. The charity of Christ must conquer in all things.

Finally, while the past crimes of those who call themselves Christians should never be ignored, criticisms of them should not become an excuse to ignore the grievous transgressions of our own age. Expert modern historians estimate that in the entirety of the Spanish Inquisition, approximately two thousand people were executed. Meanwhile it is estimated that the atheist regimes of Stalin and Mao together were responsible for the collective

---

21. *Catechism of the Catholic Church*, pars. 2297–98.

deaths of approximately forty to fifty million persons. The problem of irresponsible human life-taking is not something reducible to "religious causes," nor can a singleminded focus on this facet of the Church's history be used as an excuse to ignore her sound warnings about the grave disrespect of human persons that so often takes place in modern society. The answer to misguided religion is not "no religion," but the embrace of a reasonable religious practice.

In the modern era, the Church's teaching on religious freedom has been formulated primarily in response to the rise of the modern secular state. In this context the Church has insisted upon the freedom to preach the Gospel, but also to establish religious institutions (charities, universities, schools, hospitals, institutions of religious orders) that take part actively in the public life of society. Needless to say, many secular governments as well as religious states (in India and the Muslim world) have sought to suppress various forms of public expression of Christianity in general and Catholicism in particular.

The Catholic Church has grounded her claims about this matter in both theological and philosophical principles. *Theologically*, the Church has the mandate to preach the Gospel and to establish social organizations in the public square because she is herself established by God (an institution of divine right), and is instructed by the light of divine revelation.[22] She is charged with the responsibility of bringing the message of salvation to all human beings so as to make possible an authentic encounter with the grace of Christ. No human government can legitimately suppress the least aspect of the divinely revealed truth or its lived expression in public society. *Philosophically*, the Church appeals in the public square to a truth of the natural law. Human beings are made to seek the truth, and religious truths are among the highest of truths. Consequently, any legitimate government must respect the rights of its

---

22. *Dignitatis Humanae*, nos. 9–12.

citizens to seek religious truth, to adhere to it, and to allow it to deeply inform their lives and their public actions.[23]

Based on these principles, the Church in the modern world has sought to promote religious freedom on two fronts. In the context of the secular regimes, the Church has insisted on the plenary right of the Church to advance Christian teachings in the public square. Historically this engagement has been most dramatic in communist countries where there were active attempts to suppress Catholicism almost entirely. However, it is increasingly the case that secular democratic liberalism in some places has become legally intolerant of Christian free expression due to the Church's teachings on sexual morality and her defense of unborn human life. In the context of religious regimes, especially in Islamic cultures, the Catholic Church has insisted on respect for the dignity and civic rights of minority non-Muslim populations. Muslims and Catholics have some common convictions and should seek to find ways to live peacefully side by side. However, the Islamic suppression of the free right to convert to Christianity or to debate the truth of Christianity publicly in much of the Muslim world remains a stumbling block to the development of an authentic ethos of enlightened rationality and religious freedom in the world today.

Religious freedom conceived of in the sense we have discussed above is not merely about the capacity to be religious or not, to think one thing or another is true. More profoundly it is about respect for the integrity of the search for truth in each human person. Everyone is capable of seeking God and of coming to know God progressively by way of understanding and love. The ultimate foundation for *religious* freedom is the respect for the human capacity freely to approach the truth itself. If a secular government or culture begins to believe that it has the right to control whether a human being may freely accept authentic truth

23. *Dignitatis Humanae*, nos. 2 and 5–7.

about God and divine revelation, it will shortly follow that that same government or culture will believe that it has the right to control what a human being may believe about anything and everything. Authentic worship of God is, in this sense, the ultimate safeguard of the freedom of human thought in general, not its adversary. Those who promote a rational freedom of religion in the public square, then, also promote thereby the protection of the deepest dynamic of freedom in human society: the freedom to seek the truth.

7

THE LAST THINGS

Death and Final Judgment

The primary existential certitude each person has is that he exists. That we and the world around us really exist is evident. The second existential certitude each person has is that he must die. Whatever else may happen to us in a fairly uncertain world, the fact that we will eventually die is a defining reality of our existence.

Martin Heidegger spoke in *Being and Time* of the human person as a "being towards death," that is to say, not only as a being conditioned by the reality of death, but also as a being able to think about this fact, and to live authentically (or not) in the face of death.[1] Given that we are going to die, we should live out the time we have in this world with seriousness and purposefulness, as well as with appropriate joy and grief, but not with superficiality or with a callous indifference to spiritual questions.

The reality of death can be looked upon in different ways, of course: with resignation and gloom, with stoic fatalism, or with hope and even expectation. Great Christian saints have sometimes had a mysterious desire to pass through death to eternal life with God. We see this already in St. Paul:

---

1. Heidegger, *Being and Time*, 279–311.

It is my eager expectation and hope that I shall not be at all ashamed, but that with full courage now as always *Christ will be honored in my body, whether by life or by death. For to me to live is Christ, and to die is gain.* If it is to be life in the flesh, that means fruitful labor for me. Yet which I shall choose I cannot tell. I am hard pressed between the two. *My desire is to depart and be with Christ, for that is far better.* But to remain in the flesh is more necessary on your account.[2]

Paul seems conscious in this passage of the reality of life after death, and of the continued existence of the spiritual soul, even apart from the body, prior to the final resurrection. He also seems aware of the possibility of beatitude: of the happiness that comes from life with God in the world to come.

The Second Vatican Council states things in this way:

It is in the face of death that the riddle of human existence grows most acute. Not only is man tormented by pain and by the advancing deterioration of his body, but even more so by a dread of perpetual extinction. He rightly follows the intuition of his heart when he abhors and repudiates the utter ruin and total disappearance of his own person. He rebels against death because he bears in himself an eternal seed which cannot be reduced to sheer matter. All the endeavors of technology, though useful in the extreme, cannot calm his anxiety; for prolongation of biological life is unable to satisfy that desire for higher life which is inescapably lodged in his breast. Although the mystery of death utterly beggars the imagination, the Church has been taught by divine revelation and firmly teaches that man has been created by God for a blissful purpose beyond the reach of earthly misery. In addition, that bodily death from which man would have been immune had he not sinned (Cf. Wis. 1:13; 2:23–24; Rom. 5:21; 6:23; Jas. 1:15) will be vanquished, according to the Christian faith, when man who was ruined by his own doing is restored to wholeness by an almighty and merciful Savior. For God has called man and still calls him so that with his entire being he might be joined to Him in an endless sharing of a divine life beyond all corruption.[3]

---

2. Phil 1:20–24.
3. *Gaudium et Spes*, no. 18.

The Catholic Church teaches that human death consists in the separation of the human body and the spiritual soul.[4] The spiritual soul is the core source of our personal identity, and includes our intellectual life and our free will. In this sense, the inner essence of the person lives on after death. At the same time, however, the rupture of body and soul is "substantial" because the body and soul are both essential to what the human being is. The loss of the body, then, is radical. Without my body, I am not a complete human being. The spiritual soul can exist without the body, but this existence is also incomplete. Consequently, even if we affirm the existence of the spiritual soul that continues to subsist after death (as the Catholic Church teaches), we also need to affirm the resurrection of the body in order to make sense of the future destiny of the whole human person, body and soul.[5]

The New Testament and the early Christian tradition affirm that each human soul is judged by God immediately at death. "Death puts an end to human life as the time open to either accepting or rejecting the divine grace manifested in Christ .... Each man receives his eternal retribution in his immortal soul at the very moment of his death, in a particular judgment that refers his life to Christ: either entrance into the blessedness of heaven — through purification or immediately — or immediate and everlasting damnation."[6]

What are the criteria by which we will be judged? The New Testament is clear on this point. First, have we believed in Christ

---

4. *Catechism of the Catholic Church*, par. 624.

5. Ibid., par. 366.

6. Ibid., pars. 1021–22. See scriptural references in 2 Tm 1:9–10; Lk 16:22, 23:43; Mt 16:26; 2 Cor 5:8; Phil 1:23; Heb 9:27, 12:23; and the teaching of the magisterium in Council of Lyons II (1274), Denz. 857–58; Council of Florence (1439), Denz. 1304–6; Council of Trent (1563), Denz. 1820; Pope Benedict XI, *Benedictus Deus*, Encyclical Letter, 1336, Denz. 1000–1001. For the councils referenced, see H. Denzinger, *Compendium of Creeds, Definitions, and Declarations on Matters of Faith and Morals*, 43rd ed., ed. Peter Hünermann, Robert Fastiggi, and Anne Englund Nash (San Francisco: Ignatius, 2012).

and his mystery, revealed to us in faith?[7] Second, have we been obedient to his commandments, and followed his teachings regarding the precepts of charity, as understood and taught by the Catholic Church?[8] Finally, when we have committed serious sins (grave or mortal sins) have we made an integral confession of those sins (clearly stated in species and in number), seeking out the forgiveness of Christ in the sacrament of penance?[9] The soul can "anticipate" the final judgment already in this life by the regular examination of conscience, by going to confession, and by growing in fidelity and obedience to the teachings of Christ. Our ongoing conversion is part of the way we prepare for our personal judgment before God.

This prospect of personal judgment, for eternal life or eternal damnation, may seem terrifying when we think about it seriously, but on a deeper level it is profoundly liberating. The teaching of divine revelation gives perspective to the whole of the rest of life. It teaches us that our lives in this world are lives lived *en route* toward the City of God. In this life we are on pilgrimage returning toward God, walking slowly toward the city that is heaven. Heaven is the life of beatitude that is lived by the saints. The challenge of this life is to get on the right path and to go home, to not stray from the path, nor to make others stray. The journey is communal. In the life of the Church we walk together toward God.

Hell

It is not difficult for any person to be saved by the grace of God. All we have to do is accept the offer of God's grace and mercy and cooperate with that offer faithfully. However, it is also not difficult to refuse this offer, or to forsake grace unfaithfully. Conse-

---

7. Rom 10:10.
8. Jn 15:10, 1 Jn 2:4.
9. 1 Jn 5:16, Jn 20:23.

quently, eternal damnation is a real possibility for each human being. Although modern Christian culture tends to ignore this teaching, it is no trivial fact, and is something that needs to inform the conscience of each human person.

The Church's teaching on hell was not invented in the Middle Ages but stems from Jesus Christ himself, who mentions the threat of eternal damnation at many points in his own teaching, fifteen times in the Gospel of Matthew alone. "And if your right hand causes you to sin, cut it off and throw it away; it is better that you lose one of your members than that your whole body be thrown into hell."[10] The apostles (Peter, Paul, and John) also teach clearly that this mystery is a reality. Hell is a "mystery" for two reasons. First it is mysterious that human beings choose to do evil in preference to the good, and that they reject God, life in Christ, and the offer of grace. How is it that human beings fail to know God and to love him effectively above all things? Why does sin serve over time to blind us to the reality of God? Second, hell is a mystery because it shows us something about God's truthfulness, as well as his loving respect for his creatures. God preserves all his spiritual creatures in existence for eternity, as part of the primal gift of creation. This is the case for angels and for the souls of human persons, even when those beings reject God or turn away from the divine law. However, God also maintains the reality of his divine truthfulness even in the face of human and angelic sin. Sin and injustice toward God do not have the last word, because God is himself eternal truth. Christ is the king of this world, even if there are inhabitants of the kingdom who "will not serve." In the life that is to come, each of us must confront the truth of our choices made in the face of Christ and his kingdom. Our personal responsibility will be made manifest.

Understood in the light of Christ, even the revelation of the existence of hell is part of the "good news": it underscores the im-

10. Mt 5:30.

portance of personal responsibility, and shows us the deep existential significance of our lives. Our choices matter to God. The choices we make in this life, therefore, count a great deal more than we might think. What we do or do not do can have eternal consequences. Furthermore, the teaching on hell paradoxically signals the importance of mercy. To avoid hell, we must confide ourselves radically to the mercy of God and we must show mercy to others. The surpassing remedy to the threat of eternal damnation is the truth of the Gospel and the mercy of God. Thinking about the real possibility of damnation, then, can lead each of us to seek the mercy of God effectively in our lives, to abandon ourselves to the mercy of God, and to be much more merciful to others.

What are the origins of hell? Where does it come from? Fundamentally, eternal damnation stems not from God, but from the choices of human beings, who freely turn away from God, Christ, and the moral law. The decision to freely commit actions that are morally grave ruptures our relationships with God and other human beings made in God's image. If we do not seek reconciliation with God, these ruptures leave us not in a state of grace, but in a state of gracelessness, as wounded, fallen human beings. Salvation is by the grace of Christ alone. Consequently, eternal loss occurs when we act in such a way as to forsake the grace of God.

Of course many people are unaware of the mystery of grace in Christ through no fault of their own. The Catholic Church, based on the clear revelation of scripture, teaches that Christ died for all human beings, and that God in various ways offers the possibility of salvation to all human beings.[11] Grace is mysteriously at work in the world and discreetly present in the lives of all human beings. As we noted above, Pope John Paul II suggests that this grace is frequently at work in the human conscience of each man as he ponders the moral law, helping him to see what he

11. Cf. 1 Tm 2:3–5.

must do, and ought not to do, but also what he should repent of or regret.[12] The deepest workings of the human heart frequently remain hidden from view in this life. We can estimate what might be happening in a person's life from his or her outward actions and words, but ultimately God is the judge of each human soul and of who that person is. This judgment takes place in light of the grace that a given person received and the moral knowledge that was available to him in the particular decisions he made.

The mystery of eternal damnation stems, then, from the human soul purposefully turning away from God, the mystery of Christ, and the moral law, already in this life, but with permanent consequences that endure in the next. The essence of damnation consists in the eternal loss of God. The spiritual soul of each human being is made with an inalienable desire for happiness, one that can ultimately be fulfilled only through knowledge of God and love of the infinite goodness of God. To ignore God or turn away from him results in permanent loss of the only spiritual reality that can truly grant the soul authentic beatitude. Furthermore, the service of God entails the service of those who are made in the image of God. It is possible to turn away from God permanently, then, by implicit means, when we treat other human beings unethically and act contrary to the precepts of charity. God rightly punishes those who do serious injustice to their fellow men and who refuse to repent.

The loss of God results in eternal torment for the soul, since the natural drive toward happiness is deeply inscribed in human beings by nature. This natural drive remains present in the state of damnation, but can never find authentic fulfillment apart from God. After death, the human soul loses the capacity to ignore its deeper calling by distracting itself and turning toward creatures. This is because life in the body has ceased, and confrontation with the truth of Christ has taken place. Consequently, the souls

12. John Paul II, *Veritatis Splendor*, pars. 2–3.

of the damned are made unhappy by their loss of God, through their free decision to reject the truth about God, Christ, and his grace. "They refused to love the truth and so be saved."[13] The Bible also speaks clearly of eternal torments that exist for the human body in hell after the general resurrection. Many theologians link these discomforts to the inner spiritual rejection of God. The soul is made eternally unhappy due to its refusal of the truth about God, and so the body is also forever in unrest. The "pains of fire" that Jesus Christ speaks of are outward, physical discomforts which are somehow related to, and follow from sinful inner decisions of the conscience.[14] These pains bear witness to the justice of God who rightly punishes sin: his purity is an eternal fire. They also manifest the indissoluble unity of human body and spiritual soul: the decisions of our spiritual life have a profound impact on our bodies. This is true even for those who definitively reject God.

Purgatory

St. Catherine of Genoa, a fifteenth-century mystic who had visions of purgatory, says that all of the souls in purgatory are happier than any human soul on earth.[15] Her reasoning is simple. In this life, while we might live in a state of grace, we are also subject to temptation and risk. It is possible to sin against the grace of God and to forfeit our salvation. Pilgrimage toward God in this world is characterized by hope and a kind of militancy, by which we aim with vigilance to be faithful to Christ and to arrive in heaven. Unlike people in this earthly state, however, the souls in purgatory can sin no more. They possess God once and for all. All the souls in purgatory therefore know with final certitude

13. 2 Thes 2:10.
14. Mt 13:42.
15. See Catherine of Genoa, *Treatise on Purgatory* (New York: Sheed and Ward, 1946), chap. 1.

268

that they are inevitably bound for heaven, for the eternal vision of the essence of God. They cannot *not* be saved. They cannot forfeit the gifts of grace.

The state we call "purgatory" is one of purification and expectation. The Catholic Church claims that the souls of those who die in a state of grace, but who remain morally imperfect (with some sinful attachments and egoism), are prepared to see God face to face by gradual influxes of illumination and purifications of charity. This process is spiritually painful because each soul is given to perceive its defects more perfectly, and the will of each person is progressively freed from all egoism so as to love God for his own sake in immaculate purity. This state is also liberating because this purification allows the souls in purgatory to anticipate heaven, progressively knowing and loving God with greater stability and purity. The soul becomes fully transparent to the grace of God, like a window washed clean from filth, in which sunlight shines through in sparkling clarity.

What is the biblical basis for the doctrine of purgatory? This teaching, like many others, has a liturgical origin, one denoted clearly in scripture. Belief in purgatory stems from the ancient practice of praying for the dead, asking for the forgiveness of their sins. The practice is pre-Christian and arose already in ancient Judaism, prior to the time of Christ. We find an example in scripture (2 Macc 12:40–45), where Jewish soldiers who died in battle are found to be wearing pagan amulets. Although they died heroically for the faith of Israel, their commitment to God was still imperfect. "Therefore [Judas Maccabeus] made atonement for the dead, that they might be delivered from their sin."

Jesus of Nazareth himself makes oblique reference to this belief in the forgiveness of some sins "in the age to come" (Mt 12:32). As Pope St. Gregory the Great comments on this verse: "For certain lesser faults, we must believe that, before the Final Judgment, there is a purifying fire. He who is truth says that whoever utters blasphemy against the Holy Spirit will be pardoned neither in this age nor in the age to come. From this sentence we understand that certain offenses can be forgiven in this age, but certain others in the age to come."[16] The references here to purification by fire are drawn from 1 Peter 1:7 and 1 Corinthians 3:15. These New Testament images were assembled by the early Church to refer to the process that occurs after death, in the souls of those for whom we intercede and for whom we pray. The early Church both in the East and West prayed for the souls of the faithful departed in the course of the eucharistic liturgy, interceding for the forgiveness of their sins. In the fourth century *Catechetical Lectures*, traditionally ascribed to St. Cyril of Jerusalem, the basic teaching of the Church is manifest: the sacrifice of the Mass is offered for both the living and the dead, so that those who are now undergoing purification after death may be aided by the grace of the Cross of Christ, to which the members of the Church, moved by the Holy Spirit, unite their petitions. Describing the anaphora prayer of the eucharistic liturgy to those who are preparing to enter the Church, the author writes:

Then we commemorate also those who have fallen asleep before us, first Patriarchs, Prophets, Apostles, Martyrs, that at their prayers and intercessions God would receive our petition. Then on behalf also of the Holy Fathers and Bishops who have fallen asleep before us, and in a word of all who in past years have fallen asleep among us, believing that it will be a very great benefit to the souls, for whom the supplication is put up, while that holy and most awe-filled sacrifice is set forth.[17]

Rightly understood, then, the doctrine of purgatory is a traditional teaching of the Bible and the early Church.

---

16. St. Gregory the Great, *Dial.* 4, 39 (PL 77:396); cf. Mt 12:31. The translation is taken from *Catechism of the Catholic Church*, par. 1031.

17. Cyril of Jerusalem, *Catechetical Lecture* 23 (*On the Mysteries* V); *On the Sacred Liturgy and Communion*, Number 9, in *Nicene and Post-Nicene Fathers*, vol. 7, ed. P. Schaff and H. Wace, trans. E. H. Gifford (Buffalo, N.Y.: Christian Literature Publishing, 1894); translation slightly modified.

The metaphysical basis for the doctrine of purgatory is very straightforward. In truth, anyone who believes in the mystery of heaven must implicitly affirm the reality of a "process" or state that we call purgatory. The reason is the following. Internal transformation by grace, however sudden its advent, always leads to a progressive transformation of the human person. This is not due to the character of God's grace, but due to the character of human nature. The human mind and heart are spiritual faculties, and they always only develop over time, by a movement from "potency" or capacity to a state of actuation. One *becomes* a violinist, or a lawyer or a theologian or a saint. This occurs over time. Thus even if justification by grace occurs "in an instant" as Thomas Aquinas argues, transformation and sanctification do not.[18] The process we call "purgatory" is grounded metaphysically in the progressive purification of the sinful human heart that is effected gradually over time by the working of God's grace. It begins in this life and can take on a more robust form in some than in others. It continues, however, in the spiritual lives of separated human souls after death. The souls of those who die in a state of grace are gradually purified of their egoism and freed from every stain of sin as a proximate preparation for perfect union with God in the beatific vision (heaven). To believe in the possibility of heaven is to believe in the possibility of progressive human transformation by grace. To believe that this progressive transformation frees us from our moral imperfections and sinful inclinations after death is to believe in purgatory.

Some modern Catholic theologians envisage purgatory as a mystery of Christ's own fire of love purging the soul of its stains after death. In his beautiful poem, "The Dream of Gerontius," John Henry Newman portrays the human soul's encounter with Christ after death as a moment in which the soul is wounded by the radiant intensity of Christ's holiness and purity, pierced with

18. Aquinas, *ST* I-II, q. 113, a. 7.

remorse at its own sinfulness and sent into the fires of purgatory by the irradiating splendor of Christ's overwhelming charity. As the guardian angel explains in the poem:

> It is the face of the Incarnate God
> Shall smite thee with that keen and subtle pain;
> And yet the memory which it leaves will be
> A sovereign febrifuge to heal the wound;
> And yet withal it will the wound provoke,
> And aggravate and widen it the more.[19]

Pope Benedict XVI states the idea in this way:

The fire which both burns and saves is Christ himself, the Judge and Savior. The encounter with him is the decisive act of judgment. Before his gaze all falsehood melts away. This encounter with him, as it burns us, transforms and frees us, allowing us to become truly ourselves. All that we build during our lives can prove to be mere straw, pure bluster, and it collapses. Yet in the pain of this encounter, when the impurity and sickness of our lives become evident to us, there lies salvation. His gaze, the touch of his heart heals us through an undeniably painful transformation "as through fire" (1 Cor. 3:15). But it is a blessed pain, in which the holy power of his love sears through us like a flame, enabling us to become totally ourselves and thus totally of God.[20]

It is easy to see from such passages that we can begin the process of purgation already in this life by asking God to enlighten us as to our faults and to purify us by the active power of his grace. Growth in charity progressively expands our hearts and reduces the influence of egoism in our lives. As we enter into an entirely transparent relationship with Christ, we learn to confess our sins with hope in the power of his grace to burn our souls spiritually, not so as to destroy but so as to heal and transform us. In this way, the active purification of the spiritual life in this world initiates

19. John Henry Newman, *The Dream of Gerontius* (London: Catholic Truth Society, 1953).

20. Pope Benedict XVI, *Spe Salvi*, Encyclical Letter, November 30, 2007, par. 47; available at www.vatican.va.

and anticipates the mystery of purgatory that is to take place in the next.

Heaven

Every major religious tradition seeks in some way to explain human existence and to promote a way of life having a final aim, or leading to an ultimate purpose. So one of the most significant of ways to compare religions is by considering what they propose as the final aim of human existence. Thomas Aquinas argued that Christianity is distinctively reasonable, among all the religions, precisely in this regard, due to its teaching on heaven.[21] Christianity does not propose that human existence ends at death, or that the human soul reincarnates until it is freed from the cycle of rebirth, so as to live in a permanently impersonal state. Nor does the human being aim ultimately to live in material prosperity, in a life of sensual comforts and physical pleasures. Instead, Christianity proposes that the final end of man is to see the essence of God, that the human intellect might see God face to face, "as he is" in his eternal mystery.[22] This explains why the human person is marked by longings for the infinite. Each human being has a hidden natural desire to see God inscribed within, one that moves us to desire something always greater, and ultimately to be satisfied by nothing less than the possession of God himself. This desire to see God and to love God as God is in himself is one that has enlivened the saints with spiritual hope, even as they pass through death. As St. Teresa of Avila said on her deathbed, in expectation of heaven, "Lord ... it is time to meet." Hope in heaven is hope in the ultimate encounter with God.

Traditionally Catholic theology uses the term "beatific vision"

21. Aquinas, *Reasons for the Faith*, c. 5; cf. *Summa Contra Gentiles* III, c. 147; IV, c. 54, par. 2.
22. 1 Cor 13:12, 1 Jn 3:2, Rv 22:5.

to speak of the ultimate grace of heaven. The vision in question is not sensible, as if God were to be seen with physical eyes. Rather, it is the grace given to the soul to gaze immediately upon God in intellectual contemplation. Because God is infinitely perfect and utterly transcendent with respect to his creation, the created intellect of man and angel is naturally incapable of seeing God without the help of grace. The grace of salvation ultimately terminates in the gift of this grace, that of the beatific vision, by which God gives the souls of the blessed to see God as he is, in himself. Traditionally, the theologians stipulate: this vision is "immediate but not comprehensive." That is to say, the souls of the blessed see God in himself, but they do not have a comprehensive knowledge of God. Wonder remains forever present in heaven, and a kind of peaceful ecstatic movement of the soul turned out always into the ever greater world of God's eternal life.

If heaven consists in the vision of God's essence, it also consists in the perfect love of God. We cannot love what we do not know, but also conversely, we can love most perfectly what we come to know most perfectly. In the life of heaven, the soul is thrust into the radiant fire of the life of God, and given a most perfect knowledge of God. This in turn "burns the heart"—the spiritual will of the soul—with love for God's infinite goodness. The word "ecstasy" means literally "to stand outside" (*ex-stasis*) of one's self. In the state we call heaven, the will of the human soul goes out ecstatically into the goodness of God, which is known immediately and most perfectly. The soul "rests" profoundly in the possession of God, and is eternally satiated by the love of God, rapt out of itself. However, the soul is also most perfectly "itself" in a natural way, sinless and pure, in possession of its own integrity. The soul is united with God but does not become God. It is ever active in contemplation and love of God himself, and so never bored, always fulfilled, but also always at peace and in a rest of the most profound, unspeakable sort.

This mystery has a fundamentally Trinitarian dimension. In heaven the soul is beatified by seeing the eternal Word, Jesus Christ, in his divinity, and by seeing the Father in the Word. The soul is sanctified in the heart or will by the spiration of the Holy Spirit, whose goodness burns the heart with eternal love, as he, the Spirit, proceeds from the Father through the Word within the souls of the blessed. The "deification" or union with God that occurs in heaven is one in which the mind of each created person is united with the eternal Word and Son, and in this way he becomes a perfectly adopted child of God. The soul discovers the Father "in" the Son and receives from the Father the eternal gift of the Spirit. "God has sent the Spirit of his Son into our hearts, crying, 'Abba! Father!'"[23]

The beatific vision entails knowledge not only of God himself and of his Trinitarian life. To see God is to participate in some degree (as God wishes) in the knowledge of all things that God himself knows. So to see God face to face is also to understand the mystery of Jesus Christ, the Virgin Mary and the Church "from within," in the eternal light of God. Here we are speaking of the mystery of Christ's human life, not only in his earthly existence among us but also in his continued human existence in heaven. The insight into Christ that is given to the blessed amounts to an inversion of what we experience in our earthly lives. In this life, through the grace of faith, we come to know the divinity of Christ primarily through the medium of his human actions and sufferings. We discover who Christ is through his incarnate human life, his teachings, miracles, passion, and resurrection. In the life of the world to come, however, the human soul knows the divinity of Christ immediately by the grace of the vision, and "sees" the mysteries of the life of Christ (his Incarnation, life, death, and resurrection) in the light of the glory of God. In this life we contemplate the mysteries of the life of Christ through the me-

23. Gal 4:6.

dium of the holy liturgy of the Catholic Church. In the life of the world to come we will contemplate these same mysteries through the medium of the divine essence, in the splendor of the deity of Christ. There we will perceive "the Lamb who was slain," who is now alive forever, in the glory of his resurrection.[24] What will result is the holy liturgy of heaven, a hymn of thanksgiving, where the souls of the saints praise God continually, in union with the risen Christ and with the Blessed Virgin Mary.[25] "And night shall be no more; they will need no light of lamp or of the sun, for the Lord God will be their light, and they shall reign for ever and ever."[26]

The Catholic tradition, from New Testament times onward, has always held that heaven entails a collective life of persons. It is not merely an individual experience, nor can it be. Just as hell entails a certain cold isolation of one's self withdrawn from God (first) and others (often as a result), so heaven works conversely. Everything that rises must converge. The souls of those who are united with God are also united to one another in a common life, a collective experience of the vision of God. This must be the case because the souls of those who see God also know and love each other in the light of God. Part of the process of purgatory is the gradual purification of all misguided loves, all particular hates and misgivings and all resentments, envies, rivalries, jealousies, and hard-heartedness or lack of mercy toward other persons. Heaven, by contrast, is a place of magnanimity, in which each person gives thanks for the qualities and holiness of all other persons, and sees in them the radiant presence of Christ and the work of his grace. In the collective life of praise and harmony that is heaven, the great graces of others are never causes of sadness or envy and are always causes of joy and gratitude to God for the

24. Rv 5:12.
25. Rv 7:12.
26. Rv 22:5.

beauty of his Church. The Catholic tradition has always taught that there are degrees of holiness of those who attain to heaven, based on the degree of charity that each soul attained in his or her earthly life. The intensity of the beatification of each person is based on the intensity of his charity in this world. However, the differences that result in heaven are not the source of any disharmony. Instead, each soul perceives all things in light of the eternal radiance and infinite consolation of the vision of God. Each soul gives praise to God for his eternal wisdom and predestination, which bring the soul of each to the "place" or state that it occupies, in harmony and perfect concord with others. The souls of the saints are like cups of various sizes, some very small and some very great. Each can receive a different amount of the living water of grace that pours forth eternally from the side of Christ, and yet all are filled to the brim, eternally running over.

The souls of those in heaven are "filled" with the life of God, but despite this fact, they still remain incomplete in a fundamental way. This is due to the composite character of the human person as a spiritual animal. Human beings are embodied persons, or bodies informed by souls. No matter how happy the soul of a human person is because of the vision of God, without a body, the soul is still incomplete. This is one reason the souls of the saints remain intrinsically related to the world of men. Their destiny and ours are always interrelated. Human beings in this world are headed toward judgment and so the saints in heaven pray for their conversion and growth in sanctity, that we may rejoin them in the life of the blessed. At the same time, the souls of the just remain in perpetual relation to the physical world, as they await the resurrection of their physical bodies. There is a communion of saints that exists in the heart of the Church, of prayers shared in common by the living and the dead. There is also a spiritual ecology of interdependence between our world and the world of those who have died. We can pray for the souls in purgatory. The souls in heaven can intercede for us. In this way, the universal human community that we experience in this world as a basic fact of our existence (all human beings are in some sense one) is understood mysteriously to continue after this life. The unity and cooperation of the human community extend beyond the frontiers of death and judgment, into the relations we have with the souls of those in purgatory and heaven. The "Church militant" here below, the "Church suffering" in purgatory, and the "Church triumphant" of heaven are ultimately one Church, in three distinct states.

In this life the hope of heaven and the expectation of the beatific vision are a solace and a consolation. They are not simply unseen and unfelt truths that we adhere to in a purely dark night of faith. On the contrary, the grace of faith, hope, and love already provides us with an imperfect but real experience of union with God and an anticipation of the life of heaven in the world to come. Love already possesses the mystery, because the grace of charity causes the heart to be united to God directly, in God's own self, by lifting the heart up directly into union with the Holy Trinity. Although we presently experience this grace of union with God only under the veil of faith, nevertheless the grace of infused charity already provides a real and lasting possession of God in the heart. Meanwhile, the grace of faith, even while it is obscure, is also at times luminous, punctuated by touches of supernatural insight into the mystery of God. The faith is already a kind of real "seeing," albeit in obscurity. St. Paul speaks of "seeing through a glass darkly."[27] This vision can at times take on a contemplative intensity in which the mystery of God becomes transparent and present in greater clarity, anticipating the life of heaven and the vision of God in the world to come.

This anticipation of heaven that we experience already in this life through faith, hope, and love strengthens the heart and al-

27. 1 Cor 13:12 (KJV).

lows us to live in quiet expectation. It gives us patience amidst the sorrows of this world. It does not anesthetize our capacity to love this world, or suffer intensely, or experience wonder, or undergo deep trials of understanding. But it does orient us amidst all the vagaries of human existence toward our true home. The Christian who hopes one day to see God face to face is a pilgrim in this world steadied by the firm supernatural hope of arriving at an eternal city, one where the light of God never dims and where there is the solace and consolation of perfect peace, and love without end.

Universal Resurrection

Even in heaven, in the joy of the beatific vision, the soul remains incomplete without the body. So much so that we can also say that without belief in the resurrection of the body, it is difficult to understand belief in the immortality of the soul. How can a human soul exist forever without a body? Religious cultures that have no knowledge of the resurrection of the dead have tended to answer this question in one of two ways. Either they affirm that the soul must in some way reincarnate in another body, or they claim that the soul after death is absorbed into a larger impersonal force. Both are problematic viewpoints, but each of them illustrates a central Christian truth in a negative way: it is difficult to see how a human person can live forever without the body. If the personal soul of each human being continues to exist after death, it must live on in some way in view of reunion with the resurrected body.

Of course belief in the resurrection of the dead is not something one can demonstrate philosophically or affirm merely by the power of natural reason. The fundamental reason for the Church's confession of the universal resurrection of the dead is her belief in the historical resurrection of Jesus. If Jesus is physically glorified in his physical body, alive forever to die no more, then this has implications for all of humanity and for the whole physical world. What has happened historically in Jesus is a first instantiation and anticipation of what will happen in the end times to the whole of humanity and all creation. In the resurrection of Christ, God has signaled his commitment to his creation, his promise to refashion the whole of the created order in the light of Christ.

What the physical resurrection consists of is a mystery, one that is only partially revealed. Our knowledge of it is based primarily upon the resurrection narratives of the Gospels and the Church's experience of the glorified body of Christ present in the Eucharist. By the power of God, the glorified bodies of the saints will be conformed to the model of Christ's glorified body (no longer subject to death or suffering). Their bodies will remain truly material, but will be subject to the spiritual soul in a much more perfect way, even as the soul is itself enlightened by the beatific vision, and so perfectly subject to God. That is to say, in the resurrection from the dead, the material body will be highly "spiritualized" by the dominance of the soul, and the grace of the beatific vision will irradiate the whole human subject, affecting the sensations and feelings of the resurrected body, as well as the physical integrity and material quality of the body. The human being will have the properties of "impassibility" (freedom from bodily corruption), "subtlety" (spiritual refinement of matter), "agility" (spiritual movement of the body), and "clarity" (spiritual radiance of the body).

What will happen to the whole of the physical world in the resurrection? The scriptures only provide intimations but the traditional interpretation is that in the resurrection, there will be some sort of universal reconfiguration of the physical cosmos that affects all things. The world we live in now will not be "left behind" but reformed in a more beautiful and ultimate way so as to reflect the glory of the resurrected body of Christ and of the

Church. The universe we live in currently is ordered most particularly toward the existence of life and of human beings, in view
of the goodness of human reproduction and the spiritual community of men. The universe will be refashioned in the world to
come in view of the liturgical worship of God by the blessed in
their physical bodies. The physical world will still be our home,
but the physical body will not be oriented as it is in this life primarily toward reproduction, but instead uniquely toward the life
of eternal contemplation, worship, and shared friendship among
the saints. Heaven will be physical and political, because corporeal and political life are typically human, but this physical and
political life of heaven will also be "divinized" by the vision of
God. This intimacy with God will give rise to the common praise
of the whole Church, uniting both angels and men in one shared
liturgy. The physical world will be like a "sacrament" of the presence of Christ. The universe will be like a cosmic monstrance
with Christ's resurrected body at the center, in which the rays of
his glory will shine throughout the whole physical order and illumine it with his splendor. The whole material order will burn
with the fire of his love.

One may naturally wonder, of course, if such hopes are reasonable. Is it foolish to believe in the universal resurrection of the
dead? Friedrich Nietzsche thought so. For Nietzsche, the primal
causes of the universe are ultimately impersonal. The universe is
not governed by any transcendent principle of order or wisdom.
Instead the human being is born, lives, and dies against the backdrop of an essentially meaningless world. Consequently, the human being is responsible for forging his own sense of the meaning
of life.[28] The Jewish idea that divine love is going to change the
world in the eschaton is a form of deluded religious protest, one
that should be abandoned by the clear-sighted. Sigmund Freud,

28. Friedrich Nietzsche, *Writings from the Late Notebooks*, ed. R. Bittner, trans. K.
Sturge (Cambridge: Cambridge University Press, 2003), §5 [71], 116–23.

meanwhile, claimed that belief in the God of love stems from psychological projections onto the universe of a primal father figure. This is a strategy that religious people undertake to cope with incertitude and it stems in large part from their failure to accept the real finality of death and the impersonal nature of the universe.[29]

In response to these typical secular viewpoints, we should say three things. First, belief in the universal resurrection of the dead is not based on escapist sentiment or psychological debility. It is based on realism about the nature of God. The first evident truth is that the world exists, and yet it is also entirely composed of contingent things that do not have to exist. Therefore, the world points back to something more ultimate and transcendent: the omnipotent creator. If God is the actual author of the world that exists now, and created all things from nothing, then God is omnipotent. And if God is omnipotent (which he is), then he can refashion the world radically in light of his eternal goodness if he wants to. Contrary to Nietzsche and Freud, to claim otherwise is not psychologically insightful but philosophically erroneous.

Second, God is not only omnipotent but also personal, and God has revealed in Jesus Christ that he is love.[30] This means that the ultimate forces that govern all things are forces of interpersonal love. The divine persons of the Holy Trinity created the world out of contemplation and love. They made personal creatures in order to communicate to them a share in divine life, the beatitude or happiness that God enjoys in himself. Created persons live out the drama of existence in which our choices have everlasting consequences. In the face of death, we must choose for or against divine truth and love. In the end, this same love will also refashion all that is, remaking human beings in the image of Christ in glory. In saying all this, one is only saying at base that

29. Sigmund Freud, *The Future of an Illusion,* trans. J. Strachey (New York: W. W. Norton, 1989).
30. 1 Jn 4:8.

love is what is most real and enduring in the world. Christianity follows Christ in claiming that the ultimate power in the universe is the power of divine love.

Finally, the universal resurrection is an astonishing mystery of faith, but it is also a fitting truth about the final purpose of the physical cosmos. Modern scientists estimate that the physical world began 13.8–14.5 billion years ago in an initial compression of matter that is commonly called the "Big Bang," resulting in an initial massive expansion of the universe. This initial development gave rise from its beginnings to the kind of universe in which organic life could develop (at least on earth) and evolve progressively in increasingly complex forms, from single-cell bacteria to complex organic animals with sensate features and sophisticated capacities for tool making and sensate communication. It was in this creature (*homo sapiens*) that God first created human spiritual souls, and gave them a deep experience of his grace, calling them to a life of spiritual friendship with God within the physical world. Despite the important setback of the Fall and its catastrophic effects, the history of man is a history of intellectual discovery, moral and political development, artistic innovation, and religious inquiry. It is within this history that God inspired the prophets of ancient Israel and prepared for the Incarnation of the eternal Word.

Ontologically speaking, the evolution of our cosmos reaches its summit in the Incarnation and the resurrection of Christ. In the first man, Adam, the cosmos became spiritually self-aware (due to the new creation of the human spiritual soul). In the last man, Christ, the cosmos began to live forever in God. The resurrection of Christ is like a second "Big Bang," a second creation or "re-creation" in which God begins the process of making all things new. The sacramental life of the Church expands this dynamic process by allowing us to live and die in Christ, in union with him who is already victorious over death. The sacraments—especially the Eucharist—prepare us for the life of the world to come. Consequently, the kingdom of God is already present in seed in the visible life of the Catholic Church in this world. Despite all the setbacks of death and human evil that remain present in our fallen history, that history is also marked by the mysterious presence of the victory of Christ, his saints and his physical miracles, giving hope in the eventual transformation of all things in the life of the world to come. Christ is the "Omega point" or developmental endpoint of all things, the one in whom all things reach their final goal. Seen in this light, belief in the universal resurrection does not require of us to abandon our modern scientific realism regarding the nature of the cosmos and its history. On the contrary, the truth of the resurrection invites us to resituate our understanding of the physical world within the context of a deeper and more ultimate story, the story of God's redemption of the world through the power, goodness, and beauty of the resurrection.

A final feature of the universal resurrection that we should mention concerns the universal judgment. While God judges each individual soul at death, there is a restoration of universal moral order that occurs in the end times. The truth of each is made present to all, and the truth of all is made present to each. Here we can make an analogy to human political life in this world. Consider an unjust political regime in which the leaders are eventually overthrown, after having massacred and exploited their citizens for years. If there are collective trials of such persons in the new regime, and if these trials are safe and just, then each person who was victimized may have the possibility to come forward and bring testimony about what was done to them in secret. The outcome may be one of mercy as well as justice, but if it is to be successful it must above all be one of truth. The truth of the corrupt regime should come out before everyone for all the world to see, if there is to be a deep collective healing of the society and a restoration of just order.

The final judgment is God's transparent public trial of all of us, of the corrupt regime that is the human race. This is not a trial meant to end in condemnation (though there are those who refuse the truth about God and Christ by their own decision, and so finish in the eternity of hell). Rather the goal of the process is to allow the love and mercy of God to shine through all of reality and to expose the truth about all human persons to one another as they stand before God. This unveiling is done only ever in the light of God and serves only ever to augment our collective sense of love for God and gratitude for his grace. It procures mutual forgiveness, respect, and reconciliation between persons, as well as a shared life of praise and thanksgiving. What becomes most evident in the final judgment is the omnipresence of the offer of God's life, so often at work in the hearts and minds of human beings throughout history. All of the blessed and all of the damned will be understood most clearly and radiantly in the light of God, and in the light of their acceptance or refusal of the grace of God. Those who see God face to face will have the eternal consolation of understanding all of God's ways in the light of his transcendent mercy and wisdom, his truthfulness, and his respect for his creatures. They will be fulfilled spiritually to the point of overflowing by their direct contemplation of his infinite wisdom and goodness.

We might ask what the practical importance is of thinking of the last things, as we have done in this chapter. After all, aren't our lives concerned first and foremost with temporal affairs and practical matters? In actual point of fact, however, the last things are the first things: those we should consider first and foremost in the practical order of our decision-making. What do I live for? How do I live my life rightly in view of my ultimate goals? The Christian lives in view of Christ, and so also in view of divine judgment, purgation, heaven, and the end of the world. Far from being inconsequential, this way of life is what is most human in our fallen world. Why? Because the world we inhabit is one of great goodness, to be sure, one that offers real if limited forms of happiness, peace, and intellectual discovery. At the same time, however, this same world is incomplete, deeply imperfect, marred by moral evil, and is passing away. Our time in this world is short, while eternity draws near. Amidst the changes of this life we find our deepest joy by fixing our hearts on the one thing necessary, that which endures forever: the peace of Christ and the city of God. It is God and the hope of life with God that give true stability and fortitude to the human heart. It is this desire that unites all those who are truly Christian.

It is the living hope of union with God and the love of God that give the Catholic Church on earth her greatest strength to transcend the passing epochs of human culture (with their respective qualities and failings) and the trials of various earthly regimes. It is also this love and this hope that unite most deeply the hearts of those who are true friends of God, making the Church in this world a place of deep friendship, peace, and solace. As we hope to have shown in these pages, at the center of the Catholic Church is the indwelling presence of God the Holy Trinity, and of Jesus Christ the incarnate Word. To understand Catholicism, one must approach Christ and discover the mystery of God himself. At the same time, we may also invert the line of reasoning: he who believes in God the Holy Trinity and in Jesus Christ should also believe in the mystery of the Church. For as Bossuet says rightly, the Church is "Jesus Christ spread abroad and communicated."[31] Christ is alive in the midst of his mystical body, bringing the light of the Gospel to all nations. Ultimately the light of the Church just is the light of Christ. He will remain present with the Church until the end of time, and indeed, for all eternity. "The city has no need of sun or moon to shine upon it, for the glory of God is its

---

31. Jacques-Bénigne Bossuet, *Allocution aux nouvelles catholiques*, in *Oeuvres Oratoires*, tome 6, ed. J. Lebarq (Paris: Hachette, 1922), 508.

light, and its lamp is the Lamb."[32] As the Psalmist says, "There is a river whose streams make glad the city of God, the holy habitation of the Most High. God is in the midst of her, she shall not be moved; God will help her right early. The nations rage, the kingdoms totter; he utters his voice, the earth melts. The Lord of hosts is with us; the God of Jacob is our refuge."[33] And as Christ says, "Peace I leave with you; my peace I give to you; not as the world gives do I give to you. Let not your hearts be troubled, neither let them be afraid .... In the world you have tribulation; but be of good cheer, I have overcome the world."[34]

32. Rv 21:23.
33. Ps 46:4–7.
34. Jn 14:27, 16:33.

EPILOGUE

ON PRAYER

The Natural Desire for the Truth

There is a missionary priest who works in southern India, where he helps run a home for the poor and people dying of AIDS. He also staffs an adjacent chapel where there is eucharistic adoration throughout the day. He told me the story of a young man in his twenties who had suffered a stroke in his childhood, and was paralyzed permanently on one side of his body. This man was homeless, and came to the chapel each day and stood in the doorway, sometimes for hours, looking at the Eucharist. He was Hindu, however, not Christian. One day, after months of seeing him there, the priest asked him gently, "why do you come here to stand at the back of the chapel each day? What is it that you see there?" The young man paused for a moment, and then said to him in response: "They tell me it is God, and I try to believe it."

Prayer is grounded in our natural desire for the truth. When we pray we are trying to find God, to praise him, and to see all things realistically in light of him. In a sense, then, prayer stems from a search for perspective. It helps us understand the unfolding of our own lives in the context of God's providence, and to surrender our hearts to him in trust. When we pray we are seeking to remain in the truth of Christ. Accordingly, Aquinas teaches that prayer is first and foremost an act of the intellect, because in prayer we lift up our minds to God, but this accordingly also gives rise to an inward act of the will that he terms "devotion," by which he means the turning of our hearts to God and the inward submission of our hearts to the unspeakable goodness of God and his holy will.[1] In short, in prayer we seek to know God and gain insight into his mystery, and we also seek to love God and to love others for the sake of God.

Prayer is first and foremost interior, but it is also an activity of the whole person. We are rational animals. Consequently, when we seek to cultivate a serious life of prayer, our inward actions need to be expressed outwardly through physical actions: kneeling or bowing in the presence of God, standing in praise before him, or sitting quietly in church reading the scriptures. Embodied prayer allows us to offer our whole self to God. It denotes personal humility before the holiness of Christ, and love for him in our whole person. The practice of outward acts can also help reinforce an inward disposition to contemplation as we learn to turn toward the Lord habitually throughout the day. Physical gestures of prayer (like kneeling before God) can of course be private, but they are also often corporate. Prayer with others helps strengthen our own sense of interiority and resolve. This is why liturgical prayer is just as natural as private prayer, and in a sense even more natural, since human beings are political animals (in Aristotle's sense of the word). They are meant to live in community and to draw strength from one another by cooperation in the common pursuit of the truth, including the pursuit of truth about God that is sought in prayer.

Modes of Prayer

Since the sixteenth century, Catholic spiritual authors typically have spoken of different modes of prayer: *vocal prayer, meditation,* and *contemplation.* They are deeply interconnected. When we en-

---

1. Aquinas, *ST* II-II, q. 83, a. 1; q. 82, a. 1.

gage in one form more intensely, we tend to become open to the others almost inevitably.

Vocal prayer is the outward manifestation of our inward state of self-offering to God. When we pray vocally in the liturgy we signify in our words and gestures that our minds are turned toward God in petition, gratitude, and adoration, and that our hearts are seeking to find God, and rest in him. The words of the Catholic liturgy typically are meant to give our minds and hearts focus in this process. They bring the mystery to our attention and help us lift up our hearts to Christ. The prayers of the Mass and monastic offices are forms of collective worship that allow the whole of human society to pray together, to make social acts of self-offering to God in visible form. Catholic liturgy is meant to be beautiful and solemn so as to dispose human beings to reverence, interiority, and the quiet dignity of collective worship.

Meditation is an inward activity of the human mind at prayer. In meditation we seek to understand God and to scrutinize the mystery of Christ, so as to come to understand God better and to remain in his presence. Traditional forms of meditation center around the consideration of scripture (*lectio divina* or sacred reading), the consideration of the mysteries of the life of Christ (as in the case of the rosary), or the reading of the lives of the saints and their theological teachings. Meditation can be construed as a form of reading or thinking with a view toward finding the presence of God. It can take on very simple forms, including short prayers of repetition, such as the well-known Jesus prayer of Eastern Hesychasts: "Lord Jesus Christ, Son of God and my savior, have mercy on me a sinner." When meditation is practiced in this latter way, by the practice of mindfulness through repetitive prayer, it bears an analogy to methods found in non-Christian Eastern religious traditions. Christian monks seek to cultivate an enlightened state of consciousness based on a mystical discovery of the presence of Christ. Their prayer, however, is always focused upon a particular person: the Son of God who has lived a true human life among us, and who is now raised from the dead. It is the resurrected Lord who enlightens us. The meditative prayer of Christians, therefore, is not meant to lead to a dissolving of personal identity (reaching a state of pure selflessness). It entails a radical purification and intensification of personhood through communion with God. In Christian meditation we seek to encounter the three eternal persons of God: Father, Son, and Holy Spirit.[2]

If meditation is a more active process, one that we undertake regularly by our own initiative, contemplation is typically a more receptive or passive process, one that God initiates in us. We can choose to adore God and to meditate. We cannot choose to contemplate, though we can dispose ourselves to it by practicing what St. John of the Cross calls "mental prayer." This is the act of placing ourselves in the presence of God, drawn by the supernatural light of faith.[3] The supernatural contemplation of God is first and foremost a gift of the Holy Spirit, who indwells in our souls by grace, and who can lift up our minds and hearts so as to know God more intimately and mystically, while we are at prayer. Contemplation occurs especially when God gives the human being a deeper awareness of the presence of Christ, or a particular insight into some aspect of his mystery, such as his passion or his resurrection. Teresa of Avila was subject to a profound conversion in the middle of her life when she was given a mystical intuition into the suffering of Christ in his scourging by Roman centurions.[4]

2. See the helpful theological reflection of the Congregation for the Doctrine of the Faith, "Letter to the Bishops of the Catholic Church on Some Aspects of Christian Meditation," October 15, 1989; available at www.vatican.va.

3. "Do not omit mental prayer for any occupation, for it is the sustenance of your soul .... Never give up prayer, and should you find dryness and difficulty, persevere in it for this very reason. God often desires to see what love your soul has, and love is not tried by ease and satisfaction." John of the Cross, *The Collected Works of St. John of the Cross*, trans. K. Kavanaugh and O. Rodriguez (Washington, D.C.: ICS Publications, 2010), 728–29.

4. See Teresa of Avila, *The Life of Teresa of Avila: The Autobiography of Teresa of Avila*, trans. E. Allison Peers (New York: Image, 1991), preface.

Catherine of Siena was regularly subject to ecstasies of spirit and felt herself joined to the passion of Christ when she took communion.[5]

Not all activities of contemplation are so extraordinary, however. God frequently gives discreet graces of contemplation to ordinary people who undertake a regular life of prayer. Sometimes these take the form of a habitual quieting of the soul in profound peace, especially in the course of the sacrifice of the Mass. Others experience a stable joy even in the darkness of faith, so that their inward possession of God is not compromised even in the midst of turbulent outward events. God often gives those who pray deeper insights into his own goodness, as well as an acute sense of their own sinfulness. Such "wounds" of divine charity allow them to progress in the love of God and in the purification of their own selfishness. God can work in the soul to deepen its contemplation of him even in the midst of great darkness, whether this consists in a lack of sensate consolation or in spiritual aridity. Sometimes God is closest to a person and acting upon him most deeply precisely when he longs for God's presence and is acutely aware of God's seeming absence. This divine "pedagogy" is not meant to torment the human being, but to stir him to seek God in a more unconditional manner, so that God can in turn give the soul a deeper, unshakable union with him in the order of grace.

Trial and Perseverance

Prayer takes place in the quiet of a church, but also amidst military conflict, in the solitude of prison cells, the night that a couple is married, in classrooms, the day a child is born, when one is sick, on one's deathbed, and sometimes in remorse after an act of serious sin. Children who are very young can pray coherently and

5. See Raymond of Capua, *The Life of St. Catherine of Siena*, trans. G. Lamb (Charlotte, N.C.: TAN, 2003), 81–83, 143–73.

deeply, as can those who suffer from mental illness, drug addiction, or physically debilitating disease. Prayers can be made when we are half asleep or wide awake with concern, in the midst of joy or peacefulness, but also in anxiety or agony. Prayer can accompany us, therefore, throughout every facet of life.

This means that those who believe in God have a special possibility that others do not, but also a special burden. They can unite their lives with God continually in prayer, but they also have to sort their lives out in continual reference to God, not only in the midst of mundane things but also in the midst of trials and difficulties. There is an analogy here to remaining married to one person throughout life: the fidelity of married love presents human beings with a wonderful possibility to grow in stable love but also with a serious challenge. So too in the covenant with God: the human being is invited to consecrate all of his or her life to God, but just for this reason, he must remain in constant communion and conversation with God, even in the nights of faith or the trials of human suffering.

Catholic writers sometimes speak here of the practice of "abandonment to divine providence."[6] Abandonment in this context does not mean abdication of responsibility or an attitude of psychological infantilism. It denotes receptive availability to the initiatives of God in our life, and the desire to find God in all things. The Christian seeks to discern the will of God actively in prayer, so as to stay united with God even in the midst of changing circumstances. We do not always know what God is asking of us in a given situation, or why he permits various events in our lives. Human suffering and moral evil are sometimes deeply distressing or even agonizing. Great patience can be required of us in the face of adversity. However, the Christian faith does allow us to consecrate all of our lives to God in prayer and in love, not only when we have

6. See Jean-Pierre de la Caussade, *Abandonment to Divine Providence*, trans. D. Billy (Notre Dame, Ind.: Ave Maria Press, 2010).

grounds for gratitude but also when we are subject to the most serious difficulties. By being faithful to God in prayer, even when we
are distraught, saddened, or angered by our surrounding condition, we allow ourselves to remain connected to God, who alone
can overcome all evil, who will not abandon us, and who will wipe
every tear from our eyes.[7] Furthermore, by uniting our suffering
to the merits of Christ crucified, we allow the grace of God to take
hold of our suffering and to make use of it for the good of others.
"Now I rejoice in my sufferings for your sake, and in my flesh I
complete what is lacking in Christ's afflictions for the sake of his
body, that is, the Church."[8]

Prayer has a deeply practical side to it, since it is intimately
connected to the formation of our consciences and the process
by which we make concrete decisions. When we pray, we ask the
Holy Spirit to make us more aware of our true motives, to inspire
us to choose what is wise and honorable, and to strengthen us in
the capacity to do what is good. It is normal to pray before one
makes any major decision in life, and an error of omission not to
do so.

This practical stance does not mean that we can abdicate our
responsibility to make prudent and informed decisions, as if praying were a substitute for common sense. On the contrary: true
Christian prayer is meant to help us make complex personal decisions, and to do so with hope and trust in God. Often we cannot know with certainty what God wants of us. For example, we
typically cannot ascertain simply by praying that God wishes us
to take up residence in this city or that, to accept this job or that,
to marry this person or to enter that religious congregation. We
may see signs which suggest that God's providence is leading us
in a certain direction, but ultimately we have to live in hope that
God in his providence will allow our decisions to come to a good

7. Rv 21:4.
8. Col 1:24.

outcome. By praying in advance and by asking advice from the wise before we act, we are more likely to make decisions in peace, with the resolve that we can entrust our future to God no matter what may befall us.

Prayer helps us to forgive the sins of other people and to believe that we ourselves can obtain the forgiveness of God. The Lord's Prayer contains the momentous line: "Forgive us our sins, as we forgive the sins of those who trespass against us." One of the principal effects of original sin is that we have a very difficult time loving ourselves rightly. Our egoism and vanity are often attempts at overcompensation due to a lack of genuine love of self, and love of God. This inner wound is compounded when we commit further sins, since our errors make it harder for us to love ourselves and mark us inwardly with hidden forms of guilt and remorse. Even when people claim to have no awareness of any real "sinfulness," they are often concealing from themselves or others their own sense of moral failure, confusion, and vulnerability. Prayer helps us face all this openly in the presence of God and in the light of the mercy of Christ. By praying to Christ in honesty we are able to open up our broken hearts to the one who alone can heal them. By trusting in his mercy and forgiveness we can be strengthened in our innermost selves and in our genuine capacity to love God and others. This in turn helps us to practice active forgiveness of those who have wronged us or others. It gives us the strength to show empathy to those who are wounded and may not even realize it. Divine mercy is the true source of inner healing for human hearts, and it is a reality we can have regular contact with through daily prayer. This contact with divine mercy in turn allows us to share the mercy of God with others in ways that deeply transform human relationships.

Prayer is also something that helps us prepare for death and hope in eternal life. The Catholic Church encourages us to pray with those who are dying, and with the families of those who are dying. Each of us should pray for the grace of a good death, and entrust ourselves to the mercy of God at the hour of our death. In the universal Catholic prayer for the commendation of the dying, the Catholic priest says the following to the person who is approaching death:

Go forth, Christian soul, from this world in the name of God the almighty Father, who created you, in the name of Jesus Christ, Son of the living God, who suffered for you, in the name of the Holy Spirit, who was poured out upon you, go forth, faithful Christian. May you live in peace this day, may your home be with God in Zion, with Mary, the Virgin Mother of God, with Joseph, and all the Angels and Saints.

This beautiful prayer is expressive of the radiant hope that animates the Christian life. In praying to Christ we should "with confidence draw near to the throne of grace" and seek union with him even in and through death, in view of eternal life.[9]

Universal Forms of Devotion

The public liturgy of the Catholic Church is centered around the celebration of the seven sacraments (especially the Mass) and the reading and preaching of sacred scripture. The psalter in particular is a form of human prayer inspired by the Holy Spirit, one that informs the Church's public liturgy, especially in the "divine office" of religious orders where the psalms are prayed throughout the day.

There are other forms of devotion, however, that Catholics typically practice in addition to the public liturgy or in close association with it. One of these is called *lectio divina*, or "sacred reading." In *lectio divina* a person aspires to knowledge of the presence of Christ through meditation on the words of scripture. Here the primary point is not to read the scriptures in view of doctrinal clarification or theological understanding (though this too is im-

9. Heb 4:16.

portant and can help us pray). Instead, one treats the scriptures as a living source of the presence of God, rather like a sacramental presence. In the Gospel of John, for example, where Christ says "No longer do I call you servants . . . I have called you friends," one may rightly ask theological questions about the nature of friendship with Christ, the nature of Christian charity, and so on.[10] But in *lectio divina* we focus more on the real presence of Christ as the friend of sinners, and on his invitation to discipleship. "How can I respond more realistically to your calling? What are the obstacles in me to deeper friendship with you that I need to renounce?" This kind of reading disposes us to contemplation. The word of God pierces the soul and gives us a greater sense of the reality of the Holy Spirit dwelling within us.[11] If we allow Christ to show us our wounds and entrust ourselves to him, he can fill our hearts with the purifying fire of his charity.

The rosary is perhaps the most well-known Catholic devotion. It is medieval in origin, and was given its standard modern form in the sixteenth century by Pope Pius V. More recently Pope John Paul II added some elements. It is centered on twenty mysteries of the life of Christ. The person who prays meditates on each mystery while saying one Our Father and ten Hail Marys (aloud or in silence). The rosary is an extraordinarily flexible form of prayer. It is essentially meditative, but it makes use of vocal prayer, and can lead in turn to contemplation. It can be said in all circumstances: in a group or in private, on the subway at rush hour or in a hospital bed, in a monastery or in an office building. In this sense there is a wonderful humanity to the rosary because it allows us to consecrate all our life to the mystery of God. At the same time, the rosary is thoroughly Christocentric. It places us before the reality of the Incarnation, life, passion, death, and resurrection of Jesus. Even the Marian mysteries that come at the

10. Jn 15:15.
11. Heb 4:12.

end of the rosary (the bodily Assumption of the Virgin Mary and her coronation as queen of heaven and earth) show us the perfection of redemption in Christ, who has glorified his mother as the new Eve, the first fruits of redemption for the whole creation.

Eucharistic adoration is the highest devotion of the Catholic Church, though in a sense it is more than a devotion. This is the practice in which the Blessed Sacrament is exposed in a monstrance on the altar in a Catholic Church so that the faithful can pray in silence before the real presence of the glorified body of Christ. Here the devotion of the Church is rooted in a sacramental mystery instituted by Christ himself. Sometimes people who regularly go to adoration of the Blessed Sacrament feel no special consolation. Their prayer can be arid and difficult. At other times, and not infrequently, they experience a deep, radiant sense of the presence of Jesus. When a person is especially touched in eucharistic adoration he can have a very strong sense of the inward presence of Christ in the soul. By practicing this devotion regularly, our thoughts can be illuminated and the movements of our heart can be purified. Many receive regular consolations of supernatural peace while they are praying. One might even say that this practice can provide a faint awareness (in the obscurity of faith) of what heaven is like. In the presence of the glorified body of Christ we experience the illumination of our inmost selves and an ecstatic rest, the peaceful turning of our hearts out into God.

Interior Life

When John Henry Newman was created a cardinal in 1879 he chose as the motto for his coat of arms the expression *Cor ad Cor Loquitur*: "heart speaks to heart." He was referring to the heart of Christ who addresses our hearts, and of our human desire to turn to God in trusting friendship. At the heart of the Catholic life of prayer is the search for what is sometimes called "an interior life" of closeness to the heart of Christ.

The most important aid to the development of a genuine interior life is the frequent and right reception of the sacraments, especially those of regular confession and eucharistic communion. By making a weekly or biweekly confession of all one's sins (in accord with the authentic teaching of the Church), a person is usually helped greatly to avoid all serious sin, and to aim toward a spiritual life of union with God. By frequent communion the soul opens itself up to the presence and directives of Jesus Christ, as well as the special inspirations of the Holy Spirit. There is an organic unity to the practice of all the sacraments, so that if we practice one of them correctly (such as confession) we can reap spiritual fruits from the others (such as the sacrament of matrimony or the Eucharist), but if we fail to practice one of them rightly (such when a person marries outside the Church or fails to attend weekly Mass), it will inevitably impact the grace we receive from all the others. Consequently, we should aspire to live the sacramental life: to unite our life to Christ in and through the patient and faithful reception of the sacraments in accord with the mind of the Church.

The cultivation of an interior life with God is also greatly helped by spiritual friendships with other Christians who are seeking God. Christianity is not a closed sect whose adherents seek to avoid others, and if it were, then such behavior would be morbid. But spiritual friendships between Christians are the deepest and most noble form of friendship that human beings can experience, and such friendships "in Christ" are virtually necessary for anyone who aspires to genuine union with God in the spiritual life. To have friends is natural, and the grace of God does not destroy nature but elevates and sanctifies it. We have need, then, even in our life with Christ, for human friendship, and in a sense we have need of true friendship in this domain above all. Fellow travelers help us by their example, encouragement, and understanding. They give us good advice and the consolation of their presence and kindness. God often works through spiritual friendships in profound ways to stabilize and enlighten us in our journey toward God in this life.

The aspiration to a profound interior life of prayer does not entail the rejection of responsibility for others or the renunciation of an active engagement with the world. The Christian spiritual life is marked above all by "contemplation in action." Consider here the religious orders. Some are given more especially to contemplation and others to various active forms of evangelization or practical acts of charity. All religious orders, however, have to maintain a sense of balance between the contemplative aspiration to union with God and the active service of other human beings. Even Catholic monks and nuns in enclosed monasteries pray for the salvation of others, both day and night, and seek to serve one another in radiant fraternal charity for the sake of Christ. They are "active" in this way, in the midst of their contemplation. Members of active orders that teach or serve the disadvantaged must cultivate a life of regular prayer and contact with God in order to remain centered in Christ.

The faith in itself is inherently contemplative because it lifts up our minds to the consideration of God, who is eternal and infinitely interesting. Faith also teaches us how to find God in all things so that we can see the trace of God in his most modest physical creatures and in the ordinary workings of our everyday life. Faith gives us a God's-eye perspective on the world. It inspires in us the ambition to serve God and to make his truth known to others, but it also teaches us humility, and gives us an ever-deeper experiential awareness that we can do nothing without his help. Faith teaches us to live in the light of the absolute, and to be dissatisfied with spiritual mediocrity, but it also impels us to pay attention to the details of life so as to be faithful to God in all things.

Our interior life should also lead to a cultivation of the virtue of piety, which is the care of others performed for the sake of God. The Catholic tradition typically notes seven "spiritual works of mercy" and seven "corporeal works of mercy": counsel the doubtful, instruct the ignorant, admonish the sinner, comfort the sorrowful, forgive injuries, bear wrongs patiently, pray for the living and the dead; feed the hungry, give drink to the thirsty, shelter the homeless, visit the sick, visit prisoners, bury the dead, give alms to the poor. The love for the poor and the service of those who suffer are a constitutive part of the Christian life. St. John tells us "if any one says, 'I love God,' and hates his brother, he is a liar; for he who does not love his brother whom he has seen, cannot love God whom he has not seen."[12] Those who wish to cultivate an interior life with God should also seek to perform spiritual and corporeal works of mercy. Often when a person seeks to love his neighbor for the sake of Christ, his heart expands with the charity of Christ, and he deepens his contemplative life with the Lord. Likewise, when we open our hearts to Christ, we open our hearts to the needs of our neighbors.

The Christian life begins and ends in spiritual freedom. The truth of Christ sets us free because faith opens our hearts up to what is absolute and allows everything else to appear as it truly is, as something secondary and relative. "Indeed I count everything as loss because of the surpassing worth of knowing Christ Jesus my Lord. For his sake I have suffered the loss of all things, and count them as refuse, in order that I may gain Christ."[13] The Christian is free because he lives for the one thing necessary. Concretely it is the cultivation of the interior life that allows this transformation to take place in our lives. If we have our eyes fixed on eternity, we can live in time in a peaceful way, engaging in the world of human events without losing a sense of the prior-

12. 1 Jn 4:20.
13. Phil 3:8.

ity of God. This interior freedom also gives each of us a space to welcome all persons that God puts on our path, without defensiveness or indifference, but instead with a charity that is universal or catholic.

It is this mysterious love of Christ for humanity that sustains the Catholic Church in being down through the ages, and that inspires her saints. His love reaches out from the Cross to all of creation, and remains hidden at the center of the world as its living heart. The grace of Christ crucified is the source of the Church's life, her devotion to the truth and her freedom to love. Therein lies the essence of Catholicism: at the heart of the Church is the life of Christ. It is this life that God invites us to, and that he wants to give us, if we open our minds and hearts to him in prayer.

RECOMMENDED

READINGS

Note: In chronological order of composition.

Ignatius of Antioch. *The Letters of Ignatius of Antioch*. In *Early Christian Writers: The Apostolic Fathers*, edited by A. Louth, translated by M. Staniforth. New York: Penguin, 1987.

Irenaeus, *Against Heresies*. In *Ante-Nicene Fathers*, vol. 1, edited by A. Roberts, J. Donaldson, and A. C. Coxe, translated by A. Roberts and W. Rambaut. Buffalo, N.Y.: Christian Literature Publishing, 1885.

———. *On the Apostolic Preaching*. Translated by J. Behr. Crestwood, N.Y.: St. Vladimir's Seminary Press, 1997.

Athanasius. *On the Incarnation*. Translated by a Religious of C.S.M.V. Crestwood, N.Y.: St. Vladimir's Seminary Press, 1993.

Gregory of Nazianzus. *The Five Theological Orations*. In *On God and Christ*, translated by F. Williams and L. Wickham. Crestwood, N.Y.: St. Vladimir's Seminary Press, 2002.

Augustine. *Confessions*. Translated by H. Chadwick. Oxford: Oxford University Press, 1991.

———. *City of God*. Translated by H. Bettenson. New York: Penguin, 1982.

———. *The Trinity*. Translated by E. Hill. Hyde Park, N.Y.: New City Press, 1991.

John Damascene. *An Exposition of the Orthodox Faith*. In *Nicene and Post-Nicene Fathers*, vol. 9, edited by P. Schaff and H. Wace, translated by E. Watson and L. Pullan. Buffalo, N.Y.: Christian Literature Publishing, 1899.

Anselm of Canterbury. *Why God Became Man*. In *The Major Works*, edited by B. Davies and G. R. Evans. Oxford: Oxford University Press, 1998.

Bonaventure. *The Soul's Journey into God, The Tree of Life, The Life of St. Francis*. Translated by E. Cousins. New York: Paulist Press, 1982.

Thomas Aquinas. *Summa Contra Gentiles*. 4 vols. Translated by A. Pegis, J. Anderson, V. Bourke, and C. O'Neill. Notre Dame, Ind.: Notre Dame University Press, 1975.

Recommended Readings

————. *Compendium of Theology*. Translated by C. Vollert. London: B. Herder, 1947.

————. *Summa Theologica*. Translated by the English Dominican Province. New York: Benziger Brothers, 1947.

Catherine of Siena. *The Dialogue*. Translated by S. Noffke. New York: Paulist Press, 1980.

Raymund of Capua. *The Life of St. Catherine of Siena*. Charlotte, N.C.: TAN Books, 2011.

Catherine of Genoa. *Purgation and Purgatory, the Spiritual Dialogue*. Translated by S. Hughes. New York: Paulist Press, 1979.

Teresa of Avila. *The Autobiography of Teresa of Avila*. Translated by A. Peers. New York: Image Books, 1981.

John of the Cross. *The Living Flame of Love*. In *The Collected Works*, translated by K. Kavanaugh and O. Rodriguez. Washington, D.C.: ICS Publications, 2010.

Robert Bellarmine. *Controversies of the Christian Faith*. Translated by K. Baker. Ramsey, N.J.: KTF Press, 2016.

Francis de Sales. *The Catholic Controversy*. Translated by H. Mackey. Charlotte, N.C.: TAN Books, 1989.

Catechism of the Council of Trent. Translated by J. McHugh and C. Callan. New York: Joseph F. Wagner, 1934.

Jacques Bénigne Bossuet. *History of the Variations of the Protestant Churches*. Translator not provided. Fraser, Mich.: Real View Books, 1997.

John Henry Newman. *An Essay on the Development of Christian Doctrine*. Notre Dame, Ind.: University of Notre Dame Press, 1989.

The Baltimore Catechism. Charlotte, N.C.: TAN Books, 2010.

Therese of Lisieux. *Story of a Soul*. Translated by J. Clarke. Washington, D.C.: ICS Publications, 1996.

Elizabeth of the Trinity. *Complete Works*, vol. 1: *I Have Found God*. Translated by A. Kane. Washington, D.C.: ICS Publications, 1984.

Henri de Lubac. *Catholicism: Christ and the Common Destiny of Man*. Translated by L. Sheppard and E. Englund. San Francisco: Ignatius Press, 1988.

Reginald Garrigou-Lagrange. *The Mother of Our Saviour and Our Interior Life*. Translated by B. Kelly. Charlotte, N.C.: TAN Books, 2012.

Charles Journet. *The Mass: The Presence of the Sacrifice of the Cross*. Translated by V. Szczurek. South Bend, Ind.: St. Augustine's Press, 2008.

Yves Congar. *The Meaning of Tradition*. Translated by A. Woodrow. San Francisco: Ignatius Press, 2004.

Second Vatican Council. *Lumen Gentium*. In *Vatican II: The Essential Texts*, edited by N. Tanner. New York: Image, 2012.

Recommended Readings

Hans Urs von Balthasar. *Truth Is Symphonic*. Translated by G. Harrison. San Francisco: Ignatius Press, 1987.

G. E. M. Anscombe. *Faith in a Hard Ground: Essays on Religion, Philosophy and Ethics*. Edited by M. Geach and L. Gormally. Exeter: St. Andrews Studies, 2008.

Joseph Ratzinger. *Eschatology: Death and Eternal Life*. Second edition. Translated by M. Waldstein. Washington, D.C.: The Catholic University of America Press, 2007.

Pope John Paul II. *Veritatis Splendor: The Splendor of Truth*. New York: Pauline Books, 1993.

Catechism of the Catholic Church. Second edition. Vatican City: Libreria Edifice Vaticana, 2000.

BIBLIOGRAPHY

Anscombe, G. E. M. "Contraception and Chastity." In *Faith in a Hard Ground: Essays on Religion, Philosophy and Ethics*, edited by M. Geach and L. Gormally, 170–91. Exeter: St. Andrews Studies, 2008.

Anselm of Canterbury. *Monologion*. Translated by Jasper Hopkins. In *A New, Interpretive Translation of St. Anselm's Monologion and Proslogion*. Minneapolis, Minn.: Arthur J. Banning Press, 1986.

———. *Why God Became Man*. In *Major Works*, edited by Brian Davies and G. R. Evans. Oxford: Oxford University Press, 1998.

Aquinas, Thomas. *Summa Contra Gentiles*. 4 vols. Translated by A. Pegis, J. Anderson, V. Bourke, and C. O'Neill. Notre Dame, Ind.: Notre Dame University Press, 1975.

———. *Summa Theologica*. Translated by the English Dominican Province. New York: Benziger Brothers, 1947.

———. *Thomas Aquinas: Selected Writings*. Translated and edited by Ralph McInerny. New York: Penguin, 1999.

Aristotle. *The Complete Works of Aristotle*. Edited by Jonathan Barnes. 2 vols. Princeton, N.J.: Princeton University Press, 1984.

Athanasius. *On the Incarnation*. Translated by a Religious of C.S.M.V. Crestwood, N.Y.: St. Vladimir's Seminary Press, 1993.

Augustine. *The Literal Meaning of Genesis*. Translated by John Hammond Taylor. Ancient Christian Writers 42. New York: Newman Press, 1982.

———. *The Trinity*. Translated by Edmund Hill. New York: New City Press, 2012.

Balthasar, Hans Urs von. *Does Jesus Know Us? Do We Know Him?* Translated by Graham Harrison. San Francisco: Ignatius, 1983.

———. *The Glory of the Lord, A Theological Aesthetics*, vol. 1: *Seeing the Form*. Translated by Erasmo Leiva-Merikakis. San Francisco: Ignatius, 1982.

———. "Theology and Sanctity." In *Explorations in Theology* I: *The Word Made Flesh*, translated by A. V. Littledale and Alexander Dru, 181–209. San Francisco: Ignatius, 1989.

Bibliography

Bellarmine, Robert. *Controversies of the Christian Faith*. Translated by K. Baker. Ramsey, N.J.: KTF Press, 2016.

Benedict XII, Pope. *Benedictus Deus*. Encyclical Letter. In Denzinger, *Compendium*, 1000–1001.

Benedict XVI, Pope. *Spe Salvi*. Encyclical Letter. November 30, 2007. Available at www.vatican.va.

Bonino, Serge-Thomas. *Angels and Demons: A Catholic Introduction*. Translated by Michael J. Miller. Washington, D.C.: The Catholic University of America Press, 2016.

Carroll, William E. "Creation, Evolution, and Thomas Aquinas." *Revue des Questions Scientifiques* 171, no. 4 (2000): 319–47.

Catechism of the Catholic Church. Revised in accordance with the official Latin text promulgated by Pope John Paul II. Washington, D.C.: United States Catholic Conference, 2000.

Catherine of Genoa. *Treatise on Purgatory*. Translated by Charlotte Cornish Balfour and Helen Douglas-Irvine. New York: Sheed and Ward, 1946.

Catherine of Siena. *The Dialogue of St. Catherine of Siena*. Translated by Algar Thorold. London: Kegan Paul, Trench, Trubner and Co., Ltd, 1907.

———. *The Letters of St. Catherine of Siena*. Translated by Suzanne Noffke. Tempe: Arizona Center for Medieval and Renaissance Studies, 1998.

Congar, Yves. "Ecclesia ab Abel." In *Abhandlungen über Theologie und Kirche: Festschrift für Karl Adam*, edited by Marcel Reding, 79–108. Düsseldorf: Patmos-Verlag, 1952.

———. *Tradition and Traditions: The Biblical, Historical, and Theological Evidence for Catholic Teaching on Tradition*. Translated by Michael Naseby and Thomas Rainborough. London: Burns and Oates, 1966.

Congregation for the Doctrine of the Faith. "Doctrinal Note on Some Questions Regarding the Participation of Catholics in Political Life." November 24, 2002. Available at www.vatican.va.

———. "Letter to the Bishops of the Catholic Church on Some Aspects of Christian Meditation." October 15, 1989. Available at www.vatican.va.

———. "Letter to the Bishops of the Catholic Church on the Pastoral Care of Homosexual Persons." October 1, 1986. Available at www.vatican.va.

Council Lateran V. 1513. In Denzinger, *Compendium*, 1440.

Council of Florence. 1439. In Denzinger, *Compendium*, 1304–6.

Council of Lyons II. 1274. In Denzinger, *Compendium*, 850–61.

Council of Trent. 1563. In Denzinger, *Compendium*, 1497–1870.

Council Vatican I. *Dei Filius*. April 24, 1870. Available at www.vatican.va.

Bibliography

Council Vatican II. *Dei Verbum*. November 18, 1965. Available at www.vatican.va.

———. *Dignitatis Humanae*. December 7, 1965. Available at www.vatican.va.

———. *Gaudium et Spes*. December 7, 1965. Available at www.vatican.va.

———. *Lumen Gentium*. November 21, 1964. Available at www.vatican.va.

———. *Nostra Aetate*. October 28, 1965. Available at www.vatican.va.

Cyprian. *Letters 1–81*. Translated by Rose Bernard Donna, CSJ. The Fathers of the Church 51. Washington, D.C.: The Catholic University of America Press, 1964.

———. *The Unity of the Catholic Church*. In *Treatises*, translated by Roy J. Deferrari. The Fathers of the Church 36. Washington, D.C.: The Catholic University of America Press, 1956.

Cyril of Jerusalem. *Catechetical Lecture 23 (On the Mysteries V); On the Sacred Liturgy and Communion*, Number 9. Translated by E. H. Gifford. In *Nicene and Post-Nicene Fathers*, vol. 7, edited by Phillip Schaff and Henry Wace. Buffalo, N.Y.: Christian Literature Publishing, 1894.

Daniélou, Jean. *The Bible and the Liturgy*. No translator provided. London: Darton, Longman and Todd, 1956.

de la Caussade, Jean-Pierre. *Abandonment to Divine Providence*. Translated by Dennis Billy. Notre Dame, Ind.: Ave Maria Press, 2010.

Denzinger, Heinrich. *Compendium of Creeds, Definitions, and Declarations on Matters of Faith and Morals*. 43rd edition. Edited by Peter Hünermann, Robert Fastiggi, and Anne Englund Nash. San Francisco: Ignatius, 2012.

Ephrem the Syrian. *Hymns on Faith*. Translated by Jeffrey Wickes. The Fathers of the Church 130. Washington, D.C.: The Catholic University of America Press, 2015.

Eusebius. *Ecclesiastical History, Books 1–5*. Translated by Roy J. Deferrari. The Fathers of the Church 19. Washington, D.C.: The Catholic University of America Press, 1953.

Feser, Edward. *Aquinas: A Beginner's Guide*. Oxford: Oneworld, 2009.

Francis de Sales. *The Catholic Controversy*. Translated by Henry Benedict Mackey. Charlotte, N.C.: TAN, 1989.

Freud, Sigmund. *The Future of an Illusion*. Translated by J. Strachey. New York: W. W. Norton, 1989.

Gregory of Nazianzus. *Select Orations*. Translated by Martha Vinson. The Fathers of the Church 107. Washington, D.C.: The Catholic University of America Press, 2003.

Gregory the Great. *Dialogues*. Translated by Odo John Zimmerman. The Fathers of the Church 39. Washington, D.C.: The Catholic University of America Press, 1959.

Bibliography

Heidegger, Martin. *Being and Time*. Translated by John Macquarrie and Edward Robinson. New York: Harper and Row, 1962.

Hengel, Martin. *The Atonement: The Origins of the Doctrine in the New Testament*. Translated by John Bowden. Philadelphia: Fortress Press, 1981.

————. *The Son of God: The Origin of Christology and the History of Jewish-Hellenistic Religion*. Translated by John Bowden. Philadelphia: Fortress Press, 1977.

Heraclitus. *Fragments*. In *The Presocratic Philosophers: A Critical History with a Selection of Texts*, translated and edited by G. S. Kirk and J. E. Raven. Cambridge: Cambridge University Press, 1957.

Hippolytus of Rome. *The Apostolic Tradition*. In *The Treatise on the Apostolic Tradition of St. Hippolytus of Rome, Bishop and Martyr*. Edited by Gregory Dix. London: Alban Press, 1992.

Holmes, Michael, ed. *The Apostolic Fathers in English*. Translated by Michael Holmes. 3rd edition. Ada, Mich.: Baker Academic, 2006.

Ignatius of Antioch. *Letter to the Magnesians*. Translated by Alexander Roberts and J. Donaldson. In *Ante-Nicene Fathers*, vol. 1, edited by Alexander Roberts, James Donaldson, and A. Cleveland Coxe. Buffalo, N.Y.: Christian Literature Publishing, 1885.

Irenaeus. *Against Heresies*. Translated by Alexander Roberts and William Rambaut. In *Ante-Nicene Fathers*, vol. 1, edited by Alexander Roberts, James Donaldson, and A. Cleveland Coxe. Buffalo, N.Y.: Christian Literature Publishing, 1885.

John Chrysostom. *Homilies on the Treachery of Judas*. In *The Faith of the Early Fathers*, vol. 2, edited and translated by W. A. Jurgens. Collegeville, Minn.: The Liturgical Press, 1979.

John of the Cross. *The Collected Works of St. John of the Cross*. Translated by Kieran Kavanaugh and Otilio Rodriguez. Washington, D.C.: ICS Publications, 2010.

John Paul II, Pope. *Evangelium Vitae*. Encyclical Letter. March 25, 1995. Available at www.vatican.va.

————. *Veritatis Splendor*. Encyclical Letter. August 6, 1993. Available at www.vatican.va.

Julian of Norwich. *Revelations of Divine Love*. Translated by Elizabeth Spearing. New York: Penguin, 1999.

Leo the Great. *The Tome of Leo*. Translated by Charles Lette Feltoe. In *Nicene and Post-Nicene Fathers, Second Series*, vol. 12, edited by Phillip Schaff and Henry Wace. Buffalo, N.Y.: Christian Literature Publishing, 1895.

Levering, Matthew. *Mary's Bodily Assumption*. Notre Dame, Ind.: University of Notre Dame Press, 2014.

Lewis, C. S. *Mere Christianity*. New York: HarperCollins, 2001.

Marsden Farrer, Austin. *Love's Redeeming Work: The Anglican Quest for Holiness*. Edited by Geoffrey Rowell, Kenneth Stevenson, and Rowan Williams. Oxford: Oxford University Press, 2004.

Morerod, Charles. *Tradition et unité des chrétiens: Le dogme comme condition de possibilité de l'oecuménisme*. Paris: Parole et Silence, 2005.

Newman, John Henry. *An Essay in Aid of a Grammar of Assent*. Notre Dame, Ind.: University of Notre Dame Press, 1979.

———. *An Essay on the Development of Christian Doctrine*. Notre Dame, Ind.: University of Notre Dame Press, 1989.

———. *Apologia Pro Vita Sua*. New York: Penguin, 2004.

———. *Fifteen Sermons Preached Before the University of Oxford: Between A.D. 1826 and 1843*. London: Longmans, Green, and Co., 1909.

———. "Letter Addressed to the Rev. E. B. Pusey, D.D., on Occasion of His Eirenicon." In *Certain Difficulties Felt by Anglicans in Catholic Teaching*, vol. 2. London: Longmans, Green and Co., 1900.

———. *The Dream of Gerontius*. London: Catholic Truth Society, 1953.

Nietzsche, Friedrich. *The Anti-Christ*. Translated by Judith Norman. In *The Anti-Christ, Ecce Homo, Twilight of the Idols and Other Writings*, edited by Aaron Ridley. Cambridge: Cambridge University Press, 2015.

———. *On the Genealogy of Morality*. Translated by Carol Diethe. Cambridge: Cambridge University Press, 2008.

———. *Writings from the Late Notebooks*. Edited by Rüdige Bittner. Cambridge: Cambridge University Press, 2003.

Origen. *Homilies on Joshua*. Translated by Barbara J. Bruce. The Fathers of the Church 105. Washington, D.C.: The Catholic University of America Press, 2002.

———. *Homilies on Leviticus, 1–16*. Translated by Gary Wayne Barkley. The Fathers of the Church 83. Washington, D.C.: The Catholic University of America Press, 1990.

———. *Homily on Luke*. Translated by Joseph T. Lienhard. The Fathers of the Church 94. Washington, D.C.: The Catholic University of America Press, 1990.

———. *On First Principles*. In *An Exhortation to Martyrdom, Prayer, and Selected Works*, translated by Rowan Greer. New York: Paulist Press, 1979.

Pascal, Blaise. *Pensées*. Translated by Honor Levi. Oxford: Oxford University Press, 2008.

Bibliography

Paul VI, Pope. *Humanae Vitae*. Encyclical Letter. July 25, 1968. Available at www.vatican.va.

————. *Solemni Hac Liturgia*. Encyclical Letter. June 30, 1968. Available at www.vatican.va.

Pius IX, Pope. *Quanto Conficiamur Moerore*. Encyclical Letter. August 10, 1863. Available at www.vatican.va.

Pius XII, Pope. *Humani Generis*. Encyclical Letter. August 12, 1950. Available at www.vatican.va.

Plato. *Complete Works*. Edited by John M. Cooper. Indianapolis, Ind.: Hackett, 1997.

Ratzinger, Joseph. *Behold the Pierced One: An Approach to a Spiritual Christology*. Translated by Graham Harrison. San Francisco: Ignatius, 1986.

————. *"In the Beginning": A Catholic Understanding of the Story of Creation and the Fall*. Translated by Boniface Ramsey. Grand Rapids, Mich.: Eerdmans, 1995.

————. *Introduction to Christianity*. Translated by J. R. Foster. San Francisco: Ignatius, 2004.

————. *Jesus of Nazareth: The Infancy Narratives*. Translated by P. J. Whitmore. New York: Image, 2012.

Raymond of Capua. *The Life of St. Catherine of Siena*. Translated by George Lamb. Charlotte, N.C.: TAN, 2003.

Symmachus. "Third Relatio to the Emperor Valentinian II." Translated by John Hugo Wolfgang Gideon Liebeschuetz. In *Ambrose of Milan: Political Letters and Speeches*. Liverpool: Liverpool University Press, 2005.

Teresa of Avila. *The Interior Castle*. Translated by E. Allison Peers. New York: Image, 2013.

————. *The Life of Teresa of Avila: the Autobiography of Teresa of Avila*. Translated by E. Allison Peers. New York: Image, 1991.

Wippel, John. *The Metaphysical Thought of Thomas Aquinas*. Washington, D.C.: The Catholic University of America Press, 2000.

Witherington, Ben, III. *The Christology of Jesus*. Minneapolis, Minn.: Fortress Press, 1990.

Wright, N. T. *Jesus and the Victory of God*. Minneapolis, Minn.: Fortress Press, 1996.

Xenophanes. *Fragments*. In *The Presocratic Philosophers: A Critical History with a Selection of Texts*, translated and edited by G. S. Kirk and J. E. Raven. Cambridge: Cambridge University Press, 1957.

INDEX

Index

Index

Index